Also by Tyler Kepner

K: A History of Baseball in Ten Pitches

THE

THE *Grandest* STAGE

A HISTORY OF THE WORLD SERIES

TYLER KEPNER

DOUBLEDAY  NEW YORK

www.doubleday.com

DOUBLEDAY and the portrayal of an anchor with a dolphin are
registered trademarks of Penguin Random House LLC.

Jacket images: (baseball player) CSA-Printstock / Getty Images;
(sky) Fine Art Photographic / Stone / Getty Images
Jacket design by Michael J. Windsor

Library of Congress Cataloging-in-Publication Data
Names: Kepner, Tyler, author.
Title: The grandest stage : a history of the World Series / Tyler Kepner.
Description: First edition. | New York, N.Y. : Doubleday, [2022] |
Includes bibliographical references and index.
Identifiers: LCCN 2022005058 (print) | LCCN 2022005059 (ebook) |
ISBN 9780385546256 (hardcover) | ISBN 9780385546263 (ebook)
Subjects: LCSH: World Series (Baseball)—History. |
Baseball—United States—History.
Classification: LCC GV878.4 .K47 2023 (print) |
LCC GV878.4 (ebook) | DDC 796.357/64609—dc23/eng/20220625
LC record available at https://lccn.loc.gov/2022005058
LC ebook record available at https://lccn.loc.gov/2022005059

MANUFACTURED IN THE UNITED STATES OF AMERICA

1 3 5 7 9 10 8 6 4 2

First Edition

For Mom and Dad

Thanks for the tickets.

To be on stage when the whole world is watching, if you don't relish that, you're in the wrong business.

—Jack Morris

Contents

Introduction

The great right-hander bends at the waist and peers in for the sign. His glove—five fingers, no webbing—rests on his left knee, his socks pulled high over his calves. His jersey says BOSTON, with laces stitched up to the collar, but there is no logo on his cap or number on his back. There's no diamond anymore, either, though the setting is still a park: a grassy courtyard ringed by wooden benches and a redbrick walkway in a grove of oak trees at Northeastern University.

This is where you'll find the statue of Cy Young, by Robert Shure, commissioned by the Yawkey Foundation in 1993 on the site of the old Huntington Avenue Grounds. It's a hidden oasis amid the campus bustle, tucked between the steps of Churchill Hall and the Barletta Natatorium, home of the Huskies' swimming and diving teams. Sixty feet, six inches from the statue, on the grass, a stone marker in the shape of home plate notes the significance: on October 1, 1903, the Boston Pilgrims, now the Red Sox, met the Pittsburgh Pirates in the first modern World Series. General admission seats cost fifty cents. The leadoff man, Ginger Beaumont, took Young's first pitch for a strike, worked a full count, and flied out to Chick Stahl in center field, where Hayden Hall now stands. The next day's *Boston Globe* reported, on the front page, that 16,000 fans encircled the field, "held well back by ropes and a small army of policemen." The Pirates won the game, but Boston took the series, five games to three.

That is how it all began, when the winners of the National and American Leagues first met to crown a champion. It was called the world's championship series, "world" used as a possessive, not an adjective, the stage so grand that it must belong to the planet, not merely the 16 franchises scattered from Massachusetts to Missouri.

"In my day, growing up, the World Series was the event of the year," says Carl Erskine, who was born in 1926 and pitched in five Fall Classics for the Brooklyn Dodgers. "It was bigger than the Masters, bigger than football and basketball."

Times have changed. For several decades now, the Super Bowl has been our sporting fixation. Football wins every poll when fans are asked to name their favorite sport, but baseball is a fundamentally different product, an everyday companion for seven months, not a once-a-week spectacle for five. Americans spend countless more hours watching baseball, which has about 10 times as many games, than they do watching football, in person and at home. A Super Bowl lasts less than four hours; a World Series might go 25.

And what a treat that is for the millions of us who love baseball. Every season is an inverted pyramid, contenders whittled away as the schedule descends to that delicious denouement, in four to seven acts, beginning in late October. As the national baseball columnist for *The New York Times,* I've witnessed every World Series game for two decades, plus 21 before that. Yes, I count them all.

Only one was an afternoon game: my first, on a golden Saturday in 1983 in my hometown of Philadelphia. I was eight years old and sat with my mom on the first base side at Veterans Stadium, maybe 15 rows from the field. The Phillies lost to the Baltimore Orioles, 5–4, and the managers used almost everyone: 17 players for the Orioles, 19 for the Phillies. Gary Matthews made a leaping catch at the left field wall. Mike Schmidt got a broken-bat single. I nearly got trampled chasing a foul ball by Jim Dwyer. The Phillies brought the winning run to the plate in the bottom of the ninth, but Joe Morgan lined out to Lenn Sakata at second base.

That was Game 4, and the next day I was back with my dad for a twilight start. I watched batting practice from the front row and returned for the bottom of the ninth, dipping under the railings to see Scott McGregor finish a 5–0 shutout. Garry Maddox lined out softly to shortstop Cal Ripken Jr., who snagged the ball and shook it in his glove.

"It was all surreal, it was all new, it was all fun," says Ripken, who was 23 and never got back. "As a kid, you want to be a big league player, but part of your dream is to win the World Series. And I know what that feels like—once."

Ripken remembers fans swarming the field, grabbing at his glove to try to steal the ball. He tucked his cap in his glove, too, so nobody could snatch it off his head.

"That was still when people rushed the field," he says. "It was on the road, so it wasn't crazy-crazy, like maybe it would have been at home. But you felt like you had to get off the field."

It's funny, I had the opposite feeling: Why aren't we storming the turf? As I recall it—and video backs me up—the Orioles celebrated with no outsiders invading their space, no strangers in street clothes amid the revelers. When the Phillies won in 1980, mounted horse patrol had protected the field. This time there were no such obstacles, and none were needed. We weren't being civil; we were numb. Angry, too, or at least bitterly disappointed.

I was also confused. Maybe this was my fault. The Phillies had won the opener, and when they lost Game 2, I wasn't too upset. I had tickets to Games 4 and 5, so a split in Baltimore meant that both of my games would be played. Then weird stuff started happening: A ball skids on a wet spot on the turf in Game 3, and the Phillies lose. My brother steals my lucky hat before Game 4, and they lose again. Eddie Murray hits his name on the scoreboard (OK, just below it) with a homer in the Game 5 rout. How could my heroes lose all three at home? The men themselves were just as dumbfounded.

"I remember going back to my town house after that Game 5 and sitting there by myself going, 'How did we lose? We've got Pete Rose, we've got Joe Morgan, we've got Mike Schmidt, I can't believe we lost,'" says Marty Bystrom, who pitched that day. "It's devastating, but it happened. And not only that, but they swept us at the Vet."

Bystrom had been part of the 1980 team, taking a hero's ride down Broad Street with his teammates. Buoyant masses—including future Phillies champion Jamie Moyer, 17, who skipped class at Souderton

High School—lined the parade route to JFK Stadium, where Tug McGraw thrust his weary left arm to the sky, clutching a copy of the *Daily News* with a two-word headline: "We Win!" Bystrom hopped off the float and wandered home in a daze with Dickie Noles and Bob Walk, three kids from the farm system, none of them alive for the city's last World Series in 1950, sprinkled in with the happy throng. Somehow they'd brought joy to millions.

By 1984 Bystrom was pitching for the Yankees, where he joined a rotation with Phil Niekro, the ageless knuckleballer bound for Cooperstown. Niekro spent decades striving to reach the stage where Bystrom competed as a rookie. He never made it.

"I was 26 years old and he's 46," Bystrom says. "Think of how many years he played in the major leagues, and he never played in the World Series. So you consider: Wow, how lucky was I? It happened the first month and a half that I was in the big leagues, and then it happened again."

Willie Mays hit no homers in the World Series, but Willie Mays Aikens hit four. Justin Verlander has no World Series victories, but Jose Urquidy has three. Nobody from the 1991 Hall of Fame class—Rod Carew, Fergie Jenkins, Gaylord Perry—ever got there. Neither did Ernie Banks, Ken Griffey Jr., Roy Halladay, Ryne Sandberg, or Ichiro Suzuki.

More teams have taken part in recent years, with layers of playoffs creating more opportunities. At the turn of the twenty-first century, neither Texas team had reached the World Series, and neither Chicago team had won since the first World War. Now, every team except the Seattle Mariners has won a pennant, and half of the 30 franchises have raised a banner since 2001—with no repeats, the longest stretch ever without back-to-back championships.

"To win the World Series, it takes a lot out of you, it does," says Giants manager Bruce Bochy, who won three titles, but none consecutively, from 2010 through 2014. "Of course there's a lot of things that go with that—the celebrating, the stress it can put on some pitchers, and even the players, mentally and physically."

With pitchers training for lighter workloads than ever, an extra month of stressful innings often takes a toll the next season. In 2021, the Braves removed Ian Anderson from a Game 3 no-hitter after five innings and 76 pitches. There was no chance he was going nine, anyway, manager Brian Snitker explained, and the bullpen was rested. The Braves won.

Forty years earlier, in another Game 3, a different rookie, Fernando Valenzuela of the Los Angeles Dodgers, threw 147 pitches in a complete game. He walked seven and gave up nine hits, but lifted his team back into the World Series after two losses in New York. It was the apex of Fernandomania and propelled the Dodgers to the title.

"It wasn't Fernando's best performance," Vin Scully said on radio. "It was his *finest* performance."

Seven years later the Dodgers were back in the World Series, but Valenzuela was an afterthought; only 27, he'd already made his last All-Star team. For pitching heroics in 1988, the Dodgers turned to Orel Hershiser, using him for five starts and one relief appearance in a stretch of 17 days. He had a save and three complete games to carry his team to the top, willed his way through the next season, then blew out his arm in April 1990.

"The front of your shoulder looks like pounded veal," the surgeon, Dr. Frank Jobe, told Hershiser. "There's nothing there."

Jobe had spun a medical miracle by inventing Tommy John surgery for elbows, but he'd never tightened a major leaguer's shoulder capsule in a reconstructive operation. Hershiser would return and pitch well through the 1990s, but the surgery cost him 13 months with no precedent for recovery. He knew what he was risking in 1988, and has lived the rewards of that effort.

"My life changed," Hershiser says. "I'm a voice of the Dodgers. I'm smiled at everywhere I go. People return my emails and phone calls. You gain all this equity—smile equity, laugh equity, integrity equity, concentration equity, all this equity gets added in all these different subjects of your life."

No pitcher today would ever be allowed to match Hershiser's efforts in the 1988 postseason, which came after a superhuman stretch run: eight complete games in a row, then a 10-inning night to set a record for consecutive scoreless innings, with 59. Teams don't train pitchers to handle that much work now, cultivating instead a stable of power arms to patch games together.

By World Series time, pitchers are stretched to maximum capacity, relievers have built-in travel days for rest, and every possible matchup has been scrutinized well in advance by data-savvy front offices. With so much at stake, managers are less likely than ever to defy the odds. This aversion to risk might help a pitcher's long-term health, and probably does help a team's chances to win, but it takes a dash of wonder from the viewing experience, diluting star power and forcing us to recalibrate our definition of greatness.

It also makes the whole thing longer: relievers trotting on and off the field, hitters relentlessly working counts, pitchers and catchers furtively protecting their signs. The final five World Series of the 2010s each averaged at least 3 hours, 42 minutes per game, higher than any World Series before 2000. The third game in 2018—when the Dodgers beat the Red Sox in 18 innings—lasted 15 minutes longer than the entire 1939 World Series.

"They play these games so late that kids can't watch them during the week," laments John Wathan, the former Royals catcher and manager. "And not having any day games in the World Series, it's really sad."

In 1980, Wathan played against the Phillies in Game 6, which drew almost 55 million viewers on a Tuesday night and scored a 40.0 rating, the highest in World Series history. The 2021 finale—also Game 6 on a Tuesday night—drew about 14 million viewers, with a 7.9 rating.

Ratings for the Super Bowl, meanwhile, have held strong despite the proliferation of TV networks. The 1980 game had a 46.3 rating and more than 76 million TV viewers; the 2021 game pulled a 38.2 rating, with 91 million TV viewers.

Scott Boras, the most powerful agent in baseball, has long advocated a neutral-site World Series to help close the gap with the Super Bowl. Baseball did this in 2020, in Arlington, Texas, but only as a one-off because of the coronavirus pandemic. Boras envisions a baseball festival, with years of careful planning and promotion, that would celebrate the sport.

"We have to be forward-thinking about how we create a game that has attention above all other sports," he says. "It's already given us an indication of what the current, traditional approach has provided, and that is that baseball does not receive the attention of the Super Bowl. Well, let's create a product that does receive the attention of the Super Bowl, and let's create something that allows for a World Series week and brings commerce and corporate interaction and all those things that come to a city for the Super Bowl—but we can actually deliver four to seven games as opposed to one."

Baseball has shown no interest in Boras's plan and cares little about ratings, as long as networks keep paying handsomely for postseason rights. In its most recent deal with Fox—a seven-year, $5.1 billion extension that starts in 2022—MLB got a 40 percent bump from its previous package. With fewer and fewer people watching television in real time, live sports remain lucrative for networks. Long before television—to say nothing of modern distractions like the internet, video games, and endless in-home entertainment options—the World Series was a community touchstone, a shared experience for towns big and small.

"In my little hometown of Anderson, Indiana, people would stand there in a big crowd outside the newspaper building as they broadcast the game over a loudspeaker," Erskine says. "And we'd look at this wall and watch the World Series game by watching this little mechanical thing show where the runner moved. Radio was it. It was the magic. You made your own pictures."

The first television broadcast, in 1947, reached only New York City; Philadelphia; Washington; and Schenectady, New York, home to NBC's parent company, General Electric. By 1951 the games would be beamed across the country, though it would still be 20 years before the first World Series night game. Fans consumed the series in a wholly different way then, a bit like the early-round NCAA tournament games of today.

"The sounds of baseball fell from every window and doorway in town," Roger Angell wrote in *The Summer Game,* describing the pulse of New York each October for a decade after World War II. "Secretaries typed only between innings, with their ears cocked to the office radio down the hall, and if business drew you reluctantly into the street . . . you followed the ribbon of news via elevator men's rumors, snatches of broadcasts from passing taxi radios, and the portable clutched to a delivery boy's ear, until a sudden burst of shouting and laughter sucked you into a bar you were passing, where you learned that Campy or Duke had parked one, or that Vic Raschi had struck out Furillo with two on."

For the baby boomers in greater New York—the kids drawn to Willie, Mickey, and the Duke—it was baseball's golden era, and the World Series belonged to them. From the 1949 opener through the 1957 opener, a New York team won 47 World Series games in a row. All but four games—two in Philadelphia, two in Cleveland—were held anywhere but Yankee Stadium, Ebbets Field, or the Polo Grounds. It was quite a scene.

"It was a highly acclaimed event, like the Kentucky Derby in a way. People would dress to the hilt to go to the World Series," Erskine says. "If you look at old black-and-white photos, you see how men wore hats and shirts and ties, and women wore their finery to the World Series, including furs sometimes, if it was cool. So that atmosphere has changed dramatically; the dress code and everything has changed, the culture's changed over time. But I was always pleased to see the crowds at the World Series; they were special. It was kind of an acknowledgment that we're going to an event, and this is the top of the line right here."

When the Dodgers and Giants moved to California after the 1957 season, they kept on winning. For each of the next nine years, at least some of the World Series took place in New York, Los Angeles, or both.

To be an American was to have at least a passing familiarity with the World Series. In an episode of *The Twilight Zone* from 1961—"Will the Real Martian Please Stand Up?"—a state trooper tries to guess which patron in a diner is actually an alien in disguise. He interrogates one man with a question any human could easily answer: Who won the last World Series?

"Pittsburgh Pirates won it, took four out of seven from the Yankees," the man replies, cackling. "Didn't figure us Martians would know nothing about the great American pastime, did you?"

More than six decades later, that World Series, won on Bill Mazeroski's homer in the bottom of the ninth in Game 7, remains a signature moment in baseball history. No other seventh game has ended with a home run, though it almost happened in 2016, when the Cleveland Indians had three shots at it against the Cubs. Aroldis Chapman was tiring—which meant that his fastball was 98 miles an hour, not 100—but he retired the side in order, and the Cubs won it in the tenth.

Jason Kipnis was the second hitter in the bottom of the ninth, and Chapman struck him out with a high fastball. But the pitch that haunts Kipnis is a 1–1 slider Chapman hung in the middle of the strike zone. It could have—no, should have—turned Kipnis into Mazeroski. He swung hard and connected, pulling a high drive down the first base line. For an instant it seemed that the ball might keep climbing, might stay true, might backspin its way into history . . . and then it died, like a paper airplane, hooking harmlessly into the seats.

"It came to full effect like a week later," Kipnis says. "I'm down in the basement on my couch, watching TV. I think I'm drunk, and it probably wasn't a happy kind of drunk."

On *The Tonight Show*, Anthony Rizzo brought the World Series trophy to Jimmy Fallon's desk. On *Jimmy Kimmel Live!*, Kris Bryant showed up with a billy goat draped in a W flag as the band played "Go Cubs Go." Kipnis, it's safe to guess, took another drink.

"I turned it off," he says. "You think of that fork in the road, the way each of our lives just went, between those Cubs players and mine."

That Cubs' victory, as you may have heard, ended a championship drought that had stretched to 1908. Celebrities flocked to the team that fall—Eddie Vedder, Bill Murray, John Cusack—but the fan who personified the yearning, to me, was a man I spotted at an O'Hare McDonald's, at 5 a.m., just after they'd won the pennant. He got his food, took a seat, and pulled a Cubs flag from his suitcase, carefully unfolding it to use as a tablecloth. He ate alone, silently, at a mostly empty food court. It seemed he just wanted to be close, in some kind of tangible way, to a team that made him proud, a team that was going to the World Series.

Moments like that have made it joyous to cover the last two decades of the World Series. Twelve times in those 20 years, the winning team snapped a generational streak of futility: the Angels (42 years without a championship), the Red Sox (86), the White Sox (88), the Cardinals (24), the Phillies (28), the Giants (56), the Royals (30), the Cubs (108), the Astros (55), the Nationals (51), the Dodgers (32), and the Braves (26). There was no common trait that propelled them. Baseball takes time to reveal its truths, but a best-of-seven series overflows with peculiarity, upending any theory you can conjure. The Angels had a weak rotation and a strong bullpen; the Astros had the opposite. The Cubs' hitters struck out a lot; the Royals' hitters did not. The Phillies won all of their home games; the Nationals lost all of theirs.

The connective tissue is the meaning, the bond between franchise and fan base. It's a man named Michael Sergio parachuting into Shea Stadium during Game 6 of the 1986 World Series with a GO METS banner, slapping hands with Ron Darling as the cops lead him away. It's Steve Perry flinging his cap to Giants fans while his love song to San Francisco—"When the lights go down in the city . . ."—rings across the Bay. It's Homer Hankies in Minneapolis, Clydesdales in St. Louis, ThunderStix in Anaheim.

"When we won it with the Angels in 2002, it was electrifying," says Mickey Hatcher, the team's hitting coach. "I mean, you can't experience anything better than winning a World Series and winning it at your own stadium. Oh my, you didn't want to go home. You just didn't want to go home. You wanted to stay there all night long."

Winning on the road has its own charms. In 1971, Steve Blass pitched Game 7 for the Pirates in Baltimore. Roberto Clemente homered early in the game, Blass held the lead till the end, and though they posed for a photo in the locker room—Blass still displays it in a frame at his home—they did not get to talk until the flight back to Pittsburgh. In 15 months Clemente would be gone, lost on another airplane while delivering relief aid to earthquake victims in Nicaragua. He had been a champion before, in 1960—Clemente hit safely in every World Series game of his career—but this was his valedictory, and he wanted to show Blass what it meant.

"I'm sitting by the window with my wife, and Clemente's up ahead with Vera, and he walks back in the aisle of the airplane and says, 'Blass, come out here, let me embrace you,'" Blass says. "I'd have climbed over six elephants. I gave him a hug, he gave me a hug, and I didn't say a word. I just hung on. And I will have that singular moment with me the rest of my life."

In 1973, the Pirates' first year without Clemente, Blass would famously, and inexplicably, lose the ability to throw strikes. He went on to spend decades in the Pirates' broadcast booth and always wore his championship ring to the ballpark. If he met a young fan who was shy, Blass would ask the boy or girl to try on his ring. He delighted in the power of such a small gesture, the warmth and the comfort pulsing through that gold band.

Yet only the players can know, deep down, what it's really all about. The ring is a symbol to them of a lifetime bond, a tribute to a brotherhood.

"It represents the people," Blass says. "People ask, 'What kind of check did you get for the World Series?' We got a nice check, but I look at that and I see Danny Murtaugh and Willie Stargell and Clemente and Dock Ellis and Bob Moose, all those guys that we've lost, you go through that. We're family, we're brothers. We go through that grind—spring training, 162 games, playoffs, World Series—and you're close to those people. I think about them a lot, and every time I look at that ring, I see them."

Jim Rooker, who starred for the Pirates in the 1979 World Series, says he never grasped the magnitude of winning until the next opening day. The ring moved him to tears.

"That was the one thing that made it all real," Rooker says. "When you see that ring, it's the greatest gift as an athlete that you could ever acquire."

Lots of nonplayers get rings—team officials, owners' family members, broadcasters, ballpark personnel. When I worked for the Phillies as an intern in 1995, some people around the office still wore the NL championship ring from two years before. I knew I was meant to be a writer, but I briefly considered a front-office career, mostly for one reason: the chance to someday win a ring. I was sure I'd wear it everywhere and admire it forever—even though, of course, I wouldn't have deserved it.

What I really wanted, in the days I fell in love with baseball, was the same thing as Cal Ripken and millions of others: to be in the scrum after the last out, grinning wildly, arms upraised, forever young. Now, at least, I can tell the stories of folks who get to live that dream, or at least earn the chance. Guys like Jim Poole.

The thrill of the effort endures for Poole, a reliever for Cleveland in 1995. Poole grew up going to Phillies games and wanting to be the next Steve Carlton, just like me. Neither of us did that, but Poole got much closer, pitching for 11 seasons in the majors. When Poole was a teenager, his hero won Game 6 of the World Series. When Poole grew up, he lost it, beaten on a homer by the Braves' David Justice for the only run of the final game of the season.

Had that been me, I assume, I would have rued that moment for the rest of my life. But players are wired differently. The chance to compete, Poole says, to climb onto that stage and try, was everything.

"I just wanted to see what I would do and how would I perform," he explains. "I can't control success all the time; regrettably, the guy with the bat has something going on, too. For me, clearly, the L is next to my name in Game 6, but I've never looked back and felt I did anything but perform. I went up there and in the biggest moment I gave it everything I had. There was nothing left. So yeah, I got beat—but I didn't lose. Losing, to me, would mean that mentally I was not right. In this case, I wouldn't change a thing except I would love to have a different result."

Nearly 40 years later, that's exactly how I feel about my first time at the World Series. After a year or so, I dropped my vow to never again utter the word "Orioles." As a writer, I've spoken with many of the villains from that lost weekend—McGregor, Murray, Rick Dempsey, Jim Palmer, Ken Singleton. All have been courteous, cordial, friendly. I'm glad for them that they won.

In researching this book, I spoke with Larry David, the comic genius behind *Curb Your Enthusiasm,* about the episode he did with Bill Buckner. We talked about the first World Series game David ever saw: the Braves and the Yankees, Warren Spahn versus Whitey Ford, Game 4 in 1958. He was 11 years old and sat in the upper deck in fair territory in the Bronx. I said that it must have been one of his greatest childhood memories.

"Well," replied David, a Yankees fan, "they lost."

Understood. Maybe it's strange to remember my first World Series game as fondly as I do, since I'm sure I did not leave the Vet smiling. But at this point, in middle age, I mostly remember the feeling of that day: my stadium was now *the* stadium, the grandest stage in the game. The sun is up, the sky is blue, it's beautiful. Look around.

It's like Marty Bystrom said: How lucky was I? I was very young and got to witness a World Series game. Twice. And I've done it again and again, every game, every year, for decades now. I even get paid to go.

So here's what I've learned, with generous help from hundreds of those lucky enough to play or manage in the World Series or to build the teams that get there. There are seven chapters, one for each game of a series that goes the distance under the format used for the last century. It's not a chronology, not another recap of famous events— it's *a* history, not *the* history, a seven-sided look at the modern World Series, an ode to the most wonderful time of the year.

THE *Grandest* STAGE

Game 1

"The Whole World Knows How Bad I Am"

Handling the Pressure of the World Series

Reggie Jackson was born in Pennsylvania in the spring of 1946, just like my dad. Jackson never played for the Phillies, and in those days before interleague play, he never played against them, either. My dad was a casual fan of his, then, tied together by a loose kinship. I never grew up on stories of Reggie, except this one.

On the night of October 18, 1977, when the Yankees faced the Dodgers in Game 6 of the World Series, my dad had a work meeting in Philadelphia. He listened to the radio broadcast on his drive to our home in Flourtown, Pennsylvania, not far from Jackson's hometown of Wyncote. In the bottom of the eighth inning, Jackson launched a Charlie Hough knuckleball into the faraway black bleachers at Yankee Stadium. It was his third home run of the night, off three consecutive pitches from three different pitchers, all but sealing the Yankees' first championship in 15 years. The moment was so overwhelming that my dad pulled off to the side of Stenton Avenue, got out of his car, raised his hands over his head, and yelled, "Wow!" Reggie made him stop everything, just to cheer for greatness.

That night stamped Jackson forever as the archetype of the clutch World Series performer, the man at his best under pressure. He had worn the nickname Mr. October for only a few weeks, a throwaway line from teammate Thurman Munson that fit so perfectly it would one day be etched onto Jackson's plaque at the Hall of Fame, rendered in the same-sized type as Jackson's given name. It crowns him with a kind of halo that resonates across sports.

In 2016, after watching LeBron James lead the Cleveland Cavaliers to the championship in Game 7 of the NBA Finals in Oakland, Jackson sought out the hero in the locker room. James was tying his shoe when Jackson tapped him on the shoulder to introduce himself. He didn't need to.

"I know who you are," James said. "You're Mr. October."

Jackson lived the role James has perfected: mercenary with a mandate to fulfill a promise, a leader who cherishes the responsibility of putting rings on teammates' fingers. In five World Series for the A's and the Yankees, Jackson batted .357 with 10 home runs and 24 runs batted in. Mickey Mantle holds the career record for World Series homers, with 18, but Jackson's .755 slugging percentage is by far the highest in World Series history among players with at least 100 plate appearances.

Handling pressure, Jackson explains, does not always show in results. In one of his most famous World Series at-bats, in 1978, Jackson struck out against Dodgers rookie Bob Welch to end Game 2. But he fought Welch for nine pitches, all fastballs, power versus power, spellbinding theater. And six days later, it was Jackson who threw the knockout punch, homering off Welch to cap the Yankees' clinching victory in Los Angeles.

Jackson likes to say that as long as a hitter has a bat in his hands, he can change the narrative him. The bat, in other words, is more powerful than even the noisiest microphone—and Jackson needed that feeling of control. He was the biggest star for teams owned by Charles O. Finley and George Steinbrenner, autocrats who never understood how their decorated rosters could possibly lose. In his first World Series for each of them—in 1973* for the A's and 1977 for the Yankees—Jackson was named MVP.

Facing elimination against Tom Seaver and the Mets in '73, Jackson drilled two run-scoring doubles in a close win. Then he homered off Jon Matlack to put away Game 7. From then on, October was his favorite month.

"I started to believe that when the postseason came, I'd be better,"

---

* Jackson missed the A's–Reds World Series in 1972 after tearing a hamstring muscle in the decisive ALCS game against the Tigers—while stealing home.

Jackson says. "I started believing in the headlines. I started believing what was written and almost relied on it. It came to the point where I'm gonna be good, I'm not worried. As soon as October gets here, I'll wear the opponents down and be me."

All told, in a postseason career that stretched through age 40 with the 1986 Angels, Reggie was Reggie: his .885 on-base plus slugging percentage in 77 games was close to his .846 mark across 21 regular seasons. Given a large enough sample, that's how it typically goes for most players.

But Jackson's dominance in his five World Series seemed to be so much more than a statistical blip. To watch sports is to believe, or yearn to believe, that certain athletes can will themselves to heights we've never seen. How else to explain David Ortiz's otherworldly statistics—a .455 average and a 1.372 OPS percentage, both records for players with 50 plate appearances—in three World Series for the Boston Red Sox?

"Some people got it, some people don't," Ortiz said in 2016, near the end of his final season, and Jackson agrees. "I think it's in a player's makeup," he says. "I think it's your DNA. I don't think you can acquire it."

With it, you can acquire plenty: a nickname, a reputation, even a better car than the one you get as World Series MVP. After Game 6, *Sport* magazine awarded Jackson a Yankee-blue Thunderbird—a very nice car, he thought, and he happily signed it over to his sister, Tina. The next day, Jackson bought himself a convertible Rolls-Royce Corniche for $64,250.

Jackson drove it home to California, roof down, breezily chatting up other drivers on a CB radio. His handle: Mr. October. He got pulled over a few times, doing 90 miles an hour, but the cops didn't care about that. They just wanted to congratulate a World Series hero.

"It was enjoyable to be everybody's friend," Jackson says. "It was a great compliment the way people humbled themselves and applauded what I did. I meet people today all the time that say, 'You ruined my life,' because they're Dodger fans and I was on three teams that beat them in the World Series. But I've never met a Dodger fan that didn't also say something like, 'Man, you made it miserable for me, but I've got to shake your hand. I admire what you did.'"

A lifetime of respect and admiration, coast-to-coast cheers that never fade, all for delivering under pressure on the grandest stage in baseball.

————————

The year before Jackson reached the majors, Jim Palmer earned a distinction that will probably stand forever: youngest pitcher to throw a World Series shutout. He did it in 1966 at Dodger Stadium, nine days before his twenty-first birthday. It was the first shutout of Palmer's extraordinary career for the Baltimore Orioles, and he would keep winning until 1983, when he earned his final victory the night before his thirty-eighth birthday. That was also in the World Series.

And so that is how we remember Palmer: clutch at the start, clutch at the end, with a bunch of 20-win seasons in between. Palmer is the only pitcher with World Series wins in three decades and the only man to play for all three Orioles title teams. He strolls Baltimore with the cool self-assurance of a legend with nothing to prove, the friendly neighborhood champion who always has a table waiting at his favorite restaurant in Little Italy.

"The two worst things in baseball are if the people who see you play know you're not giving your best, and if you look in the mirror and you know you could have been better," Palmer told me a few years ago, loosely quoting Branch Rickey over lunch one afternoon. "Now, to me, that's pretty much what life's about."

There were days in October that could have been better for Palmer. He lost his only start in the 1969 World Series against the Mets. A decade later, he lost a shutout in the seventh inning with a chance to close out the Pirates at home. But usually, when it mattered most, Palmer was the Hall of Fame version of himself, even better in the postseason than he was in the regular season.

When Palmer turned 75 years old, in 2020, only one living pitcher—Andy Pettitte—had thrown more World Series innings than his 64 and two-thirds. He brought modest goals to his first nine—"All I wanted to do was not embarrass myself," Palmer says—but that day in 1966, after he'd held the reigning champion Dodgers to four hits, he insisted to reporters that he hadn't been nervous. He'd even told a coach, Billy Hunter, that he planned to throw two shutouts, not just one, in the series.

You'd think Palmer might have been intimidated. The Dodgers had been part of his earliest World Series memories; as a young boy in New York, he rushed home from school to see Sandy Amoros's famous catch in 1955. He moved to California around the same time the Dodgers did, playing Little League in Beverly Hills, chasing foul balls at the massive L.A. Coliseum, watching Sandy Koufax pitch at Dodger Stadium.

In '66, Palmer would be facing Koufax in Game 2. The Orioles' commanding performance in the opener helped him; their best hitters, Frank and Brooks Robinson, tagged Don Drysdale for homers in the first, and reliever Moe Drabowsky dominated the Dodgers with a high fastball, which was Palmer's best pitch, too.

The winner's bonus was also a powerful incentive for a rookie who painted houses in the winter for extra cash. Palmer made only $7,500 in 1966, and each share would be worth $11,683.04. (Yes, he remembers the amount, accurate to the penny.) It all put Palmer in an ideal frame of mind on the morning of Game 2, which began with his usual four-pancake breakfast.

"I wasn't saying I was gonna beat Koufax, but the whole mood of the team changed because we beat Drysdale," he says. "It's not that we weren't a good team, but I'm thinking, 'Whoa, we might have a chance to win.' So I was much more relaxed than I would have been if Game 1 had gone in another direction."

As it happened, the Dodgers never scored again after their opening 5–2 loss. They made six errors in Game 2, including three in one inning by center fielder Willie Davis, who lost two balls in the sun to spoil the last game Koufax ever pitched. Palmer cruised, and back in Baltimore, Wally Bunker and Dave McNally followed with shutouts of their own.

Palmer would start six World Series games in the 1970s, each time working seven to nine innings. He watched most of the 1983 World Series from the bullpen, grateful just to be there.

"It's not that easy to see through the plexiglass, but I thought, 'You know, there are people sitting a lot farther away than I am and paying a lot more money than I used to pay when I'd go see the Colts in the championship game for $5.75,'" he says. "But I enjoyed that World Series because most of the guys on the staff I had mentored, kind of like Robin Roberts did for me, and it was the first time that the expectations on me, from everyone else, were much less."

Palmer pitched two scoreless innings in Game 3 at Veterans Stadium, and when the Orioles took the lead in the top of the seventh—on a two-out error by Phillies shortstop Ivan DeJesus—he was the pitcher of record. Among the nine hitters Palmer faced were others bound for Cooperstown: Joe Morgan, Mike Schmidt, Tony Perez, and pitcher Steve Carlton. He retired them all.

———

Mike Schmidt went 1-for-20 in that World Series, even though he might have been the most dangerous hitter in the sport. He had belted 370 homers in the last 10 years—81 more than anyone else—and had just led the league in home runs, walks, and on-base percentage. In his last World Series, against the Royals in 1980, Schmidt had even choreographed the victory celebration.

Schmidt lived near closer Tug McGraw in suburban Media, Pennsylvania, and picked him up before Game 6, stopping for ice cream cones on the way to the Vet. He told McGraw to look for him after the final out so he could be the first to leap onto the pile.

"And sure enough, he struck out Willie Wilson and turned with his arms open toward me and said, 'Come on!'" Schmidt says. "He actually remembered our conversation, right at the end of a World Series game! And I went sprinting in there and jumped up on Tug with my arms out. That is a very popular photo."

While it didn't make the cover of *Sports Illustrated*, as he'd hoped, it became the most celebrated image in the history of Philly sports: Schmidt leaping high, smiling wide, McGraw's arm wrapped around his leg, teammates converging, fans convulsing, the scoreboard beaming a new identity for a star-crossed franchise—WORLD CHAMPIONS. Schmidt ordered a copy, enlarged to 3 by 5 feet, and hung it at his home and then at his restaurant.

Schmidt had entered that World Series with a .191 career average and no homers in four trips to the NLCS. He'd gone 0 for 5 in the finale of the breathless 1980 NLCS against Houston, when the Phillies overcame a three-run deficit to Nolan Ryan in the eighth inning at the rollicking Astrodome. The most important at-bat of his career, he likes to say, wasn't even his—it was a game-tying single by teammate Del Unser, just after Schmidt had struck out.

Without Unser's hit, the Phillies would have probably lost. Schmidt would have taken the blame, reinforcing the notion that he couldn't come through in the clutch. But with it—and the rallies that followed—the Phillies had finally broken through to their first World Series in 30 years. When Schmidt boarded the team bus after the clubhouse celebration, his teammates applauded. Unburdened and relaxed, he hit safely in all six games, homering twice and showing the kind of situational savvy that only a mentally disciplined slugger could have.

In the eighth inning of Game 3, with two outs, a tie score, and the speedy Lonnie Smith on third, Schmidt noticed the Royals' George Brett playing far behind the third base bag. He bunted toward Brett, a high-percentage play: if it stayed fair, Schmidt would be safe at first and Smith would score easily. But the ball trickled foul. The Phillies lost that night and again the next day, when Schmidt bunted for his only hit.

The payoff for those bunts came in Game 5. The Royals held a one-run lead in the ninth, three outs from taking a three-games-to-two series edge. Schmidt led off against Dan Quisenberry, but this time he had no plans to bunt. If the Phillies had trailed by two, he might have done it. But down by one with the bases empty, a homer could have tied the game, and Schmidt did that better than anyone. Yet because of those earlier bunts—once off Quisenberry, the other time leading off an inning—the Royals had to prepare for it.

"When I came up, [manager] Jim Frey came out of the dugout and was screaming at George Brett: 'Move up, move up, he might bunt,'" Schmidt explains. "So I hit a ground ball to Brett's left, which was just out of the reach of his glove. He would have made the play easily had he been playing back."

Instead Schmidt was safe on a single, starting a two-run, game-winning rally. Back at the Vet for Game 6, he had the biggest hit of his career: a humble line-drive single to right that scored two and put the Phillies ahead for good on the night they clinched the World Series.

Schmidt was known for an icy kind of intensity; it wasn't his style to pat his glove over his heart like McGraw or carom around the field like Larry Bowa, the Phillies' wayward Super Ball of a shortstop. He admired the cocksure strut of Jackson, his AL counterpart, but that wasn't Schmidt and he couldn't fake it. Still, after the Game 6 single, Schmidt knew he was going to be a champion. After rounding first base and watching the runs score, Schmidt punched the sky. He hit .381 for the series and was named MVP.

Three years later, Schmidt had every reason to be just as sure of himself. In August, when the Phillies celebrated their centennial, the fans had voted him the greatest player in franchise history. He was teammates with pillars of the Big Red Machine—Morgan, Perez, and Pete Rose—and he'd just hit .467 in the NLCS to vanquish the Dodgers, a team that had owned the Phillies in the regular season. The Orioles seemed less imposing.

Yet fear of failure stalked Schmidt. In his 2006 memoir, *Clearing the Bases,* he calls himself an "insecure psycho," merciless in his self-evaluation, unable to relish the big moments the way Rose and others did. "I was simply too afraid to fail," he wrote, "and that affected my ability to succeed under pressure." His performance in the 1983 World Series was the most painful manifestation of this fear, so dreary that even his hit was feeble: a broken-bat, bloop single off Storm Davis in Game 4.

"You do your best to make swing changes—make thought changes—as you go, and if you don't, the environment is so electric that sometimes you give in to the environment," Schmidt explains. "You're overanxious, you read headlines, you're 0 for 15, whatever the heck it was. You start to feel like: 'This is bad, the whole world knows how bad I am!' As opposed to: 'Who cares?'"

The series had opened well enough for Schmidt, with a line out and a deep fly out to the center field warning track in a 2–1 win. "Maybe another couple of feet, and the whole series might have changed, especially for me," Schmidt says, but from then on, nothing went right. He bunted—foul—with two outs in the ninth inning of Game 2, then struck out to end it. After driving balls the other way throughout the 1980 Series, he used the opposite field only twice in 1983, both for weak pop outs. He drew no walks and struck out or pulled harmless grounders in most of his at-bats. Eddie Murray was nearly as helpless for the Orioles, until the Game 5 clincher. Murray hit two home runs, while Schmidt went 0-for-4, the crowd booing after each empty at-bat. He never played again in the postseason.

How could Mike Schmidt—former World Series MVP, highest-paid player in the sport, best third baseman of all time—suffer a crisis of confidence? Rationally, he knew how good he was. How could he let himself fail repeatedly off a soft-tossing Scott McGregor, an ancient Jim Palmer, and a rumpled middle reliever named Sammy Stewart?

"I'm the guy that's supposed to lead the team—and you can't be," Schmidt says. "If you're Kareem Abdul-Jabbar, you can. That's a different kind of sport; one guy can take over the game. Baseball doesn't work that way. To take over a game in baseball, it's not going to happen. You can be a major, major part of the game, but that can only come if you allow yourself to get in mechanical position as a hitter to accept a walk, to advance a base runner, to steal a base, to make a great play defensively. That's kind of what happens, and then—boom!—all of a sudden a double in the gap comes, or a home run to the opposite field, you wrap a ball down the right field line and it hits the foul pole or something.

"That kind of thing had no chance of coming to me in the '83 World Series with my problems mechanically—based upon the environment, not allowing the game to come to me. I was trying to force the game. And for some reason, in '80, the opposite happened. I allowed the game to come to me. I hit balls to the opposite field; line drives were out of the reach of the outfielders. They were hard-hit balls, and because my mechanics were right, I could hit those balls. I didn't roll over and hit ground balls to the shortstop. I was as confident as I could have ever been."

Same man, same stage of his career. Different states of mind, vastly different outcomes.

———

I asked Schmidt if he thought certain players could be inherently clutch. He didn't answer directly but mentioned two names, Barry Bonds and Derek Jeter, to illustrate a point. Bonds played in seven postseasons, and in six of them he batted .198. Yet in 2002 he was nearly unstoppable, hitting .356 with a ridiculous .581 on-base and .978 slugging percentage.

Jeter was a completely different kind of hitter, Schmidt explained, a guy who would spray his hits to all fields. "He always played well in the postseasons, didn't he?" Schmidt asked, and I replied that, well, he did have 200 postseason hits. "Two hundred hits!" Schmidt howled. "Holy shit!" Schmidt doesn't curse much, but that was an astonishing number, even considering all the extra playoff rounds in Jeter's era.

The truth is that Jeter didn't always play well in the postseason; in 16 games when the Yankees faced elimination, he batted .262. But his postseason career is instructive because he played the equivalent of a full season—158 games—and played almost precisely to his career norms.*

Jeter in the regular season (average/on-base/slugging):
      .310/.377/.440

Jeter in the postseason: .308/.374/.465

Essentially, in an extra year consisting only of postseason games, Jeter was the exact same player as always. This is a feat, to be sure, because the quality of competition is better in October. But basically, given enough of a sample size, Jeter performed in that month just as he did in the others.

Rising to the occasion, you might say, is like the illusion of the rising fastball: it doesn't really rise, but it holds its plane longer than most fastballs. To Jeter, maintaining the same approach at all times was critical to October success. As he explained to me in 2020, when he was chief executive of the Marlins: "The approach that I've talked to our players about—since day one, the first spring training in 2018— was, 'Listen: every single pitch, every at-bat, every inning, every single

---

* Jeter's performance was comparable, in this regard, to that of Andy Pettitte. In 44 postseason starts for the Yankees and Astros, Pettitte had a .633 winning percentage and a 3.81 earned run average. In the regular season: .626 winning percentage, 3.85 ERA.

game counts, and if you take that approach, there's no added pressure. You get to the postseason, it's the same game that you played in spring training.'"

Rose was the same way, as future World Series star Jim Leyritz learned as a boy. Leyritz tagged along to spring training with his buddy Thom Brennaman, whose father, Marty, was the Reds' lead broadcaster. Rose would stay late for extra swings in the batting cage, and Leyritz helped pick up the balls.

"The other guys would be gone, and I would ask him, 'Why are you doing this?'" Leyritz says. "He said he took every at-bat from the first one in spring training to the last one of the year as if it's his last. And as I got older, I understood what that meant: that way, you don't feel like any at-bat is pressure, because they're all the same. So when you come up with the game on the line in the World Series, it should be no different."

It should be no different, maybe, but it is. After all, at Baseball -Reference.com, every player's career record comes with a separate postseason ledger beneath. When Curt Schilling met Johnny Podres, in 1992, he was pitching for his fourth organization, just another big right-hander with a good arm and not much to show for it. As a student of baseball history, Schilling knew that Podres had won Game 7 of the 1955 World Series to give the Brooklyn Dodgers their only championship. He represented greatness, and that got Schilling's attention.

"He talked about everything good that's gonna happen when you're in the postseason, so I never looked at it as a terrifying, potential failure," Schilling says. "And I realized, years later, that's exactly what the postseason was for some guys I played with: a chance to ruin everything they did during the regular season. Johnny told me, and I always said it, 'One game in the postseason can make you famous for the rest of your life.' When you say Reggie Jackson, what do you think? Three home runs in a World Series game. When you say Johnny Podres? Game 7 shutout. And so I looked at every start as an opportunity to be remembered forever."

Schilling struck out the first five batters he faced in the postseason, for the Phillies in the 1993 NLCS. Facing elimination in the World Series, he shut out a Blue Jays team that had scored 15 runs the night before. Eight years later he returned to the World Series with the Diamondbacks, facing a Yankees team with three consecutive titles. Schilling dismissed their edge.

"Mystique and aura, those are dancers in a nightclub," he sneered before the series. Then he started three times in seven games (26 strikeouts, 2 walks, 1.69 ERA) and shared MVP honors with Randy Johnson.

In 2004, Schilling was just the kind of player the Red Sox needed to silence October anxieties old and new. Their championship drought had reached 86 years after a crushing seven-game ALCS to the Yankees in 2003. But with Schilling and his stitched-up ankle, the 2004 Red Sox pulled an unprecedented comeback in the ALCS—winning four in a row against the Yankees after losing three—and then swept a loaded Cardinals team in the World Series. They had an uncommon mix of talent and bravado.

"Something takes over a team, and they see that stage as an opportunity rather than a risk," says Theo Epstein, the former Boston general manager. "That swagger, that fulfillment of a destiny—that shit's real. In '04, once we beat the Yankees, it felt like we couldn't be stopped. We had our advance meeting on the Cardinals, and we could not have handpicked a better opponent. They won 105 games, they were incredible—but they were pretty beat-up, too, a couple of their starters were out, a couple of their key lefty relievers. So when we went through our meeting, I left there so confident; I remember walking down the hall feeling, 'Oh my God, we're gonna win the World Series, we match up so well.' All their starters were righties who threw 90–91—Woody Williams, Jason Marquis, Jeff Suppan, we mauled guys like that. I bumped into [owner] John Henry as we were leaving the advance meeting, and he said, 'What do you think, how is this gonna go?' I was like, 'We got this, we're gonna crush this team.'"

In late 2011, Epstein moved on to Chicago, where the moribund Cubs had not won since 1908. For the cornerstone of his rebuild, Epstein traded for Anthony Rizzo, a talented hitter who also appealed as a leader; as an 18-year-old farmhand for Epstein's Red Sox, he had overcome Hodgkin's lymphoma.

Rizzo was fearless—by age 31, he was already the majors' active leader in hit-by-pitch—and he'd proven his toughness as a young player by challenging the entire Reds dugout to a fight after too many high-and-tight pitches. He was a proud guy, but not too proud to admit weakness or poke fun at himself. Physically drained and struggling during the 2016 NLCS, he switched to a teammate's lighter bat and came alive. And with the Cubs facing elimination before Game 5 of the World Series, Rizzo stripped naked in the clubhouse, hopped onto a couch, and exhorted the team with *Rocky* quotes, the theme song thumping in the background.

"It's just nervous energy—which is good, which is fun," Rizzo says. "That's what you want: that nervous, optimistic feeling. If you don't have that, you just quit, and that says more about you than the other side.

"The year before that, we were down 3–0 to the Mets [in the NLCS] and we ended up getting swept. So the next year when we were down 3–1, it just kind of flipped. It was like: 'No, we're not doing this, we're good, we've won three games in a row before. We're gonna take care of business and go to Cleveland.' It was just a different mentality."

The Cubs stayed loose after winning Game 5. The travel day fell on Halloween, so manager Joe Maddon let the players stay home to trick-or-treat with their families before flying to Cleveland. They rolled through Game 6 before their Game 7 thriller, and in the three elimination games, Rizzo hit .455. A year later, though, the Cubs again played three more postseason elimination games—and that time, Rizzo went 0 for 12.

We see such examples over and over. The ornery, wizardly Ty Cobb of the Tigers flopped in his first World Series, against the Cubs in 1907, finishing 4-for-20 without a stolen base. Yet the next fall, against the same opponent, Cobb batted .368.

So was he clutch or not? His career average was .366; his career average with runners in scoring position was .367. Over time, he was the same guy, whatever the situation. In a short sample, though, nearly anyone talented enough to play in the major leagues can get hot. Do it at the right time, especially early in your career, and you'll always be known as a money player.

————

Take David Freese. In October 2011, for his hometown Cardinals, Freese won MVP awards in the NLCS and the World Series. His hits in Game 6 against Texas—a down-to-the-last-strike triple and game-ending homer—are part of baseball lore. Years later, I asked Freese to recall those at-bats. How did he stay composed in the bottom of the ninth inning of Game 6 against the hard-throwing Neftali Feliz, one precious strike from winter? All he considered, he said, was his plan.

"My mind was on: 'I've never faced Feliz before, holy shit, how are we going to go about this?'" Freese said. "Not necessarily: 'What happens if I get out?' I think he started off with maybe something off-speed, but on 3–1, he went 98 or 99 low and away, and he spun me. I waved right through it.

"My thought process was still, 'Out, over, hard, stay back if he hangs a slider.' I just remember: 'Don't be late on his heater.' He threw it in the exact same spot, and that probably helped a little."

The winning home run, off Mark Lowe, was almost lucky by comparison.

"The homer was cool because [umpire] Gary Cederstrom was back there, and the 3–1 pitch was up and he called it a strike," Freese said. "I was furious, because I was leading off the inning and you just want to get on base. That call kept me in the box, and I hit the next one out."

I included all those details in a story about Freese before the 2018 World Series, when he played for the Dodgers. His performance in another World Series—in 2013, when he drove in no runs and hit .158 against Boston—got one line. What can I say? Clutch makes for great copy.

"Tell me clutch before it happens; that would be great," says Orioles executive Sig Mejdal, a longtime data analyst who worked for the Cardinals when they traded for Freese. "If it's a skill, it remains with you from year to year, and there's been so many studies that if clutch is a thing, it's so small it's beyond human observation. You didn't observe that there are clutch hitters, you felt that there were."

Freese had been a good hitter in 2011 (in 97 games, he'd slashed .297/.350/.441), but the Cardinals did not expect what they got that October.

"I wasn't thinking, 'OK, good, we're in the playoffs and we have David Freese, who somehow has the ability to hit like Babe Ruth;

he's not doing it in the regular season because he can't be bothered, but once the playoffs come he's going to have this amazing capability,'" Mejdal says. "I spent so much of my childhood playing table baseball games, and you'd have these guys where you think, 'Oh my God, another home run in extra innings, look what he's done!' But it would be absurd for me to think that this card or this disk is clutch. Yet when a human being does it, it's impossible not to attribute it to some internal capability that he has. We never say it was fortune or luck. We say he dug deep, he's a gamer, he's a winner, he's clutch. But then fast-forward to the next World Series, he's not better than a guy we would label a choker. If it's there, it's much smaller than the human brain thinks it is.

"And think of the magnitude of the skill that must change in order for you to have samples to notice the difference. The difference between the average hitter and the best hitter is something small, like one hit a week; you need a large sample. So these guys did not turn from an average hitter to a hitter that's better than Babe Ruth because the game means more or the month on the calendar has changed.

"What if we say clutch is just being good and being lucky at a time when we're paying attention?"

For the record, Freese excelled in that 2018 World Series, going 5 for 12 with a home run off David Price's first pitch in Game 5. It was Price's third appearance in five days, after a win in Game 2 and a relief outing in the ninth inning of Game 3. He had gone a decade between World Series appearances—in 2008, just a year out of Vanderbilt, Price had closed out the Rays' only win against the Phillies—but in both cases, the physical toll of a long season melted away.

"At that point, you don't feel anything," Price says. "I've never had a shot of adrenaline, but I'm sure that's what it feels like. It feels like opening day all over again."

After Freese's home run, Price shut out the Dodgers through seven innings and pitched Boston to the championship. He won the Babe Ruth Award as most valuable player of the postseason—not bad for a guy who had been reviled for his ghastly career postseason record: 2–9 with a 5.42 ERA before his pennant-clinching win, also on short rest, over Houston in the ALCS.

"I was the same guy, but I had good things happen," Price says. "I had the same mentality; I did everything the same leading up to the game. I'd failed so many times in October, but I knew I was gonna be successful at some point. It happened for me and I just ran with it. Whenever you have good things happen for you and you can do it a couple times in a row and get that feeling on the mound, you expect good things to happen, and that's huge."

Price was only the latest Red Sox pitcher to reverse a reputation in the World Series. Koji Uehara was nearly unhittable in October 2013, with a win and three saves in the ALCS and five flawless outings in the World Series. Yet just two years earlier, with Texas, Uehara had looked so shaky in the first two rounds that the Rangers dropped him from the roster for the World Series.

That's right—the same team that couldn't quite get that final strike had actually cut a reliever who would soon be untouchable in the World Series.

"It's such a great lesson about how people perceive and evaluate makeup," says Jon Daniels, the Rangers' president of baseball operations, who had traded for Uehara in the summer of 2011. "Because he really did struggle. In Detroit especially, for the ALCS, he really couldn't get through an inning. I remember one game, our players were kind of consoling him on the mound, like, 'We're still in this game.'

"So people draw conclusions off that and say, 'Well, he can't handle this or that.' And then literally 24 months later he's unhittable—he's pitching huge innings, he's the best reliever in the game for that stretch, and they win the ring. It's just so dangerous to put labels on people. You constantly make mistakes that way."

When the Yankees' Jeff Weaver allowed a homer to the Marlins' Alex Gonzalez that ended Game 4 of the 2003 World Series, he also ended his time in New York. The Yankees had traded for Weaver the summer before, and he happened to arrive on Old-Timers' Day. "My new ace!" George Steinbrenner proclaimed as he introduced Weaver to the team's legends. But that's not how it turned out.

Weaver shuffled between the rotation and the bullpen for a year and a half, and his 5.85 ERA is still the highest in Yankees history for pitchers with at least 200 innings. He hadn't pitched in four weeks before his World Series appearance, which actually began with a 1-2-3 eleventh inning. But Gonzalez lined a full-count fastball just over the wall in the left field corner, and that was it for Weaver.

"As soon as that home run was hit off him, I basically said: 'We can't retrieve this anymore, as far as staying with the Yankees, because that's all people were gonna talk about,'" says Joe Torre, who bypassed Mariano Rivera, the greatest reliever in postseason history, in a tie game on the road. "It's a shame because he had ability and he was still young, he was durable. There were a lot of things in his favor, but that home run pretty much emptied the cup."

The Yankees soon traded Weaver, and also gave up quickly on Jose Contreras, who had lost Game 5 in Miami. The Yankees had won a furious bidding war with the Red Sox to sign Contreras, a Cuban defector, for $32 million. But Contreras could not seem to handle the big moments—the Red Sox routinely pummeled him—and so the Yankees dealt him to the White Sox in July 2004.

Weaver and Contreras were both considered soft, unable to cope with the stress of Yankee life. But look what happened next. In 2005, Contreras started and won the World Series opener for the White Sox. In 2006, Weaver started and won the World Series clincher for the Cardinals.

"It's all the belief in yourself, knowing that you're going to work through it," Weaver said that night. "I've had struggles before and found it again. When you come to a team that believes in you from the get-go, it just builds your confidence."

Simply reaching the majors tends to require extraordinary self-confidence. No other sport tests you so often and demands you accept so much failure. To weather the crucible of life in the big leagues, it is reasonable to expect that anyone, at some point, could achieve some level of success under World Series pressure.

"For players, the act of playing is natural, so they're probably more comfortable being in that situation versus anticipating being in it, because what kicks in is the normal, 'I've done this a million times before' type of thing," says Bob Tewksbury, who pitched 13 years in the majors and has served as a mental-skills coach for the Red Sox, Giants, and Cubs.

"That said, you can look at performances like Carl Edwards

[pitching for the Cubs] in the 2016 World Series: two outs in the tenth and he couldn't get out of the inning. When you looked at that, you could kind of see his body language and his demeanor change; he got a little more tense. But that's a young pitcher who'd never been in that situation before, and it's the Cubs in the World Series. If you start to let the magnitude of the situation in, mentally, that's when this thing really starts to snowball."

Edwards, a rookie with two career saves, allowed a walk and a run-scoring single to the Indians with two outs and the bases empty. Mike Montgomery, with about the same experience as Edwards, replaced him for the final out, flipping two tight curveballs for his first career save. It just happened to come in Game 7 of the World Series.

"I wasn't thinking about the World Series, really," Montgomery says. "I was just thinking about being able to throw a strike in that moment. That's all I cared about."

Thinking about the circumstances can be a setup for failure. In 2021, the Astros' Framber Valdez was coming off the best playoff start of any pitcher that fall, an eight-inning gem at Fenway Park, when Dusty Baker picked him to start Game 1 against Atlanta. Yet Valdez got rocked by the Braves and acknowledged his emotions afterward.

"It was my first World Series game, so I'm not going to tell you that I didn't feel the pressure, I didn't feel any kind of tension," he said through an interpreter, adding that his adrenaline rush hurt his command. "It was maybe trying to do a bit too much, throwing a bit too hard. I was in the zone but not exactly where I wanted to be."

Duane Ward, who pitched in all eight of the Blue Jays' World Series wins in the 1990s, says it helped him to remember a fundamental rule of the sport: the odds always tilt toward the pitcher.

"You could probably go out there and tell a hitter every pitch that's coming, like you do in spring training, and you'd be surprised how often guys pop up, ground out, or swing and miss," Ward says. "It's still one of the hardest things to do: hit a round ball with a round bat square."

Ward was also used to doing it; that's what Rollie Fingers told himself, too. Fingers, the Hall of Fame closer, says he was more nervous onstage in Cooperstown than he ever was in getting there, because he is not a trained public speaker. (He forgot to thank Gene Tenace, who caught him more than anyone else, in his speech.) As a pitcher, Fingers knew what he was doing.

"I loved getting out of jams," says Fingers, who converted all six of his save chances for Oakland in the World Series. "Relief pitchers are a little crazy in the first place. You've gotta be crazy to want to come into a ballgame with the bases loaded and nobody out. I did it for 17 years, so I'm certifiable. But it just got to the point where I got used to it and I didn't mind it. I figured there's more pressure on the hitter when they're batting against me, because I was successful. You know that feeling in your gut. You feel like you've got one strike against that hitter when you first walk out there. That's a big deal. I'd been in every situation you could possibly imagine and gotten out of it. So if you get out of it once, you know you can get out of it again."

Lance Berkman had a similar thought. Berkman went 2-for-12 in his first postseason, with the Astros in 2001. In the decade to follow, he played in two World Series and hit .410 for Houston and St. Louis. He compared the feeling to the shock of seeing a rattlesnake on your kitchen floor. The first time you see it, you'd be very nervous. If you knew it would be there and saw it every day, you'd still be alert but you'd know how to handle it.

Berkman, an aw-shucks kind of guy, handled it by assuming another persona: "When I played in the World Series, this sounds kind of cheesy but I would view myself as a cold-blooded assassin—emotion has no impact on me one way or the other," he says. "That helped me really stay focused and not let those situations get out of control."

Some players do that without knowing how. In Game 6 of the 1991 World Series—the game that ended with a Kirby Puckett home run—the Twins called for Carl Willis in the seventh inning with the bases loaded, one out, and a one-run lead. The Metrodome was so loud that a coach, Rick Stelmaszek, couldn't hear the bullpen phone; he had to rest his foot on it to feel the vibrations when it rang.

Willis had been cut from the Twins' 40-man roster at the end of spring training. He'd started the season with the Portland Beavers, his seventh stop in Triple-A, after Evansville, Denver, Nashville, Vancouver, Edmonton, and Colorado Springs. Now he was here, with the Braves sensing a title, trying to save the Twins' season—and doing it. The Braves managed one harmless single off Willis in two and two-thirds innings, tying the game on a force out but never scoring again, in the game or in 1991.

It was the finest night of a workmanlike career for Willis, a future pitching coach who was so zoned in that he remembers almost nothing about it.

"It's what you dream about when you're a kid—and even once you get to the major leagues, the odds are against you to play in a World Series—but the strange thing about that night, the frustration for me, is that I don't even know what it felt like when I came off the field," he says. "I've watched videos of the game and people say, 'What were you thinking?' and I have no idea. I can tell you things I was thinking in other games, but that one, you're so locked in, focus-wise, that you really don't enjoy the moment until you're a ways beyond it."

―――――

Indeed, for many players, appreciation only comes with time. In 1924, at age 18, Senators third baseman Freddie Lindstrom became the youngest player in World Series history. He played every inning and batted .333.

"Was I nervous? No, honestly I wasn't," he told author Donald Honig in *The October Heroes.* "I was so young I think I was unconscious of the seriousness of the whole thing. Sometimes a person's innocence can work to his advantage. I was simply unawed by the glamour and unaware of the excitement and unaffected by the tensions that were building up. I was much more excited and emotionally wrought up in the '35 Series when I was with the Cubs, because by that time I was much more familiar with all the trappings and all the seriousness."

Sometimes it helps to lift yourself from that cauldron, if only for a moment, to consider the wider world. Ron Darling felt terrible in the bullpen before Game 4 of the 1986 World Series at Fenway Park, where he'd grown up watching the Red Sox. Rattled and filled with doubts, he'd blocked out the fact that his father would be on the field, representing the Air Force Reserve for the color guard during the national anthem. Ron Sr. spotted his son and called out to him—just a simple "hey" that settled Darling's nerves. Standing there with his father, he thought of their journey together, of Ron Sr.'s endless encouragement.

His mentality transformed, Darling hung tough through an early jam and fired seven shutout innings.

At another Game 4 involving the Red Sox, in 2013 in St. Louis, Boston's Jonny Gomes also got a jolt of reality at just the right time. That was the game best remembered for David Ortiz's fiery dugout speech before the top of the sixth inning, which helped snap the Red Sox into focus. But another thing happened before that inning that meant even more: Major League Baseball's annual "Stand Up To Cancer" ceremony, when everyone in the ballpark is asked to stand and hold signs for cancer victims. Gomes held two: one for his late high school coach, Bob Leslie, and another for Brady Wein, a toddler he had met by chance the year before. Gomes had grown close to the family, bringing the boy to Fenway throughout the 2013 season to hang with the team. Thinking of Brady's struggle, in particular, gave the excitable Gomes an emotional grounding.

"It totally calmed me down," he says. "Every single person's holding up a sign, I'm holding up a sign, and it was like, I'm trying to hit a baseball here in about four minutes. It just brought me back to reality—relax, stick with the basics; you did your homework, now turn it in."

With two out and two on, the Cardinals called for a reliever, Seth Maness, who threw the kinds of sinkers that Gomes often struggled to handle. Gomes moved away from the on-deck circle during the pitching change—"So even if he whistled for me, I could pretend I didn't hear him," he said, referring to manager John Farrell—and studied Maness. He reminded him of Luke Gregerson, a pitcher who had served up a walk-off homer to Gomes in July. With a clear mind and a sound plan, Gomes connected for a three-run bomb. The Red Sox never trailed again, in the game or the series, and won it in six.

Gomes was known for outward intensity; Anthony Rendon, now with the Angels, projects an almost casual nonchalance. Yet his ability to stay cool—to have a slow heartbeat, in the sports vernacular—was exactly what the Nationals needed in October 2019. After his homer off Houston's Zack Greinke in Game 7 of the World Series, this is what Rendon had done across seven postseason plate appearances in the seventh inning or later while facing elimination: walk, double, homer, double, homer, double, homer.

It was a riveting run of clutch play, yet general manager Mike Rizzo said Rendon looked the same as he did in spring training—carefree, just doing his thing. I tracked down Rendon in the dugout after the trophy presentation and a round of network interviews. Just one question, I said: How could he be so composed when it mattered most?

Rendon rarely gives insights beyond the banal. But this—after the most important game of his life, a performance that would help him earn a $245 million contract within a few weeks—struck me as meaningful:

"I feel like there's bigger things going on in this world," Rendon said quietly. "A baseball game might get magnified because it's the World Series, but we're not taking bullets for our country in Afghanistan or wherever it might be. This should be a breeze."

That attitude hardly ensures success under pressure. In an earlier stretch of 13 playoff games over several seasons, Rendon had hit just .128. But it cannot hurt to have such a foundation, as Buster Posey also showed in helping lead the Giants to three championships before his twenty-eighth birthday.

"I think you have to imagine yourself being in those situations from a young age; that would be number one," Posey says. "Number two, you need to relish those moments, because who knows? You're not ever promised another day. And then, number three, you've got to keep perspective. I'm very fortunate to come from a family that will love me whether I'm successful in baseball or not, and I think that's given me a sense of freedom that even if I fail, the people that really care about me are still going to be there."

———

When he switched from starting to closing, Dennis Eckersley accepted fear as an occupational hazard. He used the stark responsibilities of the job—if I fail, we lose—to sharpen his focus.

"It felt like life or death, because it's so devastating when you don't do well: it's over, no chance to come back," Eckersley says. "And that motivation just plays to the adrenaline—in a good way, for me, because I had been around the block. It's not like I was young. It could have been overwhelming if you're just a kid, but I could handle it. It made me better, because you had to execute."

The Cardinals' Adam Wainwright was a rookie in 2006, when he capped his first full season in the majors by saving the clinchers of the NLCS and the World Series. Rewatching those games, he says, he is much more nervous than he was in real time.

"When I'm pitching, I'm in my element and it doesn't even factor into the equation," Wainwright says. "I never allow myself to think about failure. Some people are driven by that. Dennis Eckersley told me he was so great because he was afraid to fail. I'm the opposite. I don't ever think of failure."

Another Cardinals icon, Bob Gibson, talked about fear in *Sixty Feet, Six Inches,* his conversational book with Reggie Jackson. Gibson mentions a spare outfielder who sat and stared blankly into his locker after seeing the lineup for Game 5 of the 1968 World Series. The player had the chance of a lifetime, Gibson said, but he was scared. It angered Gibson.[*]

"I was nervous, too, in situations like that, but never scared," he said. "Hell no. And as soon as the game started, the nervousness left me. I might have played with more adrenaline than usual, but that's different than being nervous. A lot different."

Yet what do we make of this, from a center fielder describing his emotions in the ninth inning of his first Game 7? He wrote in his book that he could hear his heart beating, even over the roaring fans: "For the first and last time in my career, I was pleading that the ball not be hit to me. I was terrified I'd make a critical mistake."

The player? A Hall of Famer, Kirby Puckett, famous for thriving in the clutch. The first batter of the inning hit a fly ball to Puckett, who told himself, "Don't miss it, don't miss it!" Then he clutched the ball with both hands for the out.

Or how about this from Heinie Groh, who played in five World Series for the Reds, Giants, and Pirates from 1919 to 1927: "Do you know that I was scared to death every time I went into a World Series?"

---

[*] Likely Ron Davis, who batted .177 for the Cardinals that season and went 0-for-7 in two World Series starts.

he told Lawrence S. Ritter in *The Glory of Their Times*. "Every single one, after I'd been in so many. It's a terrific strain."

As soon as he made his first play in the field, Groh said, he was able to relax. He did well enough, helping his teams to two championships and hitting .474 for the Giants in 1922. From then on, he said, he put "474" on his license plate.

Harvey Dorfman, the influential sports psychologist, wrote that "fear is a monstrous liar," tricking people into thinking they are fated to fail. If a bat boy were asked to rescue his team with the World Series on the line, his fear would be real—pitching is not his job. When that task fell to Jack Billingham, it was no big deal. He pitched for a living.

Facing elimination in Game 5 of the 1972 World Series, Reds manager Sparky Anderson called for Billingham with one on and one out in the ninth inning in Oakland. The Reds held a one-run lead, but a home run would lose the World Series. Billingham was a starter; he hadn't been called from the bullpen to protect a ninth-inning lead in more than three years.

"I was nervous, I was scared and everything else," he says. "But I also learned you've gotta throw strikes for something to happen, so— whatever. I threw my shit up there and whatever happened, happened."

Billingham understood who he was: a league-average pitcher, more or less, with a sinker, a curveball, and a great defense behind him. As Anderson paced in the Reds' dugout, Billingham calmly went to work. He gave up a single on a curveball but used the same pitch for a pop foul to Joe Morgan, an all-time great, who stumbled, recovered, and fired home for a game-ending double play.

The year before, in his first postseason start, the Pirates' Steve Blass had tried to be a different kind of pitcher, thinking he needed to blow hitters away. He got his share of strikeouts—11 in seven innings—but the Giants hit him hard in the NLCS. With a chance at redemption in his first World Series start, against the Orioles, Blass threw his sinkers and sliders for a complete-game victory.

His next scheduled start was for Game 7, in the afternoon. Blass woke up at 4 a.m. and paced the streets around the Lord Baltimore Hotel. Even after his Game 3 gem, he was equal parts anxious and eager—unsure if he could do it again, but in a hurry to find out.

"The worst part is that you think you're capable, but you don't know," Blass said. "You'll do anything to kill time because you want to get going and find out the answer: Hey, am I good enough to handle this? Am I good enough to get this done?"

Blass was plenty good enough: he subdued the Orioles again, clinching the title with another complete game. The baffling loss of control that would cruelly end Blass's career, in 1974, brought a different kind of pressure: a fight to save his livelihood, not to win a game. Perspective came with time.

"I'd be in my backyard, very near the end, tears coming down my eyes, thinking, 'I'm not going to be a Pittsburgh Pirate anymore,'" Blass says. "But the thing that helped me, and it's a cliché, was knowing that this was what I did, not who I was. I said, 'Yeah, I can't pitch anymore, but I'm not destroyed.' The family was great, the Pirates were great, the city of Pittsburgh was great to me. I went to an All-Star Game, pitched in a World Series, played on a field with Hall of Famers. In the big picture, I don't know why I agonized over it for years.

"People always say: 'What happened?' *I. Don't. Know.* I've thought of all these things, but I temper it with the fact that I lived all those dreams. I kept my sanity intact—although at times I didn't think I did—and when I look back now, if I'm strong enough to handle that, I can pretty much handle anything."

———

In the movie *Bull Durham,* the wise old catcher, Crash Davis, gives some valuable guidance to the hotheaded young pitcher, Nuke LaLoosh: "Don't think, it can only hurt the ball club." For a real-life version, there's this from Ray Knight, the 1986 World Series MVP, who told George Will: "Concentration is the ability to think about absolutely nothing when it is absolutely necessary."

A year before Knight's heroics, George Brett went 4-for-5 in the Royals' clinching victory over the Cardinals; he remains the last player with four hits in Game 7 of the World Series. He said he focused on breathing as a way to relax. He tried to hit the ball hard, not far.

"I've always believed that when the game's on the line, and you've got a good hitter and a good pitcher, whoever's heart beats the lowest is probably gonna win that battle," he says. "Try easier, not harder."

A certain kind of professional detachment helps in times of stress.

"The whole key to performing is to do it like you don't care," says Tewksbury, the mental-skills coach and former pitcher. "When you have that amateur with a three-foot putt with his buddies, he'll go, 'Screw it, I'm already 10 over par,' and he'll make it without even thinking. But if that was to win $100, he'd be thinking about it a little differently, because he'd be overthinking it."

Some of this stuff, admittedly, sounds like standard inspirational platitudes you'd find on tacky home decorations. Jeremy Affeldt, who pitched in 12 World Series games for the Rockies and Giants and allowed only one run, apologizes for sounding that way. But Affeldt grew up idolizing Dave Stewart, the Oakland ace, marveling at how he seemed "present with the energy" in the big moments—that is, how he used the heightened atmosphere to sharpen his competitiveness.

Early in his career, Affeldt said, he feared failing so much that he failed over and over. In time, though, he started using that fear to change his work habits, absorbing himself in preparation. Intellectually, Affeldt knew that every player fails—a lot. In his mind, though, he eliminated failure as an option.

Stewart was much the same way. Growing up in Oakland, he played ball in the yard with his brother, Greg, who was five years older. Keeping up was a constant challenge, he said, made more intense by the scenarios the boys would imagine: Willie Mays at the plate, bases loaded, bottom of the ninth. Big games in the majors felt the same, Stewart said, but he coughed up his first taste of the postseason with the 1981 Dodgers.

Working in relief in the opener of the division series, Stewart allowed a walk-off homer to Alan Ashby at the Astrodome. The next day, Stewart lost again. The Dodgers survived and won the World Series, but Stewart was bumped to mop-up relief.

"I put my team one game before elimination," Stewart says. "I told myself if I ever have the opportunity again, I would never, ever get beaten like that."

The opportunity came late in the decade in Oakland, where pitching coach Dave Duncan encouraged Stewart to revive the forkball he had learned from Sandy Koufax.* As the A's climbed back to respectability, in 1987, they used Stewart often against the other team's number one starter. He thrived in that role—career record in matchups with Roger Clemens: 9–0—and applied the same mentality in October.

"You practice the opportunity to pitch in big games," Stewart says. "And I did."

The A's used Stewart as their Game 1 starter for seven postseason series in a row. After those first two losses in 1981, he went 10–4 with a 2.58 ERA in the postseason, and opponents hit .200. Stewart won championships with three teams—the Dodgers, A's, and Blue Jays—and earned MVP honors for Oakland in the 1989 World Series, when he beat the Giants twice in a four-game sweep.

Often a pitcher wins two starts but still has more work to do. If his team wraps things up early, he might win MVP. But winning for a third time can be asking too much—the pitchers have already shown they can handle pressure, but after two starts, they've also shown hitters their arsenal. And often they are physically spent, leaving a bitter final impression.

This scenario has played out three times in the playoff era, with St. Louis's John Tudor in 1985, Boston's Bruce Hurst in 1986, and Cleveland's Corey Kluber in 2016. All three took the mound for Game 7 seeking their third victory of the World Series, but all three were drained. When a pitcher is tired, he may throw as hard as usual but lacks his pinpoint mechanics. That leads to mistakes out of the zone (walks) or in the zone (hits). Mental fortitude can't help if the body isn't willing.

In 2016, for the first time in his career, Kluber failed to record a strikeout. He and Andrew Miller, the Indians' best reliever, combined to give up three homers and six runs to the Cubs.

"They proved they're human," manager Terry Francona said later, a sentiment often applied in that era to Clayton Kershaw, whose very human October frailty threatened to swallow his legacy.

––––––––

* The Dodgers traded Stewart in 1983 to the Rangers, whose manager, Doug Rader, would not let him use the forkball.

Kershaw won 95 more games than he lost in the 2010s. He earned an MVP award, three Cy Youngs, and eight All-Star selections. Among pitchers with at least 200 starts from 2010 through 2019, Kershaw had by far the lowest ERA—2.31, a staggering 72 points better than the next-best figure, Chris Sale's 3.03. It is the widest gap between the top two ERAs for any decade.*

But while most pitchers in his class won a championship in the '10s (Sale, Justin Verlander, Max Scherzer, Madison Bumgarner, Jon Lester, David Price), Kershaw did not. Starting in 2013, he led the Dodgers to a division title each season, but something always went wrong in October. For the decade, Kershaw was 9–10 with a 4.28 ERA in the postseason, and the ending summed it up. Protecting a two-run lead against Washington in the decisive fifth game of a 2019 division series, Kershaw served up homers on consecutive pitches to Anthony Rendon and Juan Soto. He crouched on the mound and hung his head after Soto connected.

Later, encircled by reporters in the middle of the clubhouse, Kershaw brought up the past before anyone asked: "Everything people say is true right now about the postseason, I understand that," he said. "Nothing I can do about it right now. It's a terrible feeling."

In that moment, Kershaw seemed a portrait of a beaten man, glumly resigned to the inevitable. All of the other Dodger starters to win the Cy Young—Don Newcombe, Don Drysdale, Sandy Koufax, Fernando Valenzuela, Orel Hershiser—had also won a World Series. That validation eluded Kershaw and gnawed at those around him, especially after revelations of the Astros' 2017 cheating scandal.

Kershaw twice pitched brilliantly against the Astros in that World Series, as a starter in the opener and a reliever in Game 7. In between was a clunker: six runs across four and two-thirds innings in Game 5. The good games came at home and the bad one in Houston, where the Astros deployed a system of electronic sign stealing, decoding the catcher's signals off a monitor near the dugout and banging a trash can to tell hitters what was coming. Kershaw threw 51 sliders or curveballs that night, and not once did the Astros swing and miss.

---

* The next closest: a 50-point gap in the 1910s between Walter Johnson at 1.59 and Grover Cleveland Alexander at 2.09.

"They didn't swing and miss because they knew what was coming," Hershiser says. "He went from, I don't know, 30 swings and misses to zero. That's impossible."

The Astros were known to be skilled at sign stealing, though few knew the scope of it in 2017. One Dodgers pitcher, Alex Wood, changed signs constantly for his start in Houston, and pitched well. Kershaw did not vary his sequences, and paid for it. In early 2020, when the extent of the cheating had been revealed, Hershiser contemplated everything the Astros had taken from Kershaw and his teammates.

"I talk to the guys and say, 'Can you tell me what your conversations are like with fans?' And all of them, to a man, come back to: 'I'm still waiting for you guys to win one.' So they become sympathetic figures instead of champions: 'You're my favorite player—but. You guys are the best team, seven division titles in a row—but.' I mean, the Astros put a 'but' at the end of every conversation they have with fans, and that's ridiculous."

I called Hershiser again in late October, from the press box in Texas before Game 6 of the World Series. Kershaw had beaten the Rays in Games 1 and 5 to put the Dodgers on the verge of the title. His World Series ERA was 2.31, precisely his regular-season mark for the decade of the 2010s, as if to underscore that Kershaw, at last, was himself.

"I think baseball needs him to win," Hershiser said. "I don't think we need another Ernie Banks. The greatest players in the game should be part of a world championship—for baseball, and for the fans."

A few hours later Kershaw was a champion, romping joyously from the bullpen after the final out. He was watching from there out of instinct; ever a model teammate, Kershaw wanted to be available in relief, just in case. But this October was different in a fundamental way: for the first time in his 10 career trips to the postseason, Kershaw had not started on short rest or made a relief appearance. He was not asked to carry an extra burden. He was asked to be himself, and he was.

I wanted Kershaw to contextualize this afterward, to explain the meaning of the moment after all that came before. He had done this in defeat 12 months earlier, and this was his chance to revel in victory. I had asked a version of the question to Price in 2018, after he'd won the finale for the Red Sox—beating Kershaw, in fact—and he seemed to savor the opportunity. Price said he held the "trump card" now, and he delighted in waving it at those who had doubted him.

Kershaw had a different reaction. Criticism had never seemed to motivate him, nor had his place in history. There was no way to change the past, anyway, so why not live in the moment?

"I don't care about legacy, I don't care about what happened last year, I don't care about what people think, I don't care at all, man," he said. "We won the World Series. The 2020 Dodgers won the World Series. Who cares about all that other stuff?"

For Kershaw, it almost seemed meant to be. The neutral site for this pandemic World Series was Arlington, of all places—a suburb of his Dallas hometown. Attendance was limited to 11,500 or so, but Kershaw scored extra tickets for family and friends in the upper reaches of Globe Life Field. He thought of them after the final out, he went on to say. They'd supported him through all those empty Octobers and wanted this as badly as he did. He was thankful and overwhelmed on a sprint to the mound that took decades.

"It was a content feeling, just like: job is done, we won, we won our race, and it's over," Kershaw said. "We completed our mission."

————————

The Dodgers won 98 more games in the 2010s than the San Francisco Giants. But while the Dodgers always fell short in October, the Giants held three parades. It helped to have the greatest pitcher in World Series history on their side.

In his first World Series start, in 2010, Madison Bumgarner tossed eight shutout innings to beat the Rangers. In his second, in 2012, he spun seven shutout frames to beat the Tigers. In his third, Game 1 against the Royals in 2014, he actually gave up a run but won anyway. Then he threw a complete-game shutout in Game 5.

After the Royals won Game 6, a few of the writers asked Bumgarner what his pitch count might be if he needed to work in Game 7.

"Maybe 200, as long as you're getting outs," he told us. "I don't know; I feel like pitch counts are overrated."

It was such a badass reply—two days' rest, 200 pitches—that left no doubt about what would happen in Game 7: Bumgarner was going to pitch, and when he took the mound, he wasn't coming out. Sure enough, he saved it—with five shutout innings. That made Bumgarner 4–0 with a save over 36 World Series innings, with a record 0.25 ERA.

"I hope he gets traded to a contender and pitches about three innings in the World Series and gives up two runs," Jack Billingham says with a laugh; his 0.36 ERA for the 1970s Reds used to be the record. "I'd like to go back into first place, because they don't talk about me anymore. I'm a has-been!"

Sorry, Jack, but Bumgarner may have the record for a while. In 2020 he joined the Arizona Diamondbacks, an undermanned team that finished in last place. That spring, I sought him out in the D-backs' clubhouse for the secrets to his steely-eyed mastery of the World Series. We'd talked before about his epic confrontation with Salvador Perez for the last out in 2014, in Kansas City: two outs, bottom of the ninth, man on third, World Series–winning run at the plate, that rare and exquisite Game 7 scenario in which any pitch could win or lose the championship. Bumgarner had an average fastball but uncommon conviction in it, and he baited Perez with six in a row, up in the zone, until Perez fouled out to end it.

Bumgarner, at 25, was a three-time champion. In his 30s, with his San Francisco era behind him, he could reflect on his mind-set in the moments that define his career.

"Something is wired different in a lot of people," he says. "I'm not saying me, necessarily, but I don't know; it's just different. I remember feeling like that since I was a little kid. It didn't matter what I was doing, I just had this feeling of wanting to win—not like, 'I wish I win,' but finding a way to make it happen."

As a senior in high school, Bumgarner pitched the South Caldwell Spartans past the Ashley Screaming Eagles to clinch the North Carolina 4A championship at the minor league park in Zebulon. It was the Spartans' first title in a quarter century, and it avenged their loss in the finals the year before. Three years later, as he prepared for his World Series debut, Bumgarner said he doubted there could be any more pressure in that game than he had faced in Zebulon.

"I remember it got twisted around; people tried to say I thought it was the same, and that's not what I meant," Bumgarner said. "But to a high school kid, at that point in his life, that's just as big a game to him as the World Series is to a grown man."

As we talked, Bumgarner noticed a few teammates nearby, easily within earshot. Like many who play a humbling game for a living, Bumgarner is wary of sounding boastful or arrogant. He beckoned me to a quiet spot in the room.

"I didn't want to say this right there, because I don't want to sound cocky, but you asked me about pressure and I want you to know the real answer," he said. "Ever since I was a kid, when people would say there was pressure, I just didn't buy it. I am the pressure. That was the thought in my head."

I asked if he meant that nobody could put as much pressure on him as he puts on himself, a fairly common statement. I misunderstood.

"What I mean is, I am the pressure on you," he said. "I believed that then, and I still do. It's easier now to believe it, but I always did."

It sounded like that chilling line from *Breaking Bad,* when Walter White tells his wife that people fear him, not the other way around: "I am the danger." In the World Series, Madison Bumgarner is the one who knocks, the one who leaves hitters trembling. He transforms by transferring, shifting the pressure to become the absolute best version of himself when it matters most. I cannot imagine a more fitting embodiment of greatness.

Game 2

A Wiffle Ball Plunking

*The Sidebar Stories to the Greatest
Moments in World Series History*

Leave it to the wisest of American philosophers, Homer J. Simpson, to crystallize our process of information intake: "Every time I learn something new, it pushes some old stuff out of my brain."

Learning is like that, isn't it? As a student, you spend weeks carefully crafting a detailed term paper. You feel like an expert on the subject, intimately familiar with its nuances. Time passes, and you're lucky to remember a few basic facts.

It's the same way with sports. No matter how invested you get in a game or series, you tend to remember just a snapshot or two of what really happened. Since you're reading this, I suspect you're familiar with the most famous moments in World Series history: the Black Sox scandal in 1919; Bill Mazeroski's walk-off homer in 1960; Joe Carter's in 1993; and so on. But the sidebar stories, the ones you forgot or never knew, can be just as fascinating.

Take the seventh game in 1997, the Indians and Marlins in Miami. You may remember that Cleveland's Jose Mesa blew the save in the ninth inning and Florida's Edgar Renteria later won it with a single.* But most of that game was about Jaret Wright, the hard-throwing Cleveland rookie who carried a one-hit shutout into the seventh inning stretch.

How did the Marlins finally get to him? The answer traces to

---

* Renteria flinched at a first-pitch slider from Charles Nagy, expertly setting up another slider for the second pitch, which he lined to center field to win the game.

another Game 7, at Ebbets Field in 1952, and a different rookie right-hander, Joe Black of the Brooklyn Dodgers. With one out in the sixth inning of a 2–2 game, Mickey Mantle came to bat for the Yankees. Black had retired Mantle twice with inside fastballs, but here Mantle moved back from the plate, too subtle for Black or catcher Roy Campanella to notice. In better position for the inside pitch, Mantle homered to put the Yankees ahead for good.

Forty-five years later, Black attended Game 7 with his friend Leonard Coleman, the president of the National League. Bobby Bonilla was due to lead off the bottom of the seventh against Wright. Coleman picks up the story from there:

"We were sitting in the seats by the first base dugout, and the batter's circle was very close to the front row. Some players you'd talk to, some you left alone, but Bobby was talkative. The first couple of times, Wright had jammed him, and Joe and I were sitting there talking about it. Joe says, 'This guy thinks he's going to get him out just by jamming him all night.' So when Bobby was coming up for the third time, Joe called him over and said, 'Look, Bobby, he's gonna try and jam you with a high fastball in tight. Take a step back from the plate. He's not gonna pick up that you adjusted your stance.' I remember Bobby kind of put his hand on his chin and gave a quizzical look for a second and said, 'All right, Joe, I'm gonna try that.' And he backed up and boom! Next thing I knew the ball was in the right field bleachers. And then when Bobby crossed home plate, he stuck his finger right at Joe and said, 'Thank you.'"

Black actually guessed wrong about the pitch—Wright tried a high changeup that floated over the middle, not an inside fastball—but his suggestion put Bonilla in position to clobber it, finally getting the Marlins into the game. To me, that's an irresistible angle: faded a bit over time, but essential to the story we remember best.

In that spirit, here are nine sidebars to some of the most famous moments in World Series history.

What you know: The 1919 White Sox
conspired to throw the World Series.

———

What you might not know: The Reds
were the better team anyway.

For someone who spent his life twirling, not typing, Christy Mathewson sure knew how to write a baseball column. In 1919, three years after the end of his glorious pitching career, Mathewson analyzed the World Series for *The New York Times*. He was quite familiar with the Cincinnati Reds, having managed them for most of the past three seasons, and suspected that their opponents, the Chicago White Sox, were trying to lose the opening game. In describing a 9–1 laugher for Cincinnati, Mathewson ended his column this way: "The White Sox are supposed to be a great ballclub, but no team to my knowledge was ever defeated by so large a score in an opening game of the world's series *when each contender was trying its best.*" The emphasis is mine, but I'm sure Mathewson closed that way for a reason. He could not come right out and accuse the White Sox of treachery, yet with a deftly worded qualifier, he could bury them for those in the know.

Mathewson had left his job as Reds manager to serve the U.S. Army in France in World War I. A chemical warfare officer, he was exposed to poison gas and died of tuberculosis in 1925. He was only 45 then, with so much left to contribute to baseball. The Reds of 1919—still largely his team—showed that Mathewson might have had a strong second act as a builder and manager of winning clubs.

Of course, only one World Series winner is viewed with more skepticism than the 1919 Reds—the 2017 Houston Astros, who cheated by stealing signs electronically. Yet the Reds were the victims, not the perpetrators, of a scam. They won the championship, but the White Sox' actions robbed them of the legitimacy that should have come with it.

That's a shame, because a vital part of the story is largely forgotten: the Reds were better than the White Sox. The 1919 Reds had a .686 winning percentage, a franchise record for the World Series era, and at 96–44, they won eight more games than the White Sox. They allowed the fewest runs in the National League and scored the second most.

"I don't think we could have beaten Cincinnati anyway," said Grover Lowdermilk, a Chicago reliever, as quoted in his *Sporting News* obituary in 1968. "The Reds had a great ballclub."

The Reds' rotation was so deep that five pitchers made at least 18 starts, each with an ERA well below the league average of 2.91. They were the first team ever to use five different starters in the first five games of a World Series, while the White Sox were missing the great Red Faber, who had won three times in the 1917 Series. Faber was stricken by the flu, leaving Chicago with only Dickey Kerr, who was brilliant, and Eddie Cicotte and Lefty Williams, who took bribes to lose.

"Red Faber was ill during the Series," White Sox catcher Ray Schalk said, in his *Sporting News* obituary in 1970. "But if he'd been able to play, we'd have beaten the Reds despite the gamblers."

Maybe so, but with Chicago's staff depleted and Cincinnati's loaded, the Reds had a decisive edge. For that they could thank Mathewson and his successor, Pat Moran. Mathewson pitched his entire career with the Giants until his very last game, for Cincinnati on September 4, 1916. The Giants had traded him that July with two other future Hall of Famers: Bill McKechnie, who would win two titles as a manager, and Edd Roush, a young center fielder who had angered the Giants' imperial manager, John McGraw, for insisting on using a massive 48-ounce bat.

In Roush—whose potential McGraw had endorsed, despite their differences—Mathewson arrived with a defensive marvel who would win two of the next three NL batting crowns. He inherited a few other position players with staying power, including third baseman Heinie Groh and outfielder Greasy Neale, who went on to coach the Philadelphia Eagles to two NFL titles. But Mathewson remade the entire rotation, snagging Dutch Ruether off waivers from the Cubs and drafting Hod Eller and Jimmy Ring off minor league rosters. The trio won 48 games in 1919, plus four more in the World Series.

With Mathewson in France early that year, the Reds' owner, Garry Herrmann, hired Moran to succeed him. Moran had left the Phillies after four years and one pennant to coach McGraw's pitchers in New York. A former catcher, Moran had shown his keen eye for arms by recognizing the potential of the Phillies' Grover Cleveland Alexander, encouraging his sidearm delivery. With the Reds, he found Ray Fisher and Slim Sallee on waivers, and under his guidance, Sallee, Ruether, and Eller had the best seasons of their careers.

The Reds had another, more subtle, advantage over the White Sox: they actually liked each other. The White Sox were largely split into factions over education and salary lines. Yes, they had won in 1917, but infielders Eddie Collins and Chick Gandil hadn't spoken in years. Collins, the Columbia-educated captain, was part of a well-mannered group—with Schalk, Faber, Kerr, and manager Kid Gleason—seen as favorites of owner Charles Comiskey. Gandil led a group of renegades "who openly expressed dislike for management and felt underpaid and underappreciated," wrote Susan Dellinger, Roush's granddaughter, in *Red Legs and Black Sox,* an engrossing, meticulously researched account of the Reds and the series.

Gamblers preyed upon the White Sox players' resentment. The infamous "eight men out"—Gandil, Cicotte, Williams, Shoeless Joe Jackson, Happy Felsch, Swede Risberg, Fred McMullin, and Buck Weaver—had various degrees of culpability, as historians have chron-icled for more than a century. The Black Sox are a part of the cultural firmament now, referenced in literature (*The Great Gatsby*), film (*The Godfather: Part II*), and television (*Mad Men,* as part of Roger Ster-ling's acid trip). But in the context of the time, fixing a World Series was not as shocking as it would be today. In some ways it was merely a natural outgrowth of the era—as the Reds knew, intimately.

Consider Mathewson's reaction when his friend Hugh Fullerton, a longtime Chicago columnist, told him before Game 1 that some of the White Sox had been scheming with gamblers to throw the series. Mathewson doubted they could really pull it off, but not that they would try. He also believed baseball deserved it.

"They have it coming," Mathewson told Fullerton. "I caught two crooks and they whitewashed them."

He was referring to first baseman Hal Chase and infielder Lee Magee, players he had managed with the Reds the year before. Chase was a well-known scoundrel—"the most notoriously corrupt player in baseball history," his Society for American Baseball Research bio calls him—and Mathewson accused him in affidavits of throwing games. The National League ruled for Chase, citing inconclusive evidence, and he moved on to the Giants in 1919.

If they had won the pennant, Dellinger wrote, Chase's presence would have made them "easy pickings" to throw the World Series. But while the Giants trailed the Reds by just a half game entering August, a 10-game Cincinnati winning streak late in the month swelled the deficit to nine. That would be the final margin.

The White Sox won the AL crown easily—they had an eight-game lead in mid-September—and when Cicotte arrived at the Hotel Sinton in Cincinnati for Game 1, he found $10,000 on his pillow, placed there by Abe Attell, a former boxing champion and associate of Arnold Rothstein, the famed New York mobster. With his second pitch in the bottom of the first inning, Cicotte drilled the Reds' Morrie Rath in the middle of the back. Cicotte was the best control pitcher in the American League, and had hit just two of the 1,176 hitters he had faced that season. The message was unmistakable: the fix was in.

The true intentions of the White Sox for the full eight-game series (in a best-of-nine) will always be one of baseball's enduring mysteries. But the illegitimacy of the opener has never been in doubt. Cicotte served it up to the Reds—he allowed a walk and a triple to his counterpart, Ruether, in the opening blowout—but when others did not receive the payments they'd been promised, much of the scheme unraveled.

"Well, maybe the White Sox did throw it," Groh told Lawrence S. Ritter in *The Glory of Their Times*. "I don't know. Maybe they did and maybe they didn't. I didn't see anything that looked suspicious. But I think we'd have beaten them either way; that's what I thought then and I still think so today."

In 1985, Roush told *The Cincinnati Post* that the Reds had won "fair and square," adding, "Sure, there were gamblers trying to fix the Series. But they didn't pay the money up front like they promised, and after the first game the Sox played 100 percent."

Roush had his suspicions at the time. He first heard of the fix after Game 2 from Jimmy Widmeyer, a Reds booster club member who ran a Cincinnati newsstand. The Reds took two of three in Chicago and returned home needing one victory for the title—but lost twice at Redland Field. Now there were rumors that the Reds had thrown games to prolong the series, which would increase the gate receipts and, thus, enrich the winner's share.*

Roush never quite let go of that suspicion. Late in life, he told Dellinger that Ruether and Sallee—who combined to allow 15 hits and eight runs in nine and a third innings in Games 6 and 7—were often seen talking with gamblers. "We should have won that sixth game in the '19 Series," Roush said. "Mighty funny pitchin' goin' on out there."

To his credit, Roush acted on his doubts in the moment. His account of a meeting before Game 8 in Chicago is a highlight of Ritter's masterpiece. Roush told Moran what he'd heard, that gamblers had gotten to some of the Reds players. Moran consulted the team captain, Jake Daubert—an upstanding veteran who replaced the crooked Chase at first base—and asked Eller, the Game 8 starter, about the rumors:

"Has anybody offered you anything to throw this game?"

"Yep," Eller replied, and Roush said the room went silent. "After breakfast this morning a guy got on the elevator with me and got off at the same floor I did. He showed me five thousand-dollar bills and said they were mine if I'd lose the game today."

"What did you say?" Moran asked.

"I said if he didn't get damn far away from me real quick he wouldn't know what hit him. And the same went if I ever saw him again."

The game was a mismatch. Maybe Williams was rattled by shadowy threats from gamblers. Maybe he just had a bad day. Whatever the reason, the Reds chased him in the first inning with four hits in a row, and Eller went the distance in a 10–5 win. Shoeless Joe grounded to second for the final out.

Jackson had the most hits in the series, 12, including the only home run by either team. He batted .375. But he took money to lose—$5,000 in an envelope from Williams—and while a grand jury acquitted Jackson and his teammates of conspiracy in August 1921, the new baseball commissioner, Judge Kenesaw Mountain Landis, banned them all for life. Only in *Field of Dreams,* when they came in from the cornfields, did the Black Sox play together again.

---

* The players' pool of prize money now comes from 60 percent of the gate receipts from the first four games only.

Filming for that movie started in the spring of 1988, just after Edd Roush died. He was 94 years old, the last living player from the most notorious World Series ever. He had gone to the ballpark in Bradenton, Florida, for a spring training game and died in an ambulance as it cut across center field. Roush had been wearing a Reds cap when he collapsed in the press room, forever a true believer.

"Sure, the 1919 White Sox were good," he told Ritter. "But the 1919 Cincinnati Reds were better. I'll believe that till my dying day."

What you know: Babe Ruth called his
shot in the 1932 World Series.

———

What you might not know: Charlie Root
gave it up—and never lived it down.

In the long history of the Chicago Cubs, no pitcher has logged more innings or earned more victories than Charlie Root. He was the last major leaguer born in the nineteenth century, retiring in 1941 with 201 wins, all for the Cubs. He died 30 years later, at age 71, in Hollister, California.

"I was holding his hand," his daughter Della remembered, fighting back tears as she spoke in a clip on YouTube from 2009. "And he looked at me and said, 'You know, Della, I gave my life to baseball, and I'll be remembered for something that never happened.'"

He was referring to the most celebrated home run in the outsized life of Babe Ruth, whose name is forever linked with Root's. The aging Bambino indeed walloped a homer off Root at Wrigley Field in the fifth inning of Game 3 of the 1932 World Series. It was his second off Root that day and his fifteenth and final World Series blast. His theatrical flair in doing it is part of Ruth's legend.

"I looked out to center field and I pointed!" Ruth bellows, in a clip that still plays on the scoreboard before every game at Yankee Stadium. "I said, 'I'm gonna hit the next pitched ball right past the flagpole!' Well, the good Lord must have been with me."

Then comes the crack of the bat. Ruth's house, Ruth's story.

Four days after the homer, Lou Gehrig appeared on an NBC radio show, *The Fleischmann's Yeast Hour with Rudy Vallee,* and gave his account of the homer. In a clip unearthed in 2020 by his biographer, Dan Joseph, Gehrig says he had just spent the day fishing on the South Shore of Long Island Sound with Ruth. Then he delivers a monologue that sounds like he's reading from a script:

"I've played a lot of baseball but I have never seen so much nerve on display before," Gehrig says. "Babe had two strikes on him. There were 50,000 Cub fans giving him the old Bronx cheer, and the Cub players were riding him from the field. So what does he do? He stands up there and tells the world that he's going to sock the next one, and not only that, but he tells the world right where he's going to sock it, into the center field stands. A few seconds later, the ball was just where he pointed, in the center field stands. He called his shot, and then made it. I ask you, what can you do with a guy like that?"

I ask *you*, dear reader: If the scene had unfolded as Gehrig described it, what would Root have done? If Ruth had brashly pointed to the center field stands, clearly telling "the world" that he would hit the next pitch there, he would have been obviously and directly taunting Root. No pitcher with a hint of competitiveness—especially in that era—would have stood for it.

"He did not point to the center field stands," Root told Bill Roeder of *The New York World-Telegram* in 1956, when he was coaching for the Milwaukee Braves. "If he had, I'd have knocked him on his fanny with the next pitch, believe me. He just held up two fingers to show there were only two strikes and he still had one coming."

By 1932 Root had earned a reputation for toughness. He nearly died from diphtheria at age six. By 13 he was working at a steel mill in Ohio, and eventually starred for the company baseball team. At 21 he faced the touring St. Louis Browns, who signed him and brought him to the majors in 1923. The first time he faced Ruth, at Sportsman's Park that July, Root struck him out.

Within a few years he was ace of the Cubs, helping them win four pennants in a 10-year stretch starting in 1929. Trying to even the series in Game 4, Root took an 8–0 shutout into the seventh, when the A's erupted for 10 runs as Hack Wilson lost two balls in the sun. It was the biggest inning—and the biggest single-game comeback—in World Series history.

Root got another chance three years later, with help from an old

Yankee. At the end of July, the Cubs were five and a half games back in the standings. By the end of August, they were seven and a half games up—and their new shortstop, Mark Koenig, was batting .408.

Koenig had played for the fabled 1927 Yankees, hitting .500 in their World Series sweep of the Pirates, but by 1932 he had drifted to the Pacific Coast League. As it happened, the Cubs' shortstop, Billy Jurges, had been shot in the hand and ribs by a showgirl in early July. Jurges was back by the end of the month, but the Cubs wanted depth for his spot and signed Koenig, who wound up in the starting lineup for Game 1 at Yankee Stadium.

Still, Koenig struggled to fit in with the Cubs. His World Series guests had seats behind a post at Wrigley. His teammates voted him only half a share, a decision that would cost Koenig more than $2,000 and so irked Commissioner Landis that he told the manager, Charlie Grimm, that he would not issue payments until January.

Mostly, though, the Cubs had riled up Koenig's old teammates, especially Ruth, who roasted them for being cheap and reveled in his role as the heel. He captured the fans' imagination in batting practice, belting nine home runs before Franklin Delano Roosevelt, the Democratic nominee for president, tossed the ceremonial first pitch. Then, in the top of the first inning, Ruth slammed a three-run homer. The fans were frothing when he came to bat with a 4–4 tie in the fifth, and the players picked up on the cue.

"The Cub bench jockeys came out of the dugout to shout at Ruth," wrote Edward Burns in the next day's *Chicago Tribune*. "And Ruth shouted right back. Root got a strike past Babe, and did those Cub bench jockeys holler and hiss! After a couple of wide ones, Root whizzed another strike past the great man. More hollering and hissing and no small amount of personal abuse.

"Ruth held up two fingers, indicating the two strikes in umpire fashion. Then he made a remark about spotting the Cubs those two strikes."

On that, there is consensus: Ruth was telling the Cubs that, yes, he had two strikes, but it only takes one to hit it out. He was holding his hand out—like an umpire, as Burns astutely noted, and so the bench could clearly see the gesture. Even without pointing to the flagpole, then, Ruth was making sure the Cubs knew he heard them, the showman's signal for *Watch this!*

But while that surely was his underlying thought, Ruth also likely heard the taunting of Cubs pitcher Guy Bush, who'd been thrashed by the Yankees in Game 1 and was due to pitch again the next day. Some of Ruth's contemporaries in the all-white major leagues believed he was part African American; and even if they didn't believe that, they knew Ruth hated to hear about it.

"One of the nicknames he didn't like was 'Big Monkey,'" wrote Charlie Grimm, the Cubs' manager, in his 1968 memoir, "and I'm sure Guy included it."

The way Grimm saw it, Ruth was not pointing to the faraway stands. He was pointing to the mound, where Bush would be facing him in Game 4. Grimm said he heard Ruth growl: "You'll be out there tomorrow—so we'll see what you can do with me, you so-and-so tightwad."

Joe Williams covered the game for *The New York World-Telegram*, and while most writers present did not reference Ruth's gesture in their stories, Williams did. He wrote that Ruth "even went so far as to call his shot," by pointing to center field. In 1950, though, Williams wrote that Gehrig, the on-deck batter, had once shared a different explanation, which contradicted the radio interview he gave in the afterglow of the series.

"He was jawing with Bush," Gehrig told Williams, "and what he said was this: 'I'm going to cut the next pitch right down your throat.'"

Putting a cut on the ball, Williams explained, meant to slice a foul into the opposite dugout, a direct threat to his main tormentor. If that was true, Ruth missed his mark in grand style: he golfed Bush's low, outside changeup clear out of Wrigley Field. The fans tossed cabbages, oranges, and lemons, but all the Cubs could do was applaud with respect.

"Did Mr. Ruth chase those guys back in the dugout?" Ruth said in the Associated Press's game story, referring to himself in the third person. "I'll say Mr. Ruth did!"

It was all about the squawking dugout, not the stellar pitcher. Root was the last to give up a Ruthian blast in the World Series, but there was no shame in that; the Hall of Famers Grover Cleveland Alexander and Jesse Haines had also been October victims. In the moment, Ruth's homer was more a source of awe than anger.

"How he hit such a slow pitch that far amazed me," Root told Roeder. "I asked him about it the next day and he said, 'Here, take my bat.' I picked the thing up and could hardly lift it. It must have weighed 52 ounces."

Gehrig homered on the next pitch, Root's last of the day, and Bush started Game 4 this way: single, single, hit batter, sacrifice fly, walk, showers. The hit batter was Ruth, whom he drilled in the forearm. The Yankees won it in a rout to finish the sweep, and three years later Ruth would get his revenge on Bush. Playing at Forbes Field in Pittsburgh as a member of the Boston Braves, Ruth tagged Bush for the final two home runs of his career.

As for Root, he never did get a World Series victory. In 1935, the Tigers chased him in the first inning of Game 2, scoring four runs before Root could get an out. He pitched in relief later in that series, and again in the 1938 finale, when Gehrig and the Yankees completed a sweep in the Bronx.

For the rest of his life—and beyond—Root never escaped the shadow of the mythical, misunderstood called shot. Years after he died, his son, Charlie Jr., told *The Sporting News* about a friendly Wiffle ball game at the family ranch in California.

"I was pitching and my wife was up to bat," Charlie Root Jr. said. "She pointed to center field. I plunked her with the next pitch."

What you know: Don Larsen threw a perfect game in Game 5 of the 1956 World Series.

———

What you might not know: Clem Labine threw a 10-inning shutout the next day.

Clem Labine was the premier relief pitcher of the 1950s. This is the job he preferred, no matter how much his teammate and friend, starter Carl Erskine, urged him to join the Brooklyn Dodgers' rotation.

"Look," Labine would tell Erskine, "if I'm relieving, I could get called on any day—two days in a row, three days in a row. I've always got a chance to get in the game; I've always got a chance to get in when the money's on the line. I like that."

Labine usually got his wish: he made nearly 500 relief appearances in his career and only 39 starts. But in 1956, after Don Larsen reached perfection in Game 5, manager Walter Alston named Labine to start at Ebbets Field the next day. It would be only the fourth start of the season for Labine, though the change in role had precedent in the '50s.

Long before specialization, pitchers were pitchers, period. In the opener of the 1950 World Series, the Phillies started Jim Konstanty, who had worked exclusively in relief that season. But Konstanty was a standout pitcher—the NL's most valuable player, in fact—and he lasted eight innings in a loss at Yankee Stadium. After a day off, Konstanty faced a couple of batters in Game 3, then went nearly seven innings in relief in Game 4.

Today, of course, starters often work from the bullpen in October. But relievers never start—unless as an opener—because they train only for short stints. Labine just pitched.

"I don't remember Clem ever complaining about a sore arm," Erskine said. "The more he threw, the better he got."

Labine proved it as a rookie in 1951, when he shut out the Giants at the Polo Grounds—with the Giants stealing signs!—to force the final playoff game. When Bobby Thomson won the pennant with his famous home run, it made Labine's effort a footnote.

So it was again in 1956. Labine twirled a 10-inning shutout, one of only three in the World Series, with Christy Mathewson in 1913 and Jack Morris in 1991. But quite understandably, there was no escaping Larsen's shadow.

"That game in the '56 World Series was the best game I ever pitched," Labine told *The Providence Journal* in 1989. "The only problem was it came on the wrong day. With Don Larsen pitching his perfect game the day before, mine became one of the most anticlimactic games in the archives of baseball."

Labine had a fascinating World Series career. He threw the final pitch in 1953 to the Yankees' Billy Martin, who smacked a series-winning single in Game 6. He pitched in four more World Series, two as a star and two as an afterthought. Those three blowouts in

1960, when the Yankees clubbed the Pirates by 38–3? They scored off Labine each time.

Yet in 1956, with a chance to wrap up the championship the day after Larsen's gem, the Yankees could not touch him. Labine never allowed a runner past second base, and even doubled in the eighth (he sat on the bag to catch his breath during a mound conference). He actually batted for himself in the tenth, like his counterpart, Bob Turley, who gave up the game-winning hit to Jackie Robinson on a liner over Enos Slaughter's head in left.

"When Jackie hit that ball, I could have kissed him," Labine said. "I said, and I meant it, 'You living doll.'"

It was the final hit of Robinson's career. He went 0-for-3 in Game 7 and retired when the Dodgers tried to trade him to the Giants. Robinson went into business and used his platform to advance the cause of civil rights. But his closest white teammates, like Labine, declined his request to join him for the March on Washington in 1963.

Labine's biographer, a family friend named Richard Elliott, called it the "one irreversible regret of his entire life," a sentiment Erskine confirmed. Labine had just retired in 1963 and was running a sports-apparel company at home in Rhode Island. In a PBS documentary about Robinson, Labine said he had followed advice that marching with his friend might be bad for his business.

"So I didn't go," he said. "I'm sorry I didn't go."

Erskine also declined the invitation but said he had supported Robinson at so many other functions that he did not regret his decision. But Labine was an especially sensitive soul, Erskine said, a student of poetry, a family man whose arresting portrait in Roger Kahn's *The Boys of Summer* is a picture of an ex-athlete lamenting the toll of his glory days. He told Kahn he had sworn off religion after his son, Jay, lost a leg in Vietnam. Jay had joined the Marines after a fight with his father.

"If I hadn't been a ball player, I wouldn't have been away all the time," Labine said in the book. "But the traveling cost me all of it, Jay growing up. If I hadn't been a ball player, I could have developed a real relationship with my son. The years, the headlines, the victories, they're not worth what they cost us. Jay's leg."

Kahn wrote only one line about the shutout in 1956, and in context, that feels about right. The Dodgers lost a perfect game the day before. They lost Game 7 the day after. A year later, they packed up for California. A relief pitcher's 10-inning shutout—and a legend's final hit—had given Brooklyn one last day to dream. Life would never seem so orderly again.

What you know: Bill Mazeroski homered to win Game 7 of the 1960 World Series.

———

What you might not know: Hal Smith's home run was more important.

First, the disclaimer: Because it is played by humans, baseball is impossible to predict. But baseball also has zillions of historical data points to demonstrate the likelihood of an outcome. And when your team has runners at the corners with two outs in the bottom of the eighth inning and you're trailing by a run, there's a very strong chance you will lose.

According to Baseball-Reference.com, you'd have a 30 percent chance of winning in this spot. But if you hit a home run, as Hal Smith did for the Pirates in Game 7 of the 1960 World Series, your chances soar to more than 93 percent.

In the press box, that's the moment when you stop writing about Team A winning and start typing furiously about Team B. I remember this feeling in Game 7 of the 2016 World Series, in Cleveland, when Rajai Davis's game-tying three-run homer in the eighth inning suddenly made the Indians more likely to win than the Cubs. I felt it again in Houston three years later, in the seventh inning of another Game 7, when Howie Kendrick gave Washington the lead with a homer off the right field foul screen.

And they felt it, too, in the broadcast booth in Pittsburgh, when Smith connected off the Yankees' Jim Coates. With one swing, the Pirates had a two-run lead and would need just three outs for the championship.

"Forbes Field, at this moment, is an outdoor insane asylum," cried Chuck Thompson on NBC Radio, before addressing his partner, Jack Quinlan. "If he can hear me now, Jack, we have shared one of the all-time great moments in baseball."

That is how it seemed in real time, and it stayed that way for the rest of Smith's life. Yes, the Yankees came back to tie Game 7 in the top of the ninth, and then Bill Mazeroski homered off Ralph Terry to finish it. But statistically—for raising the odds that his team would win—Smith's home run is by far the biggest Game 7 moment ever.

"I get so many cards and stuff, it's absolutely amazing," Smith said in November 2019 from his home in Columbus, Texas, two months before he died there at age 89. "I get as many now as I did when I was playing, probably more. The people in Pittsburgh realize—now, this is what they tell me—that my home run was more important than Mazeroski's. Because we could have got a double and single and won that game, but we had to have some runs when I hit mine. And I was lucky enough to get a pitch to hit."

He was lucky enough to be batting at all. Smith was the backup catcher, a right-handed hitter who had started twice in blowout losses against Whitey Ford. The regular starter, All-Star Smoky Burgess, was back behind the plate for Game 7, but Smith took over in the eighth after Burgess had left for a pinch runner.

He knew the Yankees well. Smith was a minor leaguer in 1954 when the Yankees put him in the largest trade in major league history, a 17-player blockbuster with the Orioles that brought two future World Series MVPs—Don Larsen and Bob Turley—to New York. Later in the decade, with the Kansas City A's, Smith was teammates with 10 players who would appear for the Yankees in the 1960 World Series.

"I knew 'em all, Roger Maris—he played for Kansas City, he did everything great and all of a sudden they traded him off," Smith said. "Ralph Terry. There was a bunch of 'em. It just made me think: 'Now I know why I want to get traded.'"

He got his break in December 1959 with a deal to the Pirates, who had just finished their third decade in a row without a pennant. In their last visit to the World Series, in 1927, they'd been swept by the most storied team the Yankees had ever assembled. The 1960 Series would be the Yankees' twentieth since then, but the Pirates' first.

Though the teams were tied through six games, the Yankees had ruthlessly pummeled the Pirates in each of their wins: 16–3 in Game 2, 10–0 in Game 3, and 12–0 in Game 6. The Pirates' victories had all been close, and the Yankees would outscore them overall, 55–27.

In Game 7, the Yankees took a 7–4 lead into the bottom of the eighth inning. Smith was due up seventh and needed two freakish plays to get his chance. The first was a grounder to short, a certain double play until it struck Tony Kubek in the throat. Safe all around.

"It was a terrible infield," Kubek told George Vecsey many years later. "It was like the beach at Normandy, half sand, half pebbles, and they never dragged it."

Kubek left the game. Dick Groat singled in a run. After a sacrifice bunt and a fly out, the Pirates sent the great Roberto Clemente to the plate. He dribbled a grounder between the mound and first base. Coates broke for the ball, but so did Moose Skowron, the first baseman. Skowron fielded it, but nobody covered the bag. That made it 7–6 and brought up Smith. And that, Yogi Berra would say, is when the Yankees lost the game.

"Yogi was at a banquet a few years ago in Houston, and I walked up to him and said, 'Hey, Yog, how ya doing?'" Smith said. "And you know Yog, he says, 'You shouldn't have even been hitting! Coates, he didn't cover first base for Clemente. If he had, you wouldn't have gotten to hit!'"

Even so, Coates should have struck out Smith. On a 1–2 pitch, Smith swung and missed at a high fastball, his bat not only crossing the plate but actually whipping past his shoulders before he yanked it back. By modern standards, it was an obvious strike and should have been the third out—but umpire Bill Jackowski called a ball, keeping the inning alive.

Coates took a step toward the Yankees dugout but did not argue. His next pitch came in lower, a fastball again, and Smith swung hard and felt an unmistakable sensation. Smith had good pop—his .508 slugging percentage was better than any of the Pirate regulars—and he told reporters later that he knew the ball was gone as soon as he hit it. It sailed over Berra's head in left, just as Mazeroski's would in the ninth. Coates flipped his glove in the air. Pandemonium in Pittsburgh.

"For some reason, I didn't realize what it meant at the time," Smith said. "I was rounding first, went into second, turned second to go to third, and every person in the stadium—on the top of the dugouts, people were standing and yelling and clapping. I looked up to home plate; there was Clemente and Dick Groat waiting for me. Clemente just took me underneath my arm and lifted me up in the air, that's how strong he was, he was a strong man. We thought that would win it, you know."

They had to wait a bit, through a quirky ninth inning in which Mickey Mantle—unwittingly, he would always maintain—saved elimination by scrambling back to first instead of breaking for second on Berra's bases-loaded, one-out screamer to Rocky Nelson at first base. Nelson fielded the ball on a hop and stepped on the bag for the second out, but Mantle's desperate dive kept Nelson from attempting a truly bizarre ending: a tag play at second that would have ended the series—as long as it happened before Gil McDougald, the runner at third, crossed the plate.

As it was, McDougald scored without a throw, and a ground out by Skowron ended the inning. Seventy-seven batters had come to the plate, and none had been struck out. One more batter, Mazeroski, remained, and he would swing his way into immortality.

"We went back for an Old-Timers' Day, and we were all told to stand behind home plate in a line, let the people see you, the whole bit," Smith said. "When we were all through, Mazeroski said, 'Oh, by the way, Smitty, did you hit a home run?'"

Mazeroski got the glory—the only home run ever to end Game 7, a statue in Pittsburgh, a plaque at the Hall of Fame. But it wouldn't have happened without an even bigger blow by Hal Smith.

What you know: Carlton Fisk homered to
win Game 6 of the 1975 World Series.

———

What you might not know:
The winning pitcher was Rick Wise.

Rick Wise set a major league record when he took the mound at Fenway Park in the histrionic sixth game of the 1975 World Series. It was the twelfth inning, and Wise was the twelfth pitcher used by the Cincinnati Reds and the Boston Red Sox. No game in World Series history had ever featured so many pitchers.

Now it is rather common, especially if a game stretches well into extra innings. In 2018, the Red Sox and Dodgers used nine pitchers apiece as they slogged through 18 innings. Three years later, the Astros and Braves combined for at least 10 pitchers in all six games.

"Oh yeah, you'll see like 16 pitchers, eight on both teams, and they wonder why it goes over three hours," said Wise from his home in Oregon in 2020, the year he turned 75. "That no-hitter that I pitched, I threw 94 pitches in an hour and 53 minutes. That was it. That was against the Big Red Machine, too."

The no-hitter, for the Phillies on June 23, 1971, is Wise's unique achievement, and in some ways the greatest individual performance in major league history: not only did he throw a no-hitter, he also hit two home runs. Three months later, Wise retired 32 hitters in a row during a 12-inning complete game—and singled home the winning run.

Wise made $25,000 that year and wanted to double his salary. The Phillies offered a $10,000 raise. The Cardinals were locked in a similar dispute with a young starter of their own. The teams swapped their problems, and that is how Steve Carlton wound up in Philadelphia.

The Carlton deal not only pointed the Phillies toward their first title, in 1980, but it set up the Red Sox for a trade that would greatly influence Game 6. After two years in St. Louis, Wise was shipped to Boston with outfielder Bernie Carbo for outfielder Reggie Smith.

"I shouldn't have been surprised," Wise said. "Both times, in Philly and St. Louis, I bought a home, I made the All-Star team—and I got traded."

Wise kept his home in St. Louis, where Carlton also lived, and they hunted together in the off-seasons. He didn't resent his fate as The Other Guy, which began with his very first victory, in the second game of a doubleheader at Shea Stadium in 1964. In the opener, Jim Bunning pitched a perfect game.

The Carlton deal wasn't even the only time Wise was traded for a Hall of Famer. The Red Sox dealt him to Cleveland in 1978 for Dennis Eckersley, who was traded to the Cubs six years later for Bill Buckner. So the same trade chain produced a hero of one Game 6 (Carbo) and a goat of another (Buckner).

The 1975 World Series has been dissected so thoroughly that even Carbo's game-tying, three-run homer off Rawly Eastwick—a missile to center with two outs in the eighth, just after a meager half swing on a foul—got a mention from Robin Williams in *Good Will Hunting*.

Of course, Fisk is the man Williams pantomimed, the one whose reaction to the homer became one of the enduring images in baseball history. Fisk pulls a high, majestic drive off Pat Darcy to lead off the twelfth and hops along the first base line, frantically waving his arms to will the ball fair, leaping with joy as the foul pole rings out his answered prayer. The lore of that footage is well-known: Lou Gerard, the NBC cameraman in the Green Monster, was spooked by a rat and could not move his camera to his right, preventing him from following the flight of the ball as instructed. Instead, Gerard kept his lens trained on Fisk, unwittingly changing televised sports forever by creating the reaction shot.

It earned Gerard an Emmy. It also earned Wise the victory. He had been in the dugout for the home run, watching his catcher dance his way into the sport's collective memory.

"Everyone was doing the same thing Fisk was—except jumping, because our heads would hit the dugout roof," Wise said. "But everyone's hands were going to the right: 'Stay fair! Stay fair!' And it did. That set off one of the greatest celebrations I've ever seen."

The Reds would have the ultimate celebration by winning Game 7, their pitchers striking out Fisk in all three of his at-bats. But his home run is what lingers, and to get the chance for it, he had to navigate Wise through a dicey top of the twelfth.

It had been a strong year for Wise. He'd led Boston with a career-high 19 victories, and then, with his family in town from Oregon, he won the ALCS clincher in Oakland to end the Athletics' three-year reign as champions.

But the Reds bruised Wise in Game 3 of the World Series, with Johnny Bench, Dave Concepcion, and Cesar Geronimo all homering to chase him from the same mound where he'd thrown his no-hitter. So much transpired before he pitched again: Luis Tiant churning through 163 pitches for a complete-game victory the next night, two homers by Tony Perez in Don Gullett's Game 5 masterpiece, then a travel day to Boston and three days of rain.

Wise hoped to start Game 6, but the layoff gave Tiant a chance instead. He pitched into the eighth, trailing 6–3, and the rest of the drama could fill its own book: Carbo's game-tying rocket; Denny Doyle hearing "Go, go, go!" from third base coach Don Zimmer—who was really yelling "No, no, no!"—and getting pegged at the plate by George Foster while tagging up in the ninth; Dwight Evans's leaping grab in right field in the eleventh, robbing Morgan of a go-ahead hit and doubling Ken Griffey off first.

That play finished Dick Drago's third scoreless inning, and with no DH in the series, Drago left for a pinch hitter in the bottom of the eleventh. Wise had pitched 46 games for the Red Sox, none from the bullpen. But he was ready.

"After the rainouts for three days, I could have conceivably pitched a whole game in relief," he said. "I only went one inning, but it was not an easy inning."

Wise would face all three hitters who homered off him in Game 3. But two of them, Bench and Concepcion, had also been part of the Reds' lineup for the no-hitter, and Wise knew them well. Bench had homered off a hanging curve in Game 3, and as the leadoff man in the twelfth, he saw two fastballs, popping a high foul behind the plate with the second. Fisk overran it, losing his balance and tumbling to the dirt as he backpedaled for the catch.

In the NBC booth, Dick Stockton made a sharp observation. Stockton also called games for the Red Sox and was close with Wise; they lived in the same apartment building. He noted that Wise had come within an out of another no-hitter that July, in Milwaukee, getting several such pop outs with an exploding fastball. With extra rest in Game 6, he felt especially confident with it, using the fastball for 17 of his 19 pitches and placing it with precision, low and on the corners.

"I had a really, really good fastball, and I just kept pumping them in," he said. "Fisk was giving me the sign, and that was fine with me. I never shook him off."

Perez saw five fastballs and tapped the last one on the ground, but it rolled into center for a single. Then Wise jammed Foster with a 1–2 fastball, but Foster fisted it softly into left. Wise had made his pitches but was suddenly in trouble, the go-ahead run in scoring position with one out. Concepcion got into the box, crossed himself as he always did, and choked up.

Wise respected Concepcion's power—he had hit 14 homers the year before, the most among NL shortstops. Here he had the hardest hit off Wise, a liner to right, but Evans backed up for a routine catch.

That brought up Geronimo with Darcy on deck, only one reliever left in the bullpen—the forgotten Clay Kirby—and no remaining position players with a hit that October. Yet Wise attacked Geronimo with nothing but heat, making him swing and miss up in the zone on 2–1.

"That's a Rick Wise fastball at his best!" said Stockton, his buddy in the booth, and then Wise finished the inning with a called third strike on the inside corner.

He was still strong, clearly, while Darcy was tiring as he started his third inning. Fisk tugged at his jersey, flexed his chest, stretched his bat behind his back. He shook his head vigorously, as if waking from a dream. The first pitch was high, a ball. The second pitch soared into history.

The Fenway organist, John Kiley, played "The Hallelujah Chorus"— summer would last one more day. Rick Wise never pitched in the postseason again, forever a footnote and fine with it.

"If you went into an auditorium and said, 'Who was the winning pitcher in Game 6?' how many people would know it was Rick Wise?" he said. "I was at a banquet back home here, an old-timers' banquet we have every winter, and even though I was up onstage, no one could figure it out. They finally said, 'He's sitting right here—Rick Wise!'"

What you know: A bad call crushed the
Cardinals in the 1985 World Series.

———

What you might not know:
The Cardinals deserved to lose.

Denny Matthews has broadcast games for the Kansas City Royals since the franchise began in 1969. When you watch that much baseball, you learn to trust the unseen.

"I'm a big believer in: 'It's your turn,'" Matthews once told me, in his booth before a game at Kauffman Stadium. "If you think back to all the pennant winners, they won a lot of games in a lot of strange ways. In '85 I just felt like this was it, it's the Royals' turn to win the World Series. Everything's going your way and pointing in that direction. It's just your turn; the baseball gods have declared it to be so."

In the bible of baseball, the 1985 World Series could command its own gospel: the Book of Biancalana, let's call it, after the Royals' plucky shortstop, Buddy, who hit .188 in the regular season and .357 in his team's four victories over the St. Louis Cardinals. Just don't call it a fluke, and please don't blame an umpire, Don Denkinger, for altering the Cardinals' fate.

"Whenever I meet a Cardinals fan, I say to him, 'You know, it wasn't that big of a deal, really—all we gave Denkinger was a ring and a World Series share,'" cracks John Wathan, who was running from first at the end of Game 6 when Dane Iorg's single floated over his head to win it.

"That pisses 'em off even more, but it doesn't bother me. I always explain the things that happened in the rest of that inning. And they hit .170 or whatever it was for the series. And they had the seventh game as well."

By 1985, the Royals were due. Overdue, really. They had reached the end of a 10-year run that included seven trips to the playoffs. They'd lost in the division series, the championship series, and the World Series. They overcame a three-games-to-one deficit in the 1985 ALCS, against Toronto, and did it again in the World Series. It was their year, all right, and they made sure of it by capitalizing on every break.

That ALCS? Had it been best-of-five, the Blue Jays would have won. But the format changed in '85, and the Royals took advantage. Buoyed by that comeback, they shrugged off the 3–1 hole in the World Series. "Piss on it," manager Dick Howser told the players after Game 4, and everybody laughed.

"That cut the edge—'Piss on it, guys, we'll get this thing done,'" pitcher Mark Gubicza says. "That became our mantra."

The Cardinals badly missed their rookie leadoff man, Vince Coleman, who'd been lost to the weirdest injury in baseball history: a motorized tarp ran over his left leg and broke his fibula before a game in the NLCS. It was a horrible accident, to be sure, yet the Cardinals had speed to spare; even without Coleman's total (110), they still had more stolen bases than any other team in the majors.

In the 1985 World Series, though, the Cardinals had two steals and the Royals had seven. Coleman's replacement in left field, Tito Landrum, was their leading hitter, at .360, while the rest of the team batted .162. The Cardinals scored two runs across the final 27 innings, wasting three chances to clinch.

"We thought we were good enough to win," manager Whitey Herzog admitted after Game 7. "When you hit .185 and score just 13 runs, you don't deserve to win."

That's a succinct and accurate summary, as reported by *The Boston Globe,* but it's not how Herzog really felt. He believed in his soul that the Cardinals would have won in six if only Denkinger had made the right call in the bottom of the ninth inning.

Three outs from a championship with a 1–0 lead, Herzog called for Todd Worrell, a hard-throwing rookie who'd joined the team in late August. Worrell had been overpowering in Game 5, fanning all six hitters he faced, and seemed to pick up where he'd left off. But with two strikes on Jorge Orta, a veteran pinch-hitter, Worrell tried a breaking ball, up and off the plate. Orta chopped it into the dirt toward first base.

The Cardinals' Jack Clark, still new to first base after a decade in the outfield, broke to his right and charged it. Worrell dashed over to cover the bag. Had Clark reached the ball quicker, he could have tossed it gently to Worrell in stride. Denkinger, the first base umpire, expected that kind of play and moved close to the bag, in foul ground, to see who won the footrace.

But Clark did not get the ball until its third hop. With no time for a flip, he flung it sidearm to the base, knowing that Worrell would be there. By then, Denkinger was too close to see both Worrell's glove and Orta's right foot in his line of vision. When that happens, an umpire relies on his ears: if he hears the ball smack the fielder's glove before the runner hits the base, it's an out.

"But there isn't any sound, not in the sixth game of the World Series when 50,000 people are screaming and yelling at the top of their lungs," Denkinger explained in *As They See 'Em,* the definitive book on umpiring by Bruce Weber. "So I just did what I could do. I looked up, I saw Worrell catch the ball, looked down, and saw the runner's foot was on the bag, and I called him safe. The amount of time it took me to do that was enough to permit him to be safe. I blame myself for not having good position."

In the moment, though, Denkinger believed he had made the right call. Herzog and the Cardinals argued, to no avail, and Denkinger did not consult the other umpires. Instant replay for plays on the bases was still 29 years away. It was rotten luck, a sucker punch to the Cardinals. But they never got up off the canvas.

"When you have that first out of the inning—as a pitcher, as a catcher, as a defense—it's gonna roll from there," third baseman Terry Pendleton says. "You know it's gonna roll from there. It's a whole different dynamic when you get that first out of the inning."

That's fair, but the Cardinals had survived worse jams; they were 84–0 that season when leading after eight innings, and even with a runner on first, the odds still favored them. Statistically, the visiting team has about a 66 percent chance of winning when leading by a run with no outs and a runner on first.

That model, though, does not account for the kind of mistakes the Cardinals would make. On the very next pitch, Steve Balboni lifted a pop foul by the first base dugout, on the far end. Dugouts did not have railings then, as they do now, and as Clark hustled over from first, he took a quick peek to see where he was. When he looked up again, the ball had drifted over his head, out of reach, landing near the top of the dugout and bouncing high into the stands. Catcher Darrell Porter also converged on the play and should have taken charge; as a former Royal, he knew the ballpark much better than Clark.

The irony is that most batters would not have hit that kind of foul, because they would have been bunting. The lumbering Balboni, though, had never put down a sacrifice. He was a slugger—the team leader in homers and the major league leader in strikeouts—and another foul put him down in the count, 0–2. Yet Worrell, again, could not get the strikeout he needed, and Balboni pulled a single to left.

Jim Sundberg bunted back to Worrell, who fired to third for the force. Needing a double play for the championship, Worrell crossed up Porter on his second pitch to Hal McRae, throwing a slider when Porter expected a fastball. When the pitch skipped to the backstop (it was ruled a passed ball), the Cardinals were really in trouble.

With the tying run at third and the winning run at second, they walked McRae to load the bases for another pinch hitter, Dane Iorg. The Cardinals had seen him in October before: in 1982, Iorg had helped them win the World Series with nine hits against Milwaukee. This time he delivered for the Royals, punching a broken-bat single into right, too softly for the strong-armed Andy Van Slyke to make a quick throw home. Sundberg slid headfirst, just under Porter's tag, to force Game 7.

Herzog could not hide his bitterness after the game: "We had the damned World Series won tonight," he said to the *St. Louis Post-Dispatch.* Asked if the umpiring had been poor throughout the World Series, Herzog cited the American League umps: "It looks like they're prejudiced. We haven't gotten one call yet from those . . ."

Denkinger—one of the allegedly prejudiced AL umpires—would be working the plate for Game 7. That afternoon, in his office with a couple of trusted writers, Herzog was already a beaten man. Rick Hummel, from the *Post-Dispatch*, asked Herzog what he thought of the Cardinals' chances.

"And that's when he just shook his head and said, 'I'm not so sure,'" recalls Peter Gammons, who was there for *The Boston Globe.* Herzog remembers it in even stronger terms.

"The guys are really down," Herzog said, quoting himself in an interview with Fox in 2015. "We're going to get beat bad."

And so they did. The Royals thrashed the Cardinals, 11–0, on Bret Saberhagen's five-hitter. In the fifth inning, Denkinger ejected Herzog and then pitcher Joaquin Andujar, who had to be restrained by teammates and coaches.

The exchange between manager and umpire, as Denkinger recalled to Weber, went like this:

Herzog: "If you had gotten that play right last night, we wouldn't have to be here tonight."

Denkinger: "If you guys were hitting better than .122, we wouldn't have to be here tonight, either."

In his 1999 memoir, Herzog blamed Denkinger for keeping him out of the Hall of Fame, reasoning that the blown call cost him a second title that would have ensured his enshrinement. A few years later, he invited Denkinger to a banquet honoring the '85 team and presented him with a gift—a Braille watch. Herzog was elected to the Hall of Fame in 2010, despite the title that got away.

"I remember Whitey saying—and it'd have been interesting—that if he could do anything over again in 1985, he would have pulled the entire team off the field after that call and made them get it right," Pendleton says. "And I believe him, because he would have done that.

Whitey said, 'They could look at the TV, do whatever they want to do, the commissioner could come down on the field yelling and screaming, but we're not going back out there until they get it right.'"

We'll never know if that would have worked, just as we'll never know how the ninth inning would have unfolded if Orta had been out. What we do know is that the Cardinals didn't hit enough, didn't run enough, didn't field well enough, and didn't get enough strikeouts. The surprise is that they came as close to winning as they did.

Denkinger blew the call, obviously, but the Cardinals blew the World Series. The Royals fulfilled their destiny, and the Cardinals will never get over it.

"I asked Todd Worrell about it at an event," says Cardinals broadcaster Ricky Horton, a reliever on that 1985 team. "I was interviewing him—and I've been friends with Todd for a long time—and I said, 'Where are you with it now versus when it first happened? Have you been able to process it and put it past you and get to a different place with that?'

"He didn't say anything for a second, and then he said, 'It bothers me more now than it ever has.'"

> **What you know:** Kirk Gibson homered to
> win Game 1 of the 1988 World Series.
>
> ———
>
> **What you might not know:** It never would have
> happened without a walk to a .196 hitter.

It may be the most theatrical moment in baseball history, right there in Tinseltown. In the opener of the 1988 World Series, at Dodger Stadium, the hobbling Kirk Gibson, grizzled leader of the home team, rose from the dugout to pinch hit. Down to his last strike against the great Dennis Eckersley, Gibson planted his front foot, lifted his back foot, and swatted a backdoor slider into the seats for a game-winning home run. The blow was so astounding, it inspired two of the most indelible calls ever.

"I don't believe what I just saw!" cried Jack Buck on CBS Radio, while Vin Scully, in the NBC TV booth, gave the ball a feminine pronoun, like a ship: "She . . . is . . . *gone!*" After pausing for more than a minute, Scully added a famous flourish: "In a year that has been so improbable, the *impossible* has happened!"

It took an improbable walk for the impossible to happen; truth is, Gibson never should have gotten to the plate. With two outs and the bases empty, manager Tommy Lasorda used a different lefty pinch hitter, Mike Davis, to bat for Alfredo Griffin. Gibson, who had injured his left hamstring and right knee in the NLCS, was at the mercy of a teammate who had just batted .196.

"If Davis makes an out, Gibson never gets to bat," says Walt Weiss, the Oakland shortstop that night. "You could make the case that Gibson should have been hitting in Davis's spot. He could have tied the game, so you would think he would have used him there."

Gibson didn't think so. Watching from the trainer's room in the bottom of the eighth, he had heard Scully say flatly that he would not play. Gibson angrily started hitting off a tee and sent the clubhouse manager, Mitch Poole, to find Lasorda. When Lasorda hustled back in to see him, Gibson told him to use Davis for Griffin, and then he would hit for the pitcher.

That made sense to Lasorda, even though he did not think much of Davis, who had flopped as a free agent; only one hitter in the majors in 1988, the Phillies' Steve Jeltz, had more plate appearances than Davis with a lower batting average. When Davis told teammates that God had promised he would homer in the postseason, they laughed. They were mocking his faith in the manager, not the Lord.

"I was in Lasorda's doghouse," Davis said, "and they knew: 'For you to get in the lineup, you're gonna need a superlong bat to get to the plate, because it's gonna be hard to hit from that bench you're sitting on.'"

Davis had one thing going for him in a matchup with Eckersley: they had been teammates in Oakland the year before, when Davis slugged 20 home runs by the All-Star break. In a one-run game, Eckersley would have to respect Davis's power. But he should have remembered the reason the A's let him go: "I didn't walk," he says.

Davis had faced Eckersley nine times before the 1988 World Series without drawing a walk. That was typical of Eckersley, who had the lowest walk percentage of any starter in the National League with the

Cubs two years earlier. He was even more precise during the Athletics' three-year run of AL pennants, averaging 0.8 walks per nine innings, by far the best ratio in baseball.

Even so, Lasorda guessed that Eckersley would pitch around Davis, respecting the hitter he had been in Oakland, if the light-hitting Dave Anderson stood on deck as a decoy for Gibson. Eckersley ignored Anderson, but Lasorda's other instinct was correct: he did not think of Davis as the feeble Dodger of 1988.

"I was afraid to come in," Eckersley says. "You've gotta be careful late anyway, and right away you assess somebody. I gave him too much fucking credit, obviously. I knew the guy, I'd just played with him the year before. That had something to do with it. I wasn't looking at who was on deck or nothing; Anderson was on deck, but I wasn't even thinking about that. I just fucked up, which was unlike me, because I'm a control guy. I just got tentative."

Davis reinforced his reputation with a good cut at Eckersley's first pitch, a fastball he fouled back. None of the next four pitches were close: four balls, each well off the outside corner. Only then did Gibson get his chance.

Eckersley soon found the pitch he'd tried to use on Davis, the fast-ball on the outside corner. Davis stayed tethered to first as Gibson fouled both back. With two strikes, Davis would have the chance to steal his way into scoring position. He pinched the side of his pants, indicating his intent to the third base coach, Joey Amalfitano, who returned the gesture. Davis was free to take off.

Five years earlier, he had stolen 32 bases for the A's. Hampered by injuries in 1988—and a .260 on-base percentage—Davis had swiped just seven for the Dodgers. Still, he distracted Eckersley, who made two pickoff throws with an 0–2 count. Gibson dribbled a weak foul halfway up the first base line; had he tapped it just a bit harder, it would have ended the game. It nearly ended one pitch later, anyway, when catcher Ron Hassey tried to pick off Davis after ball one.

"My heart was beating, because if I get picked off right there with Kirk Gibson up at the plate, you just bury me on the spot," Davis said. "Same thing if I get thrown out stealing, you just bury me at second base."

He made it on the 2–2 pitch without a throw. At that point Gibson could think small and concentrate on Mel Didier's famous scouting report insisting that Eckersley would throw a backdoor slider to lefties with a full count. The A's have always sniffed at that intelligence— "How many times did he get to 3–2?" Alderson said (answer: 11 times to lefties before the World Series)—but the stolen base, at least, changed the calculation.

"Because now he could just try to flip something in for a base hit," Eckersley said. "But nothing makes sense, you know what I mean? Gibson was a lamb, and he fucking took me deep."

Davis did not think Gibson had hit the ball well enough to carry over the fence. And it shouldn't have, not with that kind of swing against that kind of pitcher. But it did, and it never would have happened without Davis doing his part first. He still wishes he'd contributed more to the 1988 Dodgers; he did get that homer God promised him, a two-run shot in the Game 5 clincher, but within a year, his career would be over.

By his early 60s, Davis was coaching kids in Las Vegas. He wears his World Series ring every now and then as a motivational tool. His motto, Davis said: "Good, better, best, never let it rest—until the good gets better and the better becomes the best."

For most of 1988, the Dodgers were not the best team in baseball. But they played that way when it mattered most, and Eckersley, for his part, would never repeat his mistake. For the rest of his postseason career—94 batters in 22 games, spread over 10 years—he never issued another walk.

What you know: Joe Carter homered off Mitch Williams to win the 1993 World Series.

———

What you might not know: The Phillies actually did have a shutdown reliever.

Roger Mason's last night as a San Diego Padre was utterly ridiculous. He pitched in both games of a soggy doubleheader in Philadelphia that stretched to 4:40 a.m., the latest a major league game had ever been played. When it finally ended, with a single by zany Phillies closer Mitch Williams, delirium took over the airwaves: "This game is over," cried Harry Kalas, the voice of the Phillies, "on an RBI hit by *Mitch-ee-poo!*"

The next afternoon, in the sleepy Padres' clubhouse, Mason got word that he'd been traded down the hall. He wasn't sure what to think. A devout Christian, Mason doubted he'd fit in with the rowdy, hard-living Phillies. In the end, he could have saved their season—but for the next three months, that sure seemed unlikely.

Mason was a mop-up man. Including the NLCS against Atlanta, the Phillies had a .361 winning percentage when Mason pitched, and a .673 mark when he didn't. One night in September he gave up three home runs in a row to the Cubs, a sequence manager Jim Fregosi never forgot.

When the Phillies were winning in the late innings, Fregosi wanted David West and Larry Andersen to set up for Williams. The formula had somehow worked for six months, even though Andersen was 40, West was out of shape, and Williams was a human slasher film; his 1.613 WHIP that season remains the highest ever for a pitcher with at least 40 saves.

By late October the trio was fried, destined to be devoured by a ravenous Blue Jay lineup. Mason felt bad for Williams, who wanted to succeed so desperately but could never find a way to settle down.

"I would see Mitch in the bullpen, and the ball would just explode out of his hand," Mason says. "He'd be nice and compact and driving through the ball. But he'd get in the game and he was overthrowing. That was why he'd fall off [to the side of the mound] the way he did. It wasn't the same guy."

Yet Williams, West, and Andersen never lost their manager's trust, despite compelling evidence before Game 6 in Toronto, with the Phillies on the brink of elimination. To that point, West and Andersen had worked nine innings in the postseason and given up 16 earned runs. Williams had blown three of six save chances, and in Game 4 of the World Series, he'd turned a 14–10 lead into a 15–14 loss.

Mason, though, had pitched two and two-thirds scoreless innings that night. He would have been the winner if Williams had converted the save. It was much more than he had hoped for; when the series started, he simply wanted to face one batter so he could say he had played.

Mason knew his place in the game. When he enrolled at Saginaw Valley State in Michigan, as a scholarship wide receiver, the school did not even field a baseball team. He signed at a tryout camp with the Tigers, who told him he could pitch batting practice at spring training. He worked his way to the majors in September 1984, a month before the Tigers won the World Series. He earned one-sixth of a share and was not given a ring.

It took until 1992, when he turned 35, for Mason to pitch a full season in the majors. He had earned the chance in the 1991 play-offs, when Pirates manager Jim Leyland called on him for a save in Atlanta. That was part of a sparkling October ledger for Mason, who had given up just one earned run in 16 career postseason innings before Game 6.

Mason worked a scoreless sixth with the Phillies trailing by four runs. Then he watched from the bench as his teammates rallied for the lead, a half-inning that consumed nearly 40 minutes. A wait like that can disrupt a pitcher's rhythm, but in that time, Mason transformed. He had always seen himself as an average pitcher, nothing more. Now he felt unhittable.

"When we took the lead, everything changed for me, because now all of a sudden it's my responsibility," Mason says. "And we were in the dugout for so long, I actually started getting nervous. I'm like, 'I can't pitch like this.' But I remembered watching Orel Hershiser on Johnny Carson after the '88 series, and Johnny asked him what he did between innings, and he said he sang hymns to himself."

Mason could not think of any hymns, so he calmed himself with Bible stories. He thought of the book of Joshua and the city of Jericho, the first place the Israelites would conquer after entering the Promised Land. It resonated powerfully.

"God said, 'I've given you this city,'" Mason says. "Now, I don't know what it was about that, but all of a sudden, it was like a promise for me: *I've given you this city*. It was like, 'All right, I'll take it,' you know? So when I went out to pitch the next inning, I was so pumped up that the first two warm-up pitches weren't even close to the strike zone. So I stepped back and was like: 'OK, breathe, get yourself under control.' Because I knew that when I was out there in Game 6, they weren't going to do anything. They weren't going to hit me. I just knew it. I had no reason to think that, not with that lineup. I wasn't blowing people away. But I knew they weren't."

And they didn't. The Blue Jays sent up the top of their order in the seventh, the same hitters who would bat again in the fateful ninth. Rickey Henderson flied to left. Devon White whiffed on a high fastball. Paul Molitor flied to center. After Joe Carter led off the eighth with a fly out to left, Mason had retired seven in a row.

And that was it. With a one-run lead and the left-handed John Olerud coming up, Fregosi strode from the dugout, extended his left arm, and tapped it with his right hand. He wanted West, the lefty, playing the percentages till the end.

To that point, West had faced 15 hitters in his World Series career, and 12 had reached base. Predictably, he walked Olerud on five pitches. Andersen then made the jam worse, hitting one batter and walking another. The Jays left the bases loaded, but neat had turned sloppy, and the bottom of the ninth would start with an epic mismatch: the active leader in walks against a pitcher called Wild Thing.

When Williams walked Henderson on four pitches, it wasn't a matter of whether the Blue Jays would win, only how. With a one-out single by Molitor and the homer by Carter, Toronto exploded and the Phillies were finished. Fregosi never spoke to Mason about pulling him, and Mason never asked. He knew that Fregosi was not the kind of guy to change partners for the last dance.

"The difference between Jim Leyland and most other guys is that [Leyland] has a feel for how everything's going, and if he feels like somebody's the right person for that time—even though it may not go with the book—it seemed like he was more apt to say, 'Well, I'm going this way,'" Mason said.

"Fregosi went with the book, and I know it's an awful lot easier to ask the question because of the way everything went. Because if I had been the one out there and I had given it up, it's like, 'You've got these guys in the bullpen and you stayed with this guy?' That would have been a pretty tough thing for him to do. So he went with the book and unfortunately it just didn't work out. All I know is the way that I felt that night."

Fregosi spent many years as a scout after his managing career ended. Over lunch in a press room one day, a few years before he died in 2014,

Fregosi explained that Mason was prone to the home run ball; sooner or later, he thought, someone was bound to connect. His best relievers were rested and ready, and he had to trust them.

Mason's career peaked in Game 6. At the Phillies' home opener the next April, he found himself in the same spot as the one in Toronto, watching from the bench as the Phillies took the lead in the seventh inning. This time, though, Mason gave up the homer Fregosi had feared, a two-run shot to lose the game. The Phillies sold Mason to the Mets a few weeks later, and he blew out his shoulder during the players' strike, ending his career.

"I actually just had shoulder-replacement surgery last year," Mason said in early 2020. He hoped to be able to play catch with his grandsons, Benjamin and Luke. "I told the surgeon that's one of the things that I wanted to do, and he said I should be able to do that. But I haven't thrown a ball overhand in probably 20-some years."

Mason keeps his baseball memorabilia at his home in Bellaire, Michigan. He does not flaunt his career, doesn't show the grandkids old videos. But they're starting to get an idea.

"Did Grandpa used to be famous?" Benjamin has asked his father. Almost.

What you know: Luis Gonzalez singled off
Mariano Rivera to win the 2001 World Series.

———

What you might not know:
Tony Womack had the bigger hit—by far.

The Yankees did not belong in the 2001 World Series. The Seattle Mariners won 21 more games that season. The Oakland A's were better, too. Yet when Oakland had the Yankees on the brink of elimination in the first round, Derek Jeter saved them with his inconceivable infield flip. After that, you might say, it was Derek and the dominoes—three wins over Oakland, four in five games over Seattle, and then on to Arizona for the World Series.

"I look back on it as this: if Jeter doesn't make that play against Oakland, it's the Diamondbacks facing the A's, maybe, in the World Series, so how historic could that be?" says Tony Womack, Arizona's shortstop that fall. "What kind of ratings are you gonna get for Arizona playing the Oakland A's? With the Yankees, I looked at it as not David and Goliath, but as new franchise versus history."

The Diamondbacks indeed were a young franchise, added to the NL in 1998, but everyone in their Game 1 lineup was at least 31 years old. They dominated the Yankees for two games in Phoenix, holding the three-time defending champions to one run behind aces Curt Schilling and Randy Johnson.

Back in the Bronx, though—well, the Diamondbacks were not going to beat the Yankees there. Not seven weeks after terrorists destroyed the World Trade Center on September 11. Not after President George W. Bush's triumphant first pitch before Game 3, with snipers on the roof of Yankee Stadium, the city both leaden with anxiety and bursting with pride.

"There was no way the man upstairs wanted us to celebrate in New York after 9/11," Womack said. "I just believe in karma, and it wasn't meant for us to win there."

The Yankees won three home games in a row, all by one run. Down to their last out and trailing by two runs in Game 4, they got a game-tying homer off Byung-Hyun Kim in the ninth and won in extra innings. The next game, it happened again. Not since 1929* had a team won a World Series game after trailing by two runs in the bottom of the ninth inning—and the Yankees did it on consecutive nights.

When Tino Martinez smashed the Game 4 homer, it felt to Arizona's Craig Counsell like an earthquake at Yankee Stadium, the ground shaking beneath his spikes at second base. Everything that followed— Jeter's "Mr. November" walk-off shot in the tenth, Scott Brosius's tying homer in Game 5, Alfonso Soriano's single to win it—made the series' denouement, back in the desert, all the more stirring.

The Diamondbacks whipped the Yankees in Game 6, 15–2, decoding Andy Pettitte's pitches by the way he moved his hands to the set position with runners on base: straight down for a fastball, in a loop for a breaking ball. But the next night, when Soriano homered off Schilling to lead off the eighth, the Yankees took a 2–1 lead with six

---

* Trailing 2–0 in the ninth inning of Game 5, the A's scored three runs to finish off the Cubs and clinch the title.

outs to go. They had scored only 14 runs in seven games, yet were poised to steal a championship.

Mariano Rivera worked a scoreless eighth with three strikeouts. This was his fifth World Series, he'd never blown a save, and the bottom of the order was coming up in the ninth. Womack was due fourth, and he swears he was not concerned.

"Listen, I know Mo's the greatest closer, I get it," he says. "But he's got six outs, dude, and we've seen him. He's still not easy to hit, but six outs is a lot in Game 7 of the World Series."

No pitcher in 75 years had gotten a save of at least six outs in Game 7 of the World Series while pitching entirely with a one-run lead. And Counsell, who was due up fifth, liked the matchups for the Diamondbacks in the ninth. The leadoff man, Mark Grace, had led the majors in hits in the 1990s and was still going strong. If Grace got on and stayed out of a double play, Womack would get to hit, too. Neither was prone to striking out.

"As hitters, we kind of knew that those were the guys with the two best chances," Counsell said. "It was just what their swings did. Mark Grace had this incredible ability to get inside baseballs, which you had to do, and Tony's swing was the opposite, actually—he was completely around the baseball, but he would pull it down the line."

Grace punched a single to center, and David Dellucci ran for him. Damian Miller bunted, but too hard—straight back at Rivera, who had made just one error in his career. It might have been a double play, but this bunt was not slowed by the grass; the Diamondbacks had a strip of dirt between the mound and the plate,* and the ball skipped quickly to the heel of Rivera's glove. He gripped it awkwardly, and his throw to second sailed. Jeter stretched, but his glove could only nick the ball as it flew by; Dellucci was barreling in on him, and Jeter wound up limping with a spike to his left ankle.

"It was a bang-bang play," Dellucci recalled two years later, after the Yankees had traded for him. "The throw was a little wide. I definitely may have added a little pressure by being as close as I was."

With two on, no outs, and Jay Bell coming up, Joe Torre met with

---

* This quirk was created by their original manager, Buck Showalter, who helped build the Yankees' dynasty as Joe Torre's predecessor.

Rivera and the infielders at the mound. Torre would often say that once Rivera came into a game, his job was done—as the greatest closer ever, Rivera almost always finished the job without drama. But here Torre made an important calculation, trusting Rivera and following his instinct to get the game back under control. He told the infielders not to take any chances.

Bell was an expert bunter, a two-time major league leader in sacrifices, but this bunt was awful—on the grass and back to Rivera. Sure-handed this time, he fired accurately to third, and Brosius settled for that out. He did not whip a throw across the infield to try for a double play on Bell, who was so slow that he hadn't stolen a base all season. At spring training the next year, Rivera was still incredulous.

"The ball hit Brosius in the chest and he just took his foot off the bag," Rivera told the *Times'* Jack Curry. "I was waiting for the ball to cross me. When you're a pitcher, you always wait for the ball to cross you. I was like, 'Where's the ball?' I saw Brosius with the ball, I said, 'Uh-oh.' I tell you what, that was a double play. Easy."

Bell had technically been in the Golden Pitch scenario—a chance to either win or lose the World Series with one swing—because a triple play was at least theoretically possible. But Bell was bunting and Womack would be swinging away, making the danger more plausible for him. A two-run hit would have won it for the Diamondbacks, but a double play would have lost it.

Womack says he did not worry at all about the double play, with good reason: he was the fastest man on the team and had grounded into just four double plays in 2001, the fewest among hitters who qualified for the NL batting title. He also finished last among those players in extra-base hits, making a game-ending hit also highly unlikely.

As Counsell expected, Rivera was actually a good matchup for Womack, who had quick hands and a plan for handling his famous cutter. Womack had faced Rivera just once before, grounding out to second on a cutter in Game 5, but that gave him a sense of how the pitch looked, how quickly it got on you.

"You have to get your hands out front and beat the ball before it cuts," he says. "I was a very good hitter inside—it was hard to bust a ball inside on me—plus if you cheat with your body, you open up, so now if you do get to that cutter, you're gonna pull it foul because you've already cheated. People will say, 'Oh, you cheated to it.' I can tell you: look at my swing, if I cheated to it, that ball would not have stayed fair. It was a no-doubter from the start."

Womack had missed the pitch before, fouling back a 2–1 cutter that had barely moved at all. The 2–2 pitch moved more, but not much, and Womack cleared his hands and drilled it down the right field line. It slowed a bit after landing on the grass, and Shane Spencer cut it off to keep the winning run from scoring. But the pinch runner Midre Cummings scored easily, and Womack pulled into second, shaking his fists and looking to the sky through the open roof at Bank One Ballpark. It was tied, 2–2, and with Bell at third, Arizona instantly became the overwhelming favorite to win.

"We've got 'em by the throat, step on 'em now," Womack remembers thinking. "We can't let these guys go to the tenth inning. We got our foot on their neck, let's just keep squeezing, keep stepping. Don't let 'em breathe."

Of all the winner-take-all games in World Series history, only Hal Smith's homer in 1960 was more impactful than Womack's double. The Diamondbacks' chances of winning rose from 35 to 85 percent with one swing, matching a situation in Game 8 (one game had ended in a tie) in 1912. Then, the Red Sox' Tris Speaker had come up against the Giants' Christy Mathewson in the bottom of the tenth, down by a run, with runners on first and second—just as Womack did in 2001. Speaker drove in the tying run with a single and wound up at second, putting Boston in the same situation as Arizona would find itself 89 years later.

Greg Colbrunn, a reserve power hitter, had been on deck to hit for Counsell. But when Womack tied the game, it meant that, at worst, the Diamondbacks would be back on defense for the tenth. They would need Counsell's glove then, so he hit—incredibly, for the second time in five seasons, in the bottom of the ninth inning of Game 7 with a chance to deliver a title. With the Marlins in 1997, he'd lashed a game-tying sacrifice fly off Cleveland's Jose Mesa.

"I was like, 'Oh my God, this is the same at-bat,'" Counsell says. "A little less pressure because it was tied, but my thought again was, 'I'm gonna swing,' because when you have the chance to win the World Series, you have to swing."

He swung once, fouling a cutter by his feet, and the next pitch hit him in the right hand. It set up a double play with Luis Gonzalez coming up, but Torre kept the infield in. In the Fox booth, Tim McCarver pointed out the danger of that strategy: lefties often fought off Rivera's cutter, he said, and hit a blooper to the shallow part of the outfield.

Torre knew that, of course, but he also knew that if a hitter grounded a ball off Rivera, he usually did so weakly; there would be no time to turn a double play, and he could not risk losing the World Series while trying for it. So the infielders played in, on the edge of the dirt.

"They could have been a couple of steps back because Jay Bell was not a good runner; they were really far in," Counsell said. "But I still don't think he would have caught that ball."

Gonzalez had hit 57 home runs that season, but all that mattered here was getting Bell home from third. He choked up for the first time all season and floated an 0–1 pitch exactly where McCarver had predicted, just onto the center field grass on the shortstop's side. Arizona had won its first title, and later, in a quiet moment in the trainer's room, emotions overcame Womack.

He had lost his father, Thomas, to a heart attack that April at age 52. Thomas Womack built mobile homes and played semipro ball on weekends, passing down the game to his son. His death shattered Tony, but he tried to honor Thomas with the way he played—first with a grand slam on Father's Day and now with the focus to produce the biggest hit of the World Series.

He had blocked out all distractions on the field, just as Thomas had taught him. Between the lines, nothing else matters, his father would say; there was no moment bigger than the one you're in now. Coming through in that final big moment had helped make him a champion, and as he savored the feeling with his double-play partner, Womack broke down in tears. Counsell was there with his father, John, proudly wearing Craig's championship ring from 1997. It was too much.

"I'm coming up on 19 years without him," Womack said, in the spring of 2020. "He's my dude."

By then Womack was coaching at a high school in Charlotte and training his son, Alsander, an infielder at Norfolk State. Tony was nearly 52 years old himself then, and said he would give his son everything his father had given him. A year later, Alsander Womack signed a pro contract with the Chicago White Sox.

What you know: David Freese's triple and homer saved the Cardinals in Game 6 of the 2011 World Series.

———

What you might not know:
Lance Berkman was the man in the middle.

It was one of the greatest nights any player could imagine. In Game 6 of the 2011 World Series, one strike from elimination against the Texas Rangers, David Freese smoked a game-tying triple in the bottom of the ninth for his hometown St. Louis Cardinals. Two innings later he homered to win the game, on his way to the series MVP award.

But what about the guy with the most hits in that World Series, the one who got his own game-tying hit in Game 6, also one strike from elimination, in the inning between Freese's heroics? Wouldn't Lance Berkman like a bigger slice of the credit for David Freese Night?

"Heavens, no, he deserved it," Berkman says. "He was huge."

Speaking of heavens, you might have noticed a theme here. From Mike Davis to Roger Mason to Berkman and Josh Hamilton in this epic game, God's in-box sure gets full during the World Series. To understand Berkman's mind-set in the bottom of the tenth, trailing 9–8 with two on and two out against Scott Feldman, we have to go back to Game 3 in Texas, when Berkman started seeking guidance for the inevitable.

"What happened in Game 3 is that Albert [Pujols] hit three homers, and he had not gotten a base hit before that in the series," Berkman says. "But he hit three homers, and of course with his sterling reputation, at that point they were like, 'We're not pitching to this dude ever,' and you could just see the change in strategy that they had when they were facing Albert. And then also in that game, Matt Holliday, who normally hit fourth, slid headfirst back into third base; the catcher tried to pick him off and he jammed his finger. So he wasn't 100 percent.

"Tony [La Russa, the manager] came to me after that game and said, 'Look, against right-handers, I'm gonna hit you fourth,' because normally it was Albert, Matt, and myself, no matter what. So from that point forward, I was like, 'OK, they're not pitching to Albert, I'm gonna be hitting behind him, there's no doubt I'm gonna have a huge at-bat.' Of course, I didn't know it was gonna be a bottom-of-the-tenth, two-out kind of deal. But I knew that at some point I'm gonna be called upon to get a big hit for us, so I actually started praying at that point. There were two more games there, the off-day and the rainout, so there were probably four or five days that I was basically in prayer for the same thing."

The Rangers started lefties in Games 4 and 5, both of which they won. By then, Berkman thought, the series had already lasted too long. The Cardinals won Games 1 and 3, and if they'd held a ninth-inning lead in Game 2, he reasons, they would have then finished off a sweep. Instead, they needed Freese's triple to rescue them from defeat in Game 6—and even that was only temporary.

In the top of the tenth, Hamilton swatted a two-run homer off Jason Motte, fulfilling a prophecy of his own. In the clubhouse later—with a thick roll of plastic above his locker for a celebration that never came—Hamilton told us that God had promised him a home run as he dug his cleats into the batter's box.

"He said, 'You haven't hit one in a while—this is the time you're going to,'" Hamilton said, adding that the message made him peaceful and relaxed. "But there was a period at the end of that. He didn't say, 'You're gonna hit it and you're gonna win.'"

It sure seemed that way entering the bottom of the tenth, though, with the Rangers up 9–7 and lefty Darren Oliver coming in to face Daniel Descalso, Jon Jay, and the pitcher's spot, with no position players remaining on the Cardinal bench. Berkman wasn't conceding the season, but he wasn't expecting to win, either.

"When Hamilton hit the two-run homer, in my mind I was thinking, 'We had a great year, it was a great run,' because you just don't come back from two two-run deficits in the ninth and tenth—that's almost unheard of in the history of baseball," Berkman said. "But I looked up at the scoreboard and noticed that I was the sixth hitter up that inning—it was 8-9-1-2-3. And I remember thinking there's a decent chance that I'm not gonna get an at-bat—but if I do, it's gonna be with runners in scoring position, and most likely two outs."

Then he got nervous. Terrified, he said. Because Berkman knew that the Rangers, who'd intentionally walked Pujols three times in Game 5, would almost certainly do it again if his spot came up here. After two singles, a sacrifice bunt, and a run-scoring ground out, that's exactly what happened. It was Berkman's turn to end the season or extend it. He was 35 years old and felt the full weight of his life in the game—childhood, college, and 8,810 professional plate appearances—as Feldman put Pujols on base.

"It's like the culmination of all of your baseball experience, and you're just pushing all your chips in on one spin of the wheel," Berkman says. "Little kids, when they're in the backyard, always pretend: 'Hey, bottom of the ninth, two outs, down a run.' If they really knew what it felt like to be in that situation, they would never pretend that."

In general terms, Berkman said, he tries to think of three B's when he hits—breathe, ball (as in "see the ball"), and back through the middle. Specific to the moment, he considered how Feldman might attack him. Berkman was glad Oliver had been pulled after the bunt; he had faced Oliver only three times in the last eight years, but had more recent intelligence on Feldman, with a single and a walk in the World Series.

As a switch-hitter, Berkman always had the matchup advantage. When he'd first picked up a bat, around age five, he swung right-handed. But he threw lefty, and his father, Larry, guessed correctly that the boy could also hit that way. So Berkman was switch-hitting before Little League, and grew up to be one of the best. Among long-time switch hitters, only Mickey Mantle has a better career OPS than Berkman's .943.

As a lefty, Berkman liked the ball away, so he'd hit Feldman well when the sinker was his primary pitch. By 2011, though, Feldman had mastered a cutter, and while Berkman expected him to use it with the title on the line, he couldn't be sure. All he knew was that the plate is 17 inches wide, and if the ball is anywhere over it, he should be able to connect if he concentrated on the middle of the field.

Berkman was right about the cutters: he fouled one back, then took one for a ball before fouling a curve. One strike away now, it was time again for Feldman's best pitch. A cutter veered too far inside for ball two, but the next one caught just enough of the plate, at 93 miles an hour, to make Berkman swing. The pitch cracked his bat, a hairline break that couldn't keep the ball from landing safely in mid–center field. With Hamilton playing near the warning track, it was an easy single all the way. Familiar, too.

"I probably got, let's say, 100 hits like that in my career where you get jammed a little but you still hit that nice little line drive," Berkman said. "It's not scalded, but it's a line-drive base hit. When I felt like my swing was good, that's what I would do on that ball in. Anything that would leak to the middle of the plate, that's the one you would barrel. But anything that was inside corner, I'm fighting that back up the middle."

For the fifth time that night—*the fifth time!*—the Cardinals had erased a Rangers lead. Yet to Berkman, his approach, not his outcome, was the answered prayer. All he wanted was a chance to compete as the best version of himself, and he did it. He retired after two more seasons and has stayed close to his original team, the Astros, in his hometown.

In 2014, looking for a dependable starter to help them climb back to respectability, the Astros gave a $30 million contract to a righty who had just won 12 games for the Cubs and Orioles: Scott Feldman. One day at Minute Maid Park, sensing the awkwardness between them, Berkman approached the pitcher he'd fought for the greatest hit of his life.

He hadn't shown him up on the field, hadn't pumped his fist, hadn't even smiled. Would he gloat about the moment? Heavens, no.

"Man," Berkman told Feldman, simply, "that was a great competition."

Game 3

A Beetle in the Snow

Unlikely Heroes of the World Series

It should have been a mismatch: Don Sutton versus John Stuper in Game 6 of the 1982 World Series. Sutton had starred for the Milwaukee Brewers after a late-season trade, still going strong on his way to the Hall of Fame. He had worked 4,000 more innings than Stuper, a St. Louis Cardinals rookie best known as a clubhouse comedian who called himself John Cosell, grilling teammates with a beer-bottle microphone after victories.

"Do I look upset?" Stuper had asked reporters after Game 2, when he'd struggled before the Cardinals rallied off Milwaukee's bullpen. "We won, and that's the bottom line."

But the Cardinals would take just one of the next three games in Milwaukee, and returned to Busch Stadium facing elimination. Their ace, Joaquin Andujar, was still hobbling from a comebacker that had smashed off his leg in Game 3. It was up to Stuper to save the season against Sutton and the highest-scoring offense in baseball.

Final score: Cardinals 13, Brewers 1.

Stuper worked all nine innings. His career would not last long, but his surprise star turn in 1982 symbolizes the unlikely heroes who can emerge in the World Series, the guys with one gilded moment and not much else.

"About seven or eight years ago, one of my players found the sixth game on YouTube and put it up on the television in the clubhouse," says Stuper, who retired in 2022 after 30 seasons as the baseball coach at Yale. "He was watching me pitch and looking at the movement on my fastball, and he says, 'Coach, you were pretty good!'"

Stuper pitched through two rain delays in Game 6, totaling two hours and 39 minutes, and a 20-degree temperature drop. He was determined to work nine innings so Whitey Herzog, a manager he revered, would have a fully rested bullpen for Game 7. Stuper was healthy the next season but rarely after that. The risk was worth it.

"Even 38 years later, people in St. Louis think that shortened my career," Stuper says, reluctantly. "Whitey even said something to me about it at a reunion, about him putting me back out there after a two-and-a-half-hour rain delay. I said, 'Whitey, knowing what I know today, if I had it to do over again, I'd freaking do it. It was the World Series and I was a rookie, are you kidding me?' I have absolutely no regrets about any of that."

Sutton would pitch more than 5,000 innings in the majors. Stuper did not even reach 500. But Sutton was never on a winning World Series roster, and Stuper has a ring. He also has a cherished memory of Sutton's grace in defeat.

"He came into our clubhouse after the seventh game, came over to my locker, and shook my hand," Stuper says. "Guys were celebrating all around and he said, 'This never would have happened without you.'"

————

Stuper is the archetype of our unlikely hero: he makes a seismic impact on a victorious World Series while barely registering otherwise in the major leagues. Plenty of others nearly fit that description—Kiko Garcia and Kurt Bevacqua, Chad Ogea and Brett Phillips—but ultimately, their teams lost. Others shined in the World Series without really starring in their careers—Donn Clendenon, Rick Dempsey, Billy Hatcher, Pat Borders, Scott Spiezio—but they were everyday guys with long careers who got hot at the right time. They don't quite qualify, either.

A player like Gene Larkin, that's who we're talking about. Larkin spent seven years in the majors, all with the Twins, arriving just in time for their first championship in 1987. He never hit 10 home runs, never stole 10 bases, never hit .300. He was the first major leaguer who had played for Columbia since Lou Gehrig, so at least he was known for something. But Gehrig he was not.

"Hey, Gene," the plate umpire Don Denkinger said to Larkin, as he came to bat at the Metrodome in the bottom of the tenth inning of Game 7 in 1991. "If he keeps bringing all those outfielders in, even you could hit one over their heads."

Larkin heard the joke, but his mouth was too dry to respond. The Braves had just issued two intentional walks to load the bases with one out in a scoreless game. A fly ball would win the World Series, and that's what Larkin hit, swatting the first pitch from Alejandro Peña to deep left field, a long single that reverberates forever.

"It's always nice to be thought of as someone who came through in the clutch," Larkin says, "as opposed to someone who's never remembered at all."

Larkin is a New York guy, but he stayed in Minnesota after his career, working as a financial planner and eventually opening a baseball academy in Edina with Tom Nevers, a former infielder. People still come up to him and thank him, Larkin says—not the kids anymore, but the parents or grandparents. It isn't for his 1.6 career wins above replacement.

"They sometimes think I was a better player than I was," Larkin says, laughing. "Just look at my stats; they weren't very good. But I came through that one time, and my 15 seconds of fame have lasted 30 years now."

Before Larkin, nobody had ended the World Series with a hit since Bill Mazeroski homered for the Pirates in 1960. Yet Larkin's was the first in a flurry of clinching hits: Joe Carter's homer for the Blue Jays in 1993; Edgar Renteria's single for the Marlins in 1997; and Luis Gonzalez's single for the Diamondbacks in 2001.

Stitching such moments together is part of the fun of an event with deep roots; nearly every feat has a historical match. John Lackey, a stalwart right-hander of the early 2000s, is the only starter to win a clincher for two different franchises: Game 7 for the 2002 Angels and Game 6 for the 2013 Red Sox. But he's not the only rookie starter to win a seventh game: Babe Adams achieved the feat for the Pirates in 1909.

Adams would have a long and distinguished career, but he was 27 in that 1909 season, winless in four career starts before a yearlong banishment to the minors. He proved he belonged in 1909 (12–3, 1.11), though he worked only 130 innings. Five teammates pitched more.

The Pirates won 110 games in 1909, a dozen more than the AL champion Tigers, but Detroit had the more compelling narrative: after losing twice in a row to the Cubs, the great Ty Cobb was bound to take his team all the way. Cobb, still just 22, had enjoyed a season unmatched in history, not just winning the Triple Crown (.377, 9 homers, 107 RBI) but also leading the majors in stolen bases (76).

Yet Cobb was nearly helpless against Adams, who did not learn he was starting Game 1 until 90 minutes before the first pitch. Adams expected Howie Camnitz, a 25-game winner, to get the assignment, but Camnitz was weak from a throat operation. Fred Clarke, the Pirates' player-manager, found Adams lounging on the bench, said, "You're it," and flipped him a ball.

"I caught it and laughed, for he could be pretty funny," Adams would tell Herbert F. McDougal of *The Chicago Daily News*. "But he repeated, 'You're it. Come on, kid.'"

Clarke remembered that Adams had shut out the champion Cubs in May, and had gotten a tip from John Heydler, the NL president, who'd watched a Washington Senators rookie, Dolly Gray, subdue the Tigers in September. Heydler told Clarke that Adams was similar to Gray, but better. With his curveball and control, Adams stood a good chance of subduing the Tigers.

He wobbled at first, walking two of the first three hitters, including Cobb, who scored. But he shut out the Tigers thereafter in a complete-game win, and worked another nine innings to take Game 5.

After Detroit evened the series back home, Adams was the only sensible choice for Clarke in Game 7. The other Pirate starters had been shaky, and Adams felt strong on two days' rest. On a cold, raw day, he shut out the Tigers to clinch Pittsburgh's first title, stifling Cobb with nothing but off-speed pitches. After the last out—Tom Jones flied to Clarke in left field—the Pirates dashed for the taxi stand to party at their hotel.

"And here came my friends from Missouri," Adams said, "pushing roses at me and screaming congratulations and saying I was the only man beside Mathewson to win three games in a World Series."

A farmboy from tiny Mount Moriah, Missouri, Adams had equaled Matty, the master of them all. He would stick in the majors until 1926, at age 44—no longer a Babe, but the oldest player in the National League.

————

To go by their nickname—the "Hitless Wonders"—the 1906 Chicago White Sox would seem to have a claim as the least likely champions in the early years of the World Series. Their sin was a .230 team batting average, worst in the American League in the statistic that persisted for decades as the definitive measure of offensive prowess.

But the White Sox scored more runs than the average team in 1906, largely because they led the league in walks. They outscored opponents by 110 runs, and their 2.13 team ERA ranked third in the majors. While their six-game triumph over the 116-win Cubs was clearly unexpected, it is not shocking through a modern lens. Pitching dominated the World Series—both teams hit under .200—and the hero was Big Ed Walsh, a Hall of Fame spitballer who won twice.

The truly unfathomable champions were the 1914 Boston Braves— the original "Miracle" champions, long before the 1969 Mets. The Braves held last place on July 4 with a 26–40 record. The rest of the way they were 72–19, including the first four-game sweep in World Series history. As *Spalding's Official Base Ball Guide* would put it, the mighty Philadelphia A's, who had won three of the previous four championships, were victims of a "slam-bang, get-at-them assault."

The imagery was appropriate. Before Game 1, Braves manager George Stallings threatened to punch the venerable Connie Mack in the nose in a dispute over workout times at Shibe Park. The Braves then routed Chief Bender, 7–1, with catcher Hank Gowdy going 3 for 3.

Mack was furious with Bender. He had dispatched Bender to New York on a scouting mission late in the season, but Bender ignored the edict and stayed in Philadelphia. The Braves did not worry him.

"They're just a bunch of misfits," Bender told Mack, as recounted by teammate Shag Thompson in research by Norman L. Macht. "I won't have any trouble with them."

Bender had spent 12 seasons in Philadelphia, with credentials that would earn him a plaque in the Hall of Fame. But he never pitched for Mack after the fiasco in Game 1. He struggled in particular with Gowdy, who had a double and a triple when his turn came up in the sixth. Mack would not allow Bender to face him again, and for the first time in his five World Series as a manager, he pulled a healthy starting pitcher from the game.

"Well, Albert," Mack told Bender on the bench, using his given middle name. "Pretty good bunch of misfits."

The lead misfit was Gowdy, who had finally earned a starting job in his fifth major league season. He led the Braves in hitting in the World Series at .545 (6 for 11) with an extra-inning homer in Game 3. He also helped the pitchers—Bill James, Dick Rudolph, and Lefty Tyler—by flashing multiple signals when a runner reached second base. Gowdy would show three signs, and the pitcher would add them together. Two fingers plus three fingers plus one finger, for example, would equal six—an even number, which meant fastball. An odd number meant curve. It was Stallings's innovation, and Gowdy swore by him.

"He had me feeling that all the other catchers in baseball were grade A dopes compared to me," Gowdy told writer Joe Williams many years later, "and I actually believe that's why I hit so well in the series."

Gowdy played 12 more seasons in the majors but never got as much playing time as he did in 1914. He became a hero on a different field in 1917, when he left the Braves during a trip to Cincinnati, in his home state of Ohio, and enlisted in the 166th Infantry Regiment of the 42nd Division. Gowdy was the first active major leaguer to enlist in World War I and saw action in the Lorraine region of France—though probably not as sportswriter Walter Trumbull described it:

> A screaming shell displaced his hat,
> But Hank showed no alarm.
> He said, "James had more speed than that
> Before he hurt his arm."

Then Gowdy grabbed some hand grenades,
And with a happy smile,
Each time a Hun essayed to run
He threw him out a mile.

Gowdy—who would also serve as a major at Fort Benning, Georgia, in World War II—returned to baseball in 1919 and played in two more World Series for the Giants. In 1924, he stumbled over his mask in the twelfth inning of Game 7, dropping a foul and giving new life to the Senators' hitter, Muddy Ruel, who doubled and went on to score the winning run.

"Show me a cheerful loser and I'll show you a lunatic," Gowdy said in his postgame column for United News wire service. "I never made an alibi in my life and I'm too old to start."

A headline in the Brooklyn *Standard Union* blamed the mask, not Gowdy, as the "innocent cause" of the Giants' defeat. The story noted Gowdy's performance in 1914, his service in the war, and his status as "the most popular player in the National League." The error didn't stick, the heroics did, and the diamond at Fort Benning is named Gowdy Field in his honor.

———————

The Braves took 43 years to win their next championship after the 1914 miracle. They did it in 1957, in Milwaukee, making the Braves the first franchise with World Series titles in multiple cities. The Dodgers were the next, taking the crown while representing Los Angeles in 1959, their second season after moving from Brooklyn.

The 1959 Dodgers went 88–68 for a .564 winning percentage—to that point, the lowest ever for a World Series champion.* In their six-game victory over the White Sox, they needed an assist from Chuck Essegian, a journeyman who belted two pinch-hit home runs, and especially pitcher Larry Sherry.

Sherry was an L.A. kid, a star at Fairfax High School (like Essegian)

* The 2006 St. Louis Cardinals, at 83–78 (.516), now hold that distinction.

who made his major league debut in the Dodgers' third game in California, in 1958. He got no outs in that game, nor in his second. But by 1959 he was ready, capping a strong season with seven and two-thirds scoreless innings of relief against the Braves in the first of a best-of-three playoff series at the end of the regular season.

In the World Series, Sherry came to the rescue again with two saves and two wins in four appearances. In the last, at Comiskey Park in Game 6, he relieved Johnny Podres with one out in the fourth and blanked the White Sox the rest of the way to clinch the title. On a staff with Don Drysdale, Sandy Koufax, and Podres, it was Sherry who threw the most innings in the World Series.

"Everything he threw, we hit at somebody," White Sox pitcher Billy Pierce told author Danny Peary. "He did nothing wrong."

In all, Sherry worked 49 relief innings in 1959, going 7–0 with five saves and a 0.73 ERA, by far the best season of a middling 11-year career. Indirectly, though, he helped the Dodgers win again after he left—Lou Johnson, the outfielder they got from Detroit when they traded Sherry, hit a homer in Game 7 of the 1965 World Series as Sandy Koufax beat the Twins.

Johnson would make the last out of the next World Series, in Baltimore, flying to Paul Blair in center to give Dave McNally a 1–0 shutout and the Orioles a sweep. McNally had allowed two early runs in the opener, but the Dodgers never scored again—in the entire series. A flaky reliever named Moe Drabowsky began a string of 33 shutout innings to end the season.

Drabowsky was 31 then, with a habit of finding himself on the wrong side of history. He had served up Stan Musial's 3,000th hit in 1958 and was the losing pitcher five years later for Early Wynn's 300th victory. He also shared a record by hitting four batters in one game.

A merry prankster, Drabowsky would slip snakes into teammates' travel bags, crank-call the manager from the bullpen phone, load goldfish into dugout water coolers. He once lit Bowie Kuhn's shoe on fire, treating the commissioner to a classic clubhouse hotfoot.

He earned his fame in the Orioles' first-ever World Series game, taking the ball in the third inning and never giving it up. Drabowsky struck out the side in the fourth and fifth, and by the end he had fanned 11—still a single-game record for a reliever.

In the clubhouse later, wrapping his arms around the future Hall of Famers Brooks and Frank Robinson, Drabowsky summed up the feelings of every bit player who has starred in the World Series: "Just what is a guy like me doing in fast company like this?"

On the eve of opening day in that 1966 season, the Orioles released a 36-year-old right-hander with a losing record but a hallowed name in the annals of baseball: Don Larsen, the only man to pitch a perfect game in the World Series.

Larsen had done it for the Yankees 10 years earlier, of course, against the Dodgers in the Bronx, where he would return many times for the pin-striped embrace of Old-Timers' Day. Larsen was 89 years old in 2019 and needed a wheelchair to get from the home dugout to the first base coach's box at Yankee Stadium. A walker waited for him there, and as Larsen rose to clutch it, three tiers of cheering wafted over him like summer breeze, gently pushing Larsen to the gathering of other former Yankees on the infield. There to greet him were David Cone and David Wells, the only other Yankees to throw perfect games.

"That's pretty impressive," says Geoff Blum, watching from above home plate in the broadcast booth of the visiting Houston Astros. Blum never pitched, but he was perfect in his own way. He batted one time in the World Series—for the White Sox in 2005, against Houston—and slugged a home run.

Three other players have homered in the only World Series at-bat of their careers: Jim Mason of the 1976 Yankees, Bobby Kielty of the 2007 Red Sox (his last major league game!), and Michael A. Taylor of the 2019 Nationals. But only Blum's homer gave his team the lead. It broke a tie in the fourteenth inning of Game 3 in Houston, and the next night Chicago completed a sweep.

The standard for one-and-done World Series homers, of course, will always be the Game 1 blast by a hobbled Kirk Gibson for the Dodgers in 1988. But Gibson had also starred for Detroit in the 1984 World

Series, with an upper-deck blast at Tiger Stadium to punctuate the clincher. This was Blum's only shot at glory.

Blum has company, though, among unheralded players who delivered the very first time they grabbed a bat on that stage. Dusty Rhodes, Del Unser, Ed Sprague, and Christian Colon all came off the bench with their teams tied or trailing, with no prior experience in the World Series. All came through, with Rhodes and Unser doing so more than once.

Rhodes was a true baseball character, born in Alabama as James Lamar Rhodes but known better for his nickname in his adopted hometown. He played for the last six New York Giants teams, through 1957, then settled on Staten Island, working for years as an engineer on a tugboat. Rhodes was dry by then, but as a player he was often called "a 12 o'clock guy in a 9 o'clock town," a reference to his minor league days in Des Moines, Iowa. He drank whiskey with the Giants' owner, Horace Stoneham, who adored him.

When Rhodes died, in 2009, Willie Mays told *The Sporting News* that he'd never had a better friend. The two shared the spotlight in the opener of the 1954 World Series against Cleveland, Mays with his game-saving catch off Vic Wertz's deep drive in the eighth, and Rhodes with his game-ending three-run homer off Bob Lemon in the tenth. His bat had Mays's spike marks on it.

"During the season, Willie borrowed my regular bat and broke it," Rhodes told writer Bill Madden, decades later. "I had to have three bats flown in airmail, special delivery, for the series. Well, Willie comes up to me and asks if he can borrow another bat. This time I tell him, 'Hell, no, you broke my other one.' Willie got so mad he kicked the bat and caught his spikes in it."

The wood was sound enough for Rhodes to turn on Lemon's hanging curve and loft a pop fly down the right field line at the Polo Grounds. It traveled only 270 feet or so but nestled just inside the foul pole to give the Giants a 5–2 victory. In Game 2, Rhodes struck again off another future Hall of Famer, ducking a brushback pitch from Early Wynn as a pinch hitter in the fifth, then scoring Mays with a game-tying single.

Rhodes homered onto the right field roof in the seventh, then lashed a two-run, pinch-hit single in Game 3. He did not play in

Game 4—"It was just as well," he told Ira Berkow, many years later. "I was drinking to everybody's health so much that I about ruined mine"—but his teammates finished a sweep, humbling the 111-win Indians to give the Giants the last of their five championships in New York.

———

The Phillies won their first in 1980, with Tug McGraw on the mound. They had gotten McGraw six years earlier in a trade that sent Del Unser, their center fielder, to the Mets. By 1978 Unser had become a frustrated reserve with the Montreal Expos, all but useless as a pinch hitter (3 for 38).

"I just went up there and hacked," he says. "I wanted to get out my aggression and show 'em I could kill the ball."

Unser wasn't fooling anyone. His career as an everyday player was finished, and he'd missed the Phillies' ascent in the standings; they were a losing team when he left, and now they were the class of the NL East. "Unser is like an actor who gets killed off just before the last act," Jayson Stark wrote in *The Philadelphia Inquirer* when Unser returned in 1979. But there was one big role still to play.

Unser was playing in a racquetball tournament in Las Vegas before that '79 season when he called his old boss, Phillies general manager Paul Owens, looking for a job. Owens teased him about his hobby: If you want to get in shape for baseball, he barked, why not go to a ballpark? Unser took Owens literally, packing his things and booking a red-eye flight. He showed up at Veterans Stadium the next morning and stayed for almost 40 years.

Unser would become a longtime executive and scout for the Phillies after a two-year master class as a pinch hitter. In 1979, he became the first player ever to homer in three consecutive plate appearances as a pinch hitter. The next fall, after his crucial pinch hit to redeem Mike Schmidt in the NLCS clincher in Houston, he delivered twice in the World Series, both times against the Royals' submarine closer, Dan Quisenberry.

Teams would never use a pitcher like Quisenberry today. Even in his time, he was something of an anomaly. He tied the Yankees' Goose

Gossage for the major league lead in saves in 1980, with 33, but Gossage was the template for the modern pitcher—throwing heat, chasing strikeouts. Quisenberry was the opposite—tossing softly, chasing weak contact. He faced 43 batters in the 1980 World Series and struck out none.

"He took so much sting out of the bat with his slow, slow changeup," says Unser, who hit left-handed. "When I went up against him, I tried to hit everything down the left field line and wound up pulling the ball down the right field line. That's how slow it was. I'm thinking, 'Wait, wait, wait, wait,' like playing slo-pitch softball."

Unser lined a double to left center off Quisenberry in the eighth inning of Game 2, helping the Phillies overcome a two-run deficit to win. He singled again off him in a Game 4 loss, then delivered the biggest hit in the series: a double down the first base line to tie Game 5 in the ninth inning. The Phillies stole that game and took the series in six.

———————

Pinch hitting was in Unser's genes; with the Tigers in 1944, his father, Al, had hit a pinch-hit grand slam to beat the Yankees in the bottom of the ninth. Ed Sprague also had a big league father—Ed Sr., a pitcher—and was familiar with high stakes: he had won the College World Series twice at Stanford, and Olympic gold for the United States in 1988.

But while Unser's heroics fulfilled his goal of mastering life on the bench, Sprague's helped him escape that fate. The Blue Jays had started to sour on him as their third baseman of the future, and told him to try catching in Triple-A. He spent most of the season there in 1992, coming to bat just 50 times for Toronto, with one home run.

Sprague made the postseason roster as an afterthought, watching from the bench as Atlanta took the World Series opener. With a 4–3 lead in Game 2, the Braves had Jeff Reardon—then baseball's career saves leader—on the mound for the ninth.

With the bottom of the order due to hit for Toronto, Sprague thought he might get a chance. He checked with Rance Mulliniks, a veteran at the end of his career who had faced Reardon often. He'll try to get you to chase a high fastball, Mulliniks told Sprague, so make sure to get him down in the zone. With one on and one out, Sprague considered taking a pitch but thought better of it. He would hunt the low fastball and belt the first one he saw.

A double play would have ended the game and sent the Blue Jays back to Toronto in an 0–2 hole, but Sprague was not thinking about that. He felt strangely calm.

"It was probably one of the most relaxed at-bats I ever had in my career, one that was completely in the moment," he says. "You think about the movie *For Love of the Game*—clear the mechanism."

Sprague freed his mind to put his plan into action. He got a first-pitch fastball down the middle, just below the belt, and hammered it into the left field seats, over a sign marking the spot of Hank Aaron's record 715th home run. The Blue Jays won, 5–4, but sudden fame as a World Series hero unnerved Sprague. In the ninth inning of Game 3, at the rollicking SkyDome, Sprague pinch hit for John Olerud—he still can't believe it—and felt as shaky as he ever would in the box.

"They actually intentionally walked me," he says. "But if they had been inside my head for that at-bat . . ."

Candy Maldonado got the winning hit this time, a single to deep center to score Roberto Alomar, who pantomimed the "Tomahawk Chop" as he trotted to the plate. The Blue Jays went on to win the first World Series title for a team in Canada, which still earned them a trip to meet President George H. W. Bush—a baseball fanatic—at the White House. Bush gave manager Cito Gaston a baseball card Topps had made of him in his Yale uniform. Gaston gave Sprague third base.

"Cito grabbed me at the airport after the White House trip and he says, 'Hey, we traded Kelly Gruber, do you want to go back to third?'" Sprague says. "And I'm like, Pat Borders is the catcher, he's the World Series MVP—'Yeah, I want to go back!'"

The Blue Jays sent their farm director and a top instructor to California, where Sprague lived, for three days of off-season training at third base. Sprague spent the rest of the decade as a regular at that position, and never forgot the gesture: he became the Athletics' farm director in 2019 and says he tries to care for Oakland prospects the same way Toronto cared for him.

———

Without the homer, perhaps, Sprague would have stalled out, buried on a roster of win-now veterans. That is how it was for Christian Colon, who never quite broke through with the other top Royals draft picks of his era. From 2004 through 2010, the Royals took Alex Gordon, Mike Moustakas, Eric Hosmer, and Colon within the first four picks of the draft. The first three started every World Series game in 2014 and 2015. Colon had one at-bat.

He was left off the roster in 2014 despite getting the game-tying hit—and scoring the winning run—in the Wild Card victory over Oakland. In the 2015 postseason, Colon sat for the first 15 games. He got his only shot in the twelfth inning of Game 5 of the World Series at Citi Field, with one on, one out, and Kansas City trying to clinch.

In the Royals' executive suite, Robert Moore smiled. Robert, the 13-year-old son of general manager Dayton Moore, sensed redemption for his father, who had passed on a future superstar pitcher to draft Colon.

"Dad," Robert said, "if CC gets a hit right here, nobody will ever give you any more crap about Chris Sale."

On the mound was the Mets' Addison Reed, a pitcher Colon had faced in college and an off-season workout partner in California. Reed threw five sliders in a row, and Colon lined the last into left field, breaking a tie and sparking a five-run rally that unplugged New York City.

"I'm in the on-deck circle and it's super loud, and I'm thinking: 'Breathe, you've done this before, talk yourself through it, let's go, compete,'" Colon says. "I get the hit—and I can literally hear myself yelling and screaming."

Colon had played in Triple-A for four years. He was 26 years old, and when the Royals lost second baseman Ben Zobrist as a free agent, Colon seemed a natural fit to take over. But a different prospect, Whit Merrifield, took advantage of the chance, and by the end of the decade Colon had bounced through four other organizations.

He never earned the salaries of the other top Royals prospects, but he has a crown tattooed on his chest, "Champs 15" inked on his left forearm, and a ring that reminds him of the opportunity he seized.

"I can lay down at night and know that I gave to the organization," Colon said in the Cincinnati Reds' clubhouse before a late-September game in 2019. "I didn't take from it—I gave, and that really makes me feel good."

———————

As for Geoff Blum, he took something from the Astros with his big swing in 2005: a win in the first World Series game ever played in the state of Texas. He had spent most of the season with San Diego, where he and his wife, Kory, had newborn triplets. The Padres were in first place on July 31, and with the children finally out of the neonatal intensive care unit, Kory was at the ballpark for the first time all season. This was what Blum had wanted all year: playing at home, with his wife and new daughters safe and sound.

Then a club official tapped him on the shoulder in the clubhouse before the game. The White Sox' manager, Ozzie Guillen, had made an impassioned plea for Blum, and the Padres had traded him to Chicago. Blum broke down in tears as he told Kory, who gave him clear instructions.

"Two things," she said. "Get your sleep and win a World Series."

Blum followed orders. He signed right back with the Padres before Thanksgiving, but made his stay in Chicago count in Game 3 of the World Series, near the end of its then-record 5 hours and 41 minutes. He had entered the game in a double switch and was due up third in the top of the fourteenth against the Astros' seventh pitcher of the game, Ezequiel Astacio. Blum quickly assessed the situation: with sluggers Jermaine Dye and Paul Konerko up before him, he would probably have to bunt.

Instead, the bases were empty after a single and a double play. Blum greeted Astros catcher Brad Ausmus, his former teammate, with some friendly banter at the plate. That relaxed Blum, who expected the Astros to pitch him away. He would try to flick a ball to left field, he thought, but Astacio missed down and in.

"Right in the sweet spot," Blum says. "That's just a natural groove for my left-handed swing, and I hammered it."

The White Sox commemorate the moment as part of a two-sided championship monument outside the main entrance to U.S. Cellular Field. Blum's home run swing is preserved in bronze, facing the glassed-in reception area. He visits every year when the Astros come to town.

"You have to go through the downstairs lobby to get to the media elevator, and I glance to my right every time and see that statue," Blum says. "I can't believe it to this day."

―――――

Forty years before Blum, the White Sox had another reserve second baseman who hit just one homer for them in the regular season. That was Al Weis, in 1965, and soon he had one of the worst hitting seasons ever. In 1968, with the Mets, Weis became the only player in the expansion era with 300 plate appearances, no more than one homer, and an average below .175.

As meager as that was, the Mets valued Weis's versatility and used him in the middle infield when the starters left for military duty. Weis was healthy again, fully recovered from the injury that had ended his White Sox career: a broken leg from a collision with the Orioles' Frank Robinson. The two would meet again in the 1969 World Series.

Mets manager Gil Hodges platooned his second basemen, which meant that the right-handed Weis started four of the five games, twice each against the Baltimore lefties Mike Cuellar and Dave McNally. He victimized McNally twice, with a go-ahead single in the ninth inning of Game 2 and a game-tying homer in the seventh inning of the clincher.

Weis had actually homered before off McNally, in 1964, but his son Danny probably did not know that. Danny turned six years old on the day of Game 5 and had a premonition about his present.

"He was riding to the ballpark with my wife and Mrs. [Jerry] Grote, and for some reason he said, 'My dad's gonna hit a home run for my birthday today,'" says Weis, who learned about it after the game. "The odds of that happening at the time were probably about 1,000 to 1."

Close enough. Weis, a wispy 6 feet, 160 pounds, homered just eight times in his 1,590 career at-bats—but these were the Miracle Mets, so anything was possible. Robinson's homer gave Baltimore an early 3–0 lead, but Weis erased it with a blast over the servicemen in the left field bleachers. He charged around the bases, a Long Island kid buoyed by the roars of his hometown crowd. It was the only homer he ever hit at Shea Stadium.

"The Mighty Mite has become the hitting star of the World Series!" Curt Gowdy exclaimed on NBC, and while Donn Clendenon was named the official series MVP, the nickname served Weis well. A few days after the World Series, a car company honored him with a sidewalk presentation at 47th Street and Lexington Avenue.

"Volkswagen had that little car, the Beetle, that was also called the Mighty Mite," Weis says. "That's why I got the Volkswagen, and I had it for about 10 years. Living in Chicago, it was a great car in the snow because the engine was in the back, and you got good traction."

———

Like Weis, Mickey Hatcher came to bat more than 200 times in his only World Series season, with the Dodgers in 1988, and hit just one home run. He'd played for a decade by then, and the series had always eluded him. At the end of spring training in 1981, the Dodgers traded Hatcher to Minnesota for Ken Landreaux. That October, Landreaux caught the final out of the World Series. In 1987, Hatcher lost his Twins roster spot to Dan Gladden. That October, Gladden ripped a grand slam in the World Series opener, sending the Twins on their way.

Back with L.A. in 1988, Hatcher finally got his chance. He sensed as much during the playoffs in New York, when he met his namesake, Mickey Mantle, at Mantle's restaurant on Central Park South. Hatcher's name is Michael but his father called him Mickey, because Mantle was his favorite player. When the Dodgers played in New York, Hatcher liked to stop by the restaurant, swapping stories with old Brooklyn Dodger fans in exchange for free drinks.

Mantle was there for the playoff visit, and Hatcher met him for the first time. Mantle signed his menu and then grabbed Hatcher around the neck.

"Your name's Mickey, right?" he said. "You better fucking start hitting some home runs!"

"OK, Mickey!" Hatcher replied—what else could he say?—and then somehow hit two in the World Series against Oakland. Ever since, Hatcher has joked, he might have made some money in baseball if only he'd met Mantle sooner.

Hatcher was a certified goofball ("the flakiest man in baseball," *Inside Sports* had called him) who once spooked a teammate by pretending to be a Martian and twice posed for baseball cards with a glove the size of his torso. In 1988, Hatcher appointed himself leader of the Stuntmen, a collection of benchwarmers who cajoled slumping teammates by practicing at their positions. A Stuntman would do anything for the team, Hatcher explained, and was always ready for action.

"I'd built that whole year on getting that group of guys to understand that we were just as important as everybody else," Hatcher says—and sure enough, when injuries hobbled the league's most valuable player for the World Series, a Stuntman came to the rescue.

It is hard to say which was more unlikely: Kirk Gibson's home run to finish Game 1 or Hatcher's laser to left to get the Dodgers started. The day before, Hatcher had told the Oakland starter—his former minor league teammate, Dave Stewart—that he would hit a home run off him. He didn't really mean it, but he swung hard and bolted from the box as the ball cleared the wall in left, circling the bases in 17 seconds, shouting and shaking his fists.

"He doesn't even know how to run out a home run," Joe Garagiola declared on NBC. "He ran like he thought they were gonna take it off the scoreboard!"

It was real, and it was no fluke. Hatcher says he never swung the bat better than he did at the end of that season, and in Game 5, he belted another two-run homer in the first inning, giving a lead to the pitcher on the roll of a lifetime. Hatcher left for defense at the end, and when he dove into the throng around Orel Hershiser after the last out, he was still wearing his batting glove as he held his fist high. A Stuntman is always prepared.

———————

That remained the Dodgers' last championship for more than three decades. A longer stretch of futility came earlier, in the Brooklyn days, when the Dodgers lost their first seven World Series before 1955.

One of those losses came in 1920 to the Cleveland Indians and Bill Wambsganss—also known as W'ganss, Wam'g'ss, Wambs's, or W'bsg'ss in box scores, according to SABR. Wamby, as he was widely known, was one of several obscure players whose flash of leather never dimmed.

"No athlete in history is linked so exclusively with one little incident as Bill Wambsganss is with that unassisted triple play in the 1920 World Series," Fred Russell wrote in 1947—and it might still be true. The unusual name fit the feat: only one player had turned an unassisted triple play before Wambsganss, and just 13 others have done so ever since. That makes the unassisted triple play rarer than a four-homer game.

This one happened at League Park in Cleveland in the fifth game of the 1920 World Series, which started with a different historical footnote: the Indians' Elmer Smith had hit the first grand slam in series history in the first inning. In the fifth, Dodgers pitcher Clarence Mitchell came to bat with runners on first and second. Mitchell was a decent left-handed hitter—his lifetime average was .252—and Wambsganss, the second baseman, expected him to swing away because the Indians led by seven runs.

"We didn't need a double play, but we wanted to get the rally stopped," Wambsganss said, in an undated interview in his file at the Hall of Fame library. "So I played deep. Way back on the grass."

Mitchell smashed a liner to Wambsganss's right. He took a step and jumped to spear it, his momentum carrying him toward second base, where he touched the bag with his toe. The runner on first, Otto Miller, was stopped in his tracks, five feet away.

"Just before I tagged him, he said, 'Where'd you get that ball?'" Wambsganss told *The Sporting News* in 1966. "I said, 'Well, I've got it, and you're out number three.' Then I trotted off the field.

"At first there was dead silence. I guess everyone was stunned or didn't realize what happened. Then, all of a sudden, straw hats and scorecards and everything came flying out of the stands."

Wambsganss recognized the oddity immediately, because history's only other unassisted triple play had also been turned by a Cleveland player: shortstop Neal Ball in 1909. It would happen five more times in the 1920s, but then just once more in Wambsganss's lifetime.

Wambsganss—who died in 1985, at age 91—became a manager in the All-American Girls Professional Baseball League, guiding the Fort Wayne Daisies and the Muskegon Lassies, and later worked as a salesman in Cleveland, where recognition from the triple play helped him. He hit .259 in his career, with just seven home runs, and once called his lucky moment the greatest thing that ever happened to him.

"For such a thing to happen in a World Series was about a million-to-one shot," he told Russell. "You can't tell, it may stand for a hundred years or more."

A century later, it remains a unique moment in World Series history.

———————

The Dodgers' next five World Series losses all came to the Yankees—in 1941, 1947, 1949, 1952, and 1953—until the sublime seventh game in 1955, when Sandy Amoros, a defensive replacement in left field, saved Johnny Podres's 2–0 shutout.

It speaks to the ubiquitous nature of Don Zimmer, who spent 66 years in baseball as a player, manager, and coach, that it was his spot Amoros took in the Brooklyn lineup in the bottom of the sixth inning that day. Zimmer, the second baseman and number nine hitter, had been lifted for a pinch hitter in the top of the inning. Manager Walter Alston moved Jim Gilliam from left field to second, and sent Amoros in to play left.

The Dodgers had signed Amoros from Cuba in 1952; his name was Edmundo, but he looked like the boxer Sandy Saddler, and the nickname stuck. He tore through the minors, where writers called him "the hitter with miracle wrists." How else to explain such a scrawny frame—5 foot 7, 170 pounds—producing a .347 average and 56 homers in two and a half seasons before 1955?

Yet it was on defense that Amoros made his indelible mark, on the kind of sun-splashed World Series afternoon that baseball long ago abandoned for prime time. With nobody out in the sixth inning and runners on first and second, Amoros shaded the left-handed Yogi Berra far toward center. Berra swung from the shadows and sliced a high drive deep into the left field corner—the sun field, a notorious spot for defenders.

"Most of them, running toward the corner where the box seats jut out to the foul line, keep one eye on the ball and one eye on the fence," wrote Dana Mozley in the next day's *New York Post*. "So often, the fence wins."

Amoros said he never looked at the fence, tracking the ball the whole way. He stretched his right arm just as he reached the foul line, snagging the fair ball and firing to shortstop Pee Wee Reese, stationed near third base. Reese had no play there, but whipped a throw to first to catch a scrambling Gil McDougald for a double play.

"It was ridiculous," Eddie Robinson, a reserve Yankees first baseman, said in 2019. "If he didn't catch that ball, we win the World Series."

In 1947, another Brooklyn left fielder, Al Gionfriddo, had back-pedaled furiously in the Bronx to rob Joe DiMaggio of extra bases in Game 6. The great and stoic DiMaggio famously kicked the dirt in frustration; the little-known Gionfriddo never played again. But while the Dodgers won that game, they lost in Game 7. Amoros's catch, at last, plunged a dagger into pin-striped hearts.

"It was a killing play for the Yanks," wrote *The New York Times*, but for Amoros, the moment could not save him from a sad fate. At home in Cuba after the 1961 season, he refused an offer to manage in Fidel Castro's national baseball league. It was less an offer than an edict, of course, and Castro decided to ruin Amoros: he detained him in Cuba, preventing Amoros from playing in the Mexican League, as he had intended. He seized Amoros's ranch, his car, his cash. Amoros was not allowed to leave until 1967; when he did, he gave his World Series ring to his brother, Heriberto.

"The state does not take that," Amoros told the writer Milton Gross, four years later. "They take everything else. 'You want to go to the United States,' they tell me, 'you go as you were born, with nothing.'"

Amoros had missed by a week qualifying for a major league pension, so the Dodgers' general manager, Buzzie Bavasi, briefly made him a coach. Amoros lived in Florida, surviving off the pension, welfare, odd jobs, and help from old teammates like Zimmer, who lived nearby and sent him clothes. In 1987, Amoros lost part of his left leg to a circulatory problem, and he died five years later, at age 62.

"Everybody talks about my catch, but for me that was not the thrill," he told *Sports Illustrated,* late in life. "It all was. I never dreamed that I would play in the big leagues."

Amoros played his last major league game in 1960, two years before the Mets took over as New York's National League team. Their first World Series, in 1969, featured its own defensive wizardry by a part-time outfielder: Ron Swoboda, whose diving catch in Game 4 is commemorated with a steel silhouette above the right field gate at Citi Field. His inelegant start to the series is not.

"First play of the game, Don Buford hits a ball towards the right field fence that I get a terrible jump on," says Swoboda, who started Game 1 in right field at Memorial Stadium. "I just walked out on the field, I'm nervous as hell. I'm clunky going back—I looked like that golden robot in the *Star Wars* movie—and I never connect with the fence. I leap and it gets over my head, and we're down 1–0 because I didn't catch a ball that should have been caught.

"So I'm yelping about it in the dugout and Ed Kranepool, with his 'Noo Yawk' bedside manner, says, 'Shut the fuck up and get the next one.' It was good advice—and we did catch all of the next ones. We made all the plays and got all the calls."

The Orioles took the opener but lost the next four games. In the ninth inning of Game 4, they trailed Tom Seaver, 1–0, with one out and runners at the corners. Swoboda played a step or two in against Brooks Robinson, preparing for a shallow fly ball. He imagined a catch in right field and a game-ending throw to the plate to nab Frank Robinson tagging from third.

Swoboda had earned the right to be trusted on defense at the end of a tight World Series game. He had made 11 errors as a rookie four years earlier, and his six errors in 1968 led all NL right fielders. But Swoboda worked in right field every day with coach Eddie Yost, making him comfortable with the background at Shea and the way line drives would behave.

"If I had to dive in practice, I would," Swoboda says. "I practiced at speed—it was a game situation for me, every ball he hit. I didn't know where it was going, but I'm reading it off the bat, and that's important because that's your first look at it, and if you don't do that right, then you're playing catch-up from the get-go."

When Brooks Robinson connected off Seaver, the smart play might have been to let it fall. As hard as the ball was hit, it would have rolled for a while had it gotten past Swoboda, and even the lumbering runner on first—Boog Powell—would have likely scored the go-ahead run. But Swoboda had only three or four strides to reach the ball. He could not pause to consider the consequences.

"It would have taken me more time to think of why I shouldn't catch it than to just go hellfire—boom!—and lay out," he says. "I got it in the web of my glove, and I knew it wasn't going anywhere."

The Mets would win in the tenth with a typically wild sequence that thrust more obscure names into World Series lore. J. C. Martin bunted, Dick Hall threw it off Martin's back, and pinch runner Rod Gaspar scampered in from second without a throw. Jerry Koosman wrapped up the title the next day, earning each Met a winner's share of $18,338.18—a bump of more than $5,000 from the previous record.

Swoboda used his bonus to buy land in Shawsville, Maryland. Every season at the All-Star break, he would gather with dozens of family members in campers and tents for a reunion. There is a creek on the property for fishing, and ample space for hunting.

"It's a place to come to," Swoboda says, and it is a place where he will someday go to rest.

"When they celebrate this 100 years from 1969," he says, "my ashes are going to be strewn up in that piece of woods in Maryland that I bought with my World Series money."

———

The Miracle Mets have an enduring legacy, largely because of the losing that came before and the decades of frustration since. Had the Mets won dozens of World Series titles, instead of just two, the impact of players like Weis and Swoboda might have faded over time.

The Yankees have comparable figures, but they make up just a few stitches in the grand pin-striped tapestry. The efforts of players like

Marius Russo, Bill Bevens, and Johnny Kucks—pitching heroes of the middle championship years, in the 1940s and '50s—can be obscured by all the banners and boldface names.

Russo threw complete game 2–1 victories over Brooklyn in 1941 and St. Louis in 1943. In the second—after an injury-marred season in which he went 5–10—Russo doubled twice and scored the winning run in the eighth inning. Today it would be considered a tour de force, but late in life, Russo said it meant little under the circumstances. Some of the Cardinals, like the All-Star center fielder Terry Moore, had gone off to serve in World War II, which loomed for Russo, too.

"It just wasn't the same," he told Bill Madden some six decades later, for the book *Pride of October*. "I went into the Army Signal Corps in February of '44 and didn't get out until December of '45. My shoulder was still bad, though. I wasn't that fancy to begin with. I had just two pitches. One was my 'Our Father' and the other was my 'Hail Mary.'"

Russo pitched briefly for the Yankees in 1946 but never won another game. Neither did Bevens after 1947, and technically he did not win in the World Series, either. But he did author the strangest pitching performance in series history, then helped his team win Game 7, which turned out to be the final appearance of his career.

Bevens was a husky right-hander from Oregon whose real name was Floyd; as Kevin Cook details in *Electric October*, he got the name Bill when, as an outfielder, a fly ball bounced off the bill of his cap and somehow landed in his glove. On the mound, he was notoriously wild but also hard to hit, especially in 1946, when only four AL pitchers allowed fewer hits per nine innings.

Bevens slipped in 1947, when his 13 losses led the team and his elbow and shoulder betrayed him. But he finished the season strong and started Game 4, when the Yankees got their first hit on the first pitch of the game, and the Dodgers got their first hit on the last pitch of the game.

The Dodgers' starter, Harry Taylor, got no outs. Bevens got 26 before he allowed a hit. By that point he had walked 10, a single-game series record, but was winning, 2–1, with two outs in the ninth. When the pinch runner Al Gionfriddo stole second—the last steal of his brief career—the Yankees' manager, Bucky Harris, ordered Pete Reiser intentionally walked.

In putting the winning run on base, "Harris violated all ten commandments of the dugout," Red Smith wrote. Harris defended himself later, saying that he feared a home run by Reiser, who was playing with a broken ankle but had once led the league in slugging. In any case, Bevens would still get the first no-hitter in World Series history by retiring Cookie Lavagetto, a surprise pinch hitter for the All-Star Eddie Stanky.

With his 137th pitch, Bevens tried to bury a fastball inside on the right-handed Lavagetto. Instead, the pitch sailed high and away, where Lavagetto could extend his arms and lash it off the right field wall. It was the final hit of his career, and it scored two runs to end the game.

Just like that, Bevens had gone from no-hitter to losing pitcher. The Yankees protected Bevens in the immediate aftermath, locking the clubhouse door as he escaped with his wife, Millie, and friends from back home. They were bound for the Upper West Side, where a tavern owner closed his bar to let Bevens absorb what had happened. "My heart and brains and everything went right down to my spikes," he said then, according to Cook. But soon he was laughing, and in any case, Bevens figured his season was over. His arm was aching again, badly, and Millie would massage it the next few nights, hoping to wring out one final major league outing.

Harris called for Bevens in the second inning of Game 7, trailing 1–0 with two on and one out. A double made it 2–0, but Bevens shut out the Dodgers in the third and fourth.

The Yankees took the lead in the bottom of that inning, and Joe Page preserved it with five scoreless frames to close out the series. By all rights, Bevens should have been credited with the victory, because he was in the game when the Yankees took the lead for good. Page, as the relief ace, should have been given the five-inning save, like Madison Bumgarner in 2014. But the save statistic was not yet invented, so Page got the win.

Bevens would pitch parts of five more seasons in the minors, with more walks than strikeouts. Medical advancements might have saved his damaged right arm, but years later Bevens still could not lift it to his shoulder. He threw his last major league pitch at age 30.

Kucks did not even make it that far; he was done at 28, in 1960 with the Kansas City A's. The Yankees had sent him there the year before in a trade for Ralph Terry—the only Yankee besides Kucks to spin a shutout in Game 7 of the World Series.

Terry, who twirled his in 1962, made six World Series starts in all while Kucks made only one. Kucks was 54–56 in an otherwise nondescript career, but his sinker made him Casey Stengel's pick for Game 7 at Ebbets Field in 1956.

Like Dan Quisenberry, Kucks has a pitching profile that has disappeared from the game. It's been decades since a pitcher has thrown as many innings as Kucks did in 1956 (224 and one-third) with such a low strikeout rate (2.69 per nine innings). In Game 7 against the Dodgers, he induced 16 outs on grounders and another five on infield pop-ups. Kucks saved his only strikeout for the series' final batter, Jackie Robinson, who never played in the majors again.

———————

That was also the last World Series appearance for the Brooklyn Dodgers, who moved to Los Angeles after the 1957 season. They would visit their old Bronx rivals in the World Series once or twice a decade through the 1980s, and their third meeting, in 1978, elevated the feeblest hitter of his era.

Brian Doyle played for the Yankees and the A's from 1978 through 1981, coming to bat 214 times. His on-base plus slugging percentage was .392, the lowest in those years for any nonpitcher with that many plate appearances. But Doyle had a pedigree—his older brother, Denny, had played eight seasons in the majors—and when Willie Randolph pulled his hamstring near the end of the 1978 regular season, the Yankees had nowhere else to turn.

Doyle started at second in the famous one-game divisional playoff at Fenway Park. When his spot came up with two on and one out in the seventh and the Yankees trailing Mike Torrez, 2–0, manager Bob Lemon removed him for a pinch hitter, Jim Spencer. Had Randolph been healthy, perhaps, Lemon would have saved Spencer to hit for Bucky Dent, who followed Doyle in the order. As it happened, Spencer flied out, Dent got to bat and lofted a pop fly—deep to left!—that cleared the Green Monster for the homer that tortured a generation in Boston.

Dent would be MVP of the World Series, hitting .417 in the Yankees' six-game triumph, but Doyle was even better, at .438. Fans tend to associate Dent with the Fenway homer and Doyle with the World Series. How often do they tell him he was the MVP?

"You could fill up this stadium about six or seven times," Doyle says with a laugh, gazing up from the dugout at the new Yankee Stadium. "When I sign autographs, they'll say, 'Could you put "MVP"?' And I'll say, 'I can't, Bucky Dent was the MVP!' It's embarrassing, but it's nice."

Doyle started two of the first four games, with one hit. But he was 6-for-9 in the final two games, with three hits coming off Sutton in the clincher at Dodger Stadium. Doyle swears that Sutton was tipping his pitches—a higher leg kick meant fastball—and the Yankees rolled to a 7–2 victory and their second championship in a row. Doyle says he wears his ring all the time; as an ordained pastor, he uses it to start conversations about faith.

"I played with the Yankees, and this is a world championship ring," Doyle will say. "Let me tell you how you can be a world champion."

Doyle had played his final career game by the time the Yankees reached their next World Series, also against the Dodgers, in 1981. It took 15 years for them to return, and when they did, another bench player saved them from defeat—and, in doing so, yanked baseball history onto a different course.

———

Two games into the 1996 World Series, the Atlanta Braves were following the precise course as the Big Red Machine of the 1970s. The Reds lost two World Series early in that decade. They were upset in the NLCS in 1973 but won the World Series in 1975 and swept the Yankees in 1976, after a long drought without a Yankee pennant.

Now look at the Braves' journey in the 1990s. They, too, lost a pair of World Series early in the decade. They were upset in the NLCS in 1993 but won the World Series in 1995 and faced the Yankees in 1996, after a long drought without a Yankee pennant.

As the series headed to Atlanta for Game 3, there was every reason to expect the Braves to complete the historical symmetry. Atlanta had won its previous five games—including the last three against St. Louis in the NLCS—by a collective score of 48–2. *Forty-eight to two.* The Yankees won Game 3 of the World Series, but things looked bleak in Game 4 when a journeyman middle reliever, Mike Bielecki, struck out three in a row to squelch their rally in the sixth.

As he left the dugout to enter the game, replacing Joe Girardi behind the plate, Jim Leyritz said he looked at teammate Pat Kelly and conceded, "At least we didn't get swept." Leyritz could spot Mark Wohlers warming in the bullpen, and at that moment, Wohlers seemed invincible. In his last World Series appearance at Fulton County Stadium, he had calmly closed out the brawny Cleveland Indians to finish Tom Glavine's 1–0 clinching masterpiece. In seven scoreless appearances in the 1996 postseason, Wohlers had allowed merely two singles, with no walks and 11 strikeouts. His fastballs hummed in around 100 miles an hour.

But this night was different. Charlie Hayes led off the eighth with a dribbler down the third base line that seemed to be trickling foul but bent back fair; it hadn't even reached the bag when it stopped rolling. Then Darryl Strawberry sliced a single to left.

The next hitter, Mariano Duncan, was badly fooled by a first-pitch slider. Wohlers spun another and got a routine grounder to short, an easy double play ball that kicked off the heel of Rafael Belliard's glove. Belliard had just entered the game for defense, and scrambled to get a force at second. Only an arcane official scoring rule—you can't assume a double play—spared him an error. With two on, instead of one, Leyritz came up next as the tying run.

Leyritz was 32 and in his seventh major league season. As a young player on also-ran Yankee teams, his swagger amused veterans like Don Mattingly, who nicknamed him Elvis, which morphed into King. Rarely can a utility player pass for royalty, but Leyritz pulled it off. He wore a Stetson hat and boots, an urban cowboy from Cincinnati who rooted hard for the Rangers and drank from the Stanley Cup at the China Club in 1994. The next year, against Seattle in his first career playoff appearance, Leyritz blasted a walk-off home run.

As a hitter, Leyritz would twirl his bat as he waited for the pitch and lean back behind a stiff front leg. The twirl was a batting-practice goof he carried over into games, but the stiff leg resulted from a youthful boast gone awry. Leyritz was convinced he could beat his high school's best tennis player, Todd Blaine, if only Blaine would let him try. When Leyritz finally got the chance, he broke his left foot going for a slam.

In baseball, Leyritz discovered a work-around to at least stay busy in the batting cage. He could not step down on the foot, but if he kept his leg straight, he could still apply pressure and swing comfortably. The injury scared off the Braves from drafting Leyritz, but they tracked his progress through the summer and offered him $5,000 to sign. Leyritz wanted double, the Braves passed, and Leyritz went to the University of Kentucky.

The extra $5,000 would have been a wise investment, because Leyritz had the most pivotal swing in the four-game losing streak that ended one budding dynasty and launched another. He borrowed a bat from Strawberry, wary of breaking one from his own dwindling supply on a Wohlers fastball. For five pitches, Wohlers toyed with Leyritz: a fastball for a foul, two high sliders well out of the zone, another fastball for a foul, then a wicked slider off the plate. Leyritz lunged for it and got just enough to tap another foul.

In the Fox booth, analysts Tim McCarver and Bob Brenly questioned Wohlers's pitch selection. Leyritz was well-known as a dead-red fastball hitter, but he still expected Wohlers to challenge him on the fateful pitch.

"As a catcher, I would have called fastball, because he had just set me up reaching outside for that slider and there's no way I would have caught up to 99 or 100 inside," Leyritz says. "I thought he was gonna come back in with a fastball, so I took maybe a half an inch more off the plate, so if he did throw in, I would just take it because it would be a ball, and I was looking out over the plate."

To Wohlers, Leyritz seemed bound to catch up with his fastball, based on the way he had fouled it straight back. So he repeated what he'd done against Duncan, doubling up on the slider after it had worked on the previous pitch. Yet this time it floated over the middle, right where Leyritz was looking, and he lifted it high over left field, about the same trajectory as Ed Sprague's blast in '92. Andruw Jones chased for it, planted his right foot in the padding, and reached in vain with his glove. Three-run homer, tie game.

The Yankees never trailed again in the series, taking the title in six. The hanging slider would haunt the Braves' dreams.

"I wake up at night with a cold sweat, still, about that," Braves general manager John Schuerholz would say, 23 years later, closing his eyes as he pantomimed a ball in flight. "I see the ball in cartoon fashion in front of my face, eyes wide with fright that it's gonna be hit forever—and it was."

If the Yankees had carried three catchers instead of two, the left-handed Wade Boggs—or the less-imposing Mike Aldrete—might have hit for Leyritz. And if Leyritz had not homered, the Yankees might have lost Game 4 and never recovered. In that scenario, Leyritz believes, the dynasty never would have blossomed. The Yankees lost to Cleveland in the first round in 1997, with Mariano Rivera blowing a potential clincher, and then started poorly in 1998. At that point, Leyritz says, the Yankees would have collapsed.

"If we had not had that '96 run, George would have fired Torre, would have gotten rid of Mariano," Leyritz says. "The Yankee world would have changed."

All we know is that the Yankees just kept winning, and Leyritz was always around the edges. He played for the Padres in 1998 and went hitless in the Yankees' sweep. Back in pinstripes the next fall, Leyritz homered in another Game 4 against the Braves, with a pinch-hit solo shot in the bottom of the eighth that extended the Yankees' lead in the clincher.

It gave Leyritz the last home run of the 1900s, a stylish bit of stat-padding that earned him—through some combination of sentiment and gratitude—a one-year, $1 million contract to return in 2000. He lasted only to June, when the Yankees began a vital reconstruction of their offense.

They dealt Leyritz to the Dodgers for infielder Jose Vizcaino, and after trading for a starting outfielder, David Justice, they continued to tweak the bench, adding outfielders Glenallen Hill, Luis Polonia, and Jose Canseco. But while the Canseco move was a misguided waiver claim, the Yankees made an inspired deal on the same August day, bringing back Luis Sojo from a brief exile with the Pirates.

Sojo was a lumpy, good-natured utility man who had played a bit for the 1993 Blue Jays and always seemed to show up on winners. In a one-game division playoff for the 1995 Mariners, it was Sojo chugging around the bases for a broken-bat, Little League grand slam—technically a double and an error—that might have saved baseball in Seattle.

Sojo joined the Yankees the next summer, grabbing a seat for their annual October joyride but starting only one of 40 postseason games in the 1996, 1998, and 1999 title runs. In 2000, though, the Yankees' starting second baseman, Chuck Knoblauch, suddenly lost control of his throws to first base. That put Sojo in the field on most October nights, giving him a chance to be more than a mascot.

And yet, Sojo filled that role so well. This was a guy who would actually be called back to the Yankees' active roster *after* appearing in an Old-Timers' Game, in 2003. Anything for the team or a smile. Late in a 2000 division-series game, in Oakland, Sojo gathered a ground ball, shuffled his feet for the throw—and caught his right spike in his left shoelace. He hit the dirt, the tying run came to the plate, and Mariano Rivera had to come in to squelch the rally.

"When we got to the bench, everybody was laughing," Sojo says. "Don Zimmer was literally crying. He said, 'Not even me! I'm 75 years old and I never tripped like that!' And that was it—the team started loosening up and the rest was history."

Yet it took another memorable Sojo moment to certify the three-peat. The Yankees had a chance to clinch the World Series in Game 5 at Shea Stadium, but they were struggling to solve the Mets' Al Leiter. With the score tied in the ninth, 2–2, Leiter fanned the first two Yankees. His pitch count was soaring, but he felt strong.

A walk and a single brought Sojo to the plate, but Leiter was not worried. Sojo was not the kind of guy to inspire fear, but he was an extreme contact hitter—"His interpretation of the strike zone extends from the nose to the toenails," Buster Olney wrote in *The New York Times*—and that made him dangerous. Sojo also knew what to expect from Leiter; he had played with him in the minors and the majors with Toronto, and gotten two hits off him for the Pirates that May.

"He's got a nasty cutter," Sojo says. "He starts off throwing strikes, and then he gets nasty, nasty, nasty, like Mariano. He wants to get ahead, and I cannot take that chance. That was my first at-bat of the game and I just let it go. It went through—75 hops."

Leiter indeed started Sojo with a cutter. It was his 142nd pitch—no pitcher since has thrown that many in a postseason game—but it did not veer as far inside as Leiter wanted. Sojo extended his arms enough to smack a grounder off the grass, just beyond the dirt. Leiter landed in a good fielding position, but the ball was too far to his right; he bent for it and fell to the ground, spinning around on his knees as the ball, and the season, skipped away.

"A 10-hop chopper past me, which I should have caught," Leiter says, ruefully reciting what he saw from his helpless view on the dirt. "Kurt Abbott doesn't get it, Jay Payton throws the ball away, it goes into our dugout, we lose the World Series."

Ten hops? Seventy-five hops? Just how many hops does it take for a Luis Sojo ground ball to win the World Series? The ball keeps bouncing as the years go by.

"We lost count on the calculator," says Sojo, who still has the bat that made him a legend.

"I went to see my bat in the Hall of Fame, but then I took it," he says. "I'm not Derek Jeter or Paul O'Neill. I'm just a Punch and Judy hitter. I gotta get my bat."

Sojo never had 400 at-bats in a season, never exceeded seven homers or stolen bases, never earned a $1 million salary. But he played for 13 seasons, and in seven of them, his teams wound up in the World Series. Some guys have all the luck.

Game 4

"If I Can't Explain This, It's Wrong"

Managing in the World Series

On the field, they processed the present. Joe Carter expected a slider, because he had just chased one for strike two. Mitch Williams shook off that pitch for a fastball, up and away. Rickey Henderson, the ultimate disruptor, led off second, daring Williams to keep him there. Williams rushed his pitch to the plate, barely lifting his right foot off the mound, a slide-step move that robbed his fastball of its power and precision. The pitch veered down and in, just where a slider would be, and Carter swung and met it squarely. Because he had waited an extra instant, his line drive stayed inside the left field foul pole and won the 1993 World Series.

In the Toronto Blue Jays' dugout, Cito Gaston missed it. For millions of fans across the United States and Canada, plus the 52,195 roaring at the SkyDome, this was the moment they had waited decades to see: a home run to end the World Series. But Gaston didn't need to see it. He just needed to anticipate what might happen next.

The inning before, trailing the Philadelphia Phillies by a run, Gaston had removed John Olerud for a pinch runner, Alfredo Griffin. Olerud, who batted behind Carter, was a skilled hitter but a slow runner. Griffin moved better but had not come to bat all postseason and would never play again in the majors. He was on deck, with one out, when Carter came up against Williams.

"I'm looking at my stats and I have Darnell Coles who's sitting on the bench," Gaston says. "And my thought was, 'OK, do I want to pinch hit for Alfredo with Darnell Coles, or do I want to let Alfredo go against Mitch?' Alfredo actually had better numbers against Mitch, but I was looking for a long ball."

Coles was more likely to hit one; he'd once had a 20-homer season. Then again, Gaston reasoned, while a homer would win the World Series—and a double might, too—a single would tie the game and send it to extra innings. So who would hit next: Griffin or Coles?

"Just as I'm thinking that, I drop my head, looking at the stats," Gaston says. "I look up and all of a sudden people are jumping in front of me because Joe Carter hit the ball out of the ballpark. So I always thank Joe for doing what he did so I didn't have to make that decision."

Managers would rather not be the focus of a World Series game. They understand, especially now, that they must explain each crucial decision and accept the scrutiny that comes with the job. But they also know that their main responsibility is to put players in position to succeed. The games should hinge on the players' performance, not the misfire or masterstroke of a manager.

"I remember leaving my house before Game 7 in 1991, and I said to myself, 'I just hope I don't have to make too many decisions that will influence the game—let the players win or lose,'" says Tom Kelly, who guided the Twins to victories in 1987 and 1991. "And lo and behold, I had to make a whole bunch of decisions. But you really want to stay out of it and let the players decide, because the game's about the players."

Kelly lived those words. When the Twins clinched their first title, he stayed in the dugout after the final out. Members of the clubhouse staff and grounds crew had been told to stay off the field when it ended, so Kelly chose to share the moment with them. They were part of the team too, Kelly felt, and it was safer, anyway, to let the players dogpile from a distance.

Like Gaston, Kelly has a perfect World Series record—two wins, no defeats—and managed in the age before Twitter, when anyone could excoriate them, worldwide, in an instant. In 2018, needing eight outs to tie the World Series at two games apiece, the Dodgers' Dave Roberts pulled starter Rich Hill with a 4–0 lead. The Red Sox stormed back off Roberts's bullpen, prompting this missive from an opinionated viewer in Washington:

"Watching the Dodgers/Red Sox final innings," read the tweet from

@realDonaldTrump. "It is amazing how a manager takes out a pitcher who is loose & dominating through almost 7 innings, Rich Hill of Dodgers, and brings in nervous reliever[s] who get shellacked. 4 run lead gone. Managers do it all the time, big mistake!"

I knew Roberts should be asked about this in his postgame news conference at Dodger Stadium. I waited for eight questions, hoping someone else would do it, but no one did. So I raised my hand and asked Roberts if he had heard about the tweet. He had not. I felt ridiculous reading the words aloud, but Roberts was a good sport.

"The president said that?" he replied with a look of bemusement. Roberts paused and chose his words carefully: "I'm happy he was tuning in and watching the game. I don't know how many Dodger games he's watched. I don't think he is privy to the conversation. That's one man's opinion."

Two years later, in his third try, Roberts finally won the World Series, helped by a different manager pulling a starter from a shutout. The Rays' Kevin Cash removed Blake Snell with a 1–0 lead in the sixth inning of Game 6, and the Dodgers pounced on the Tampa Bay bullpen to wrap up their championship. So it goes.

"If you win, you're smart; if you lose, you're dumb," says Terry Francona, who managed both Roberts and Cash with the Red Sox. "Dave Roberts was taking grief for the last two years, and now all of a sudden he's the smartest guy in the world. So a lot of it's the outcome. I think managers feel like if you follow the process—because you don't have a crystal ball—you can live with whatever happens."

Francona, who guided Boston to sweeps in 2004 and 2007, and Cleveland to Game 7 in 2016, said managers must try to seize the moment without straying too far from their usual tendencies. It is a delicate dance.

"There's got to be some urgency, but that urgency can't turn into panic, or perceived panic—and that's kind of a fine line," he says. "If you actually manage like the regular season, that's not correct. But if the players look up and see shit flying everywhere, that's going to be perceived as panic—and if you do that, you'd better win. Because if you don't, things are going to fall apart."

Francona stayed consistent in all four victories over the Cardinals in 2004. The Red Sox never trailed in that World Series and each game ended with three reserves—outfielder Gabe Kapler, second baseman Pokey Reese, and first baseman Doug Mientkiewicz—on the field for defense. Infamously, in Boston's previous trip to the World Series, against the Mets in 1986, John McNamara had kept hobbled first baseman Bill Buckner on the field in the tenth inning of Game 6 at Shea Stadium. He'd used a replacement, Dave Stapleton, at the end of every postseason win, but not that night—an oversight noted even earlier in the game by Gary Thorne on the Mets' radio broadcast: "The Red Sox are six outs away from a world championship—surprised Buckner is still playing first base. They have not brought Stapleton in, which John McNamara usually does in this position of the ballgame for defensive purposes. But he leaves Billy Buck in, wanting to keep the bat." Buckner, who had just flied out to end the top of the eighth, would soon make the most famous error in baseball history when Mookie Wilson's grounder skipped through his legs to lose the game.

"If the ball was hit to either side of him and he couldn't get in front of it, yeah, I would have questioned myself," McNamara told me, some 25 years later. "But he got to the ball."

McNamara claimed to forget the specifics of how he'd used Stapleton all month, and said Buckner was a better fielder, anyway—a curious claim, since Stapleton had committed no errors that season, his last in the major leagues, and had made a nifty play in the ninth inning of Game 1. Unless McNamara simply forgot to put him in, only one explanation makes sense: he wanted Buckner, a deeply respected veteran who had played through severe ankle trouble, to be on the field when the Red Sox clinched.

"I was standing next to Marty [Barrett] in the dugout when McNamara asked me, 'You wanna finish the game?'" Buckner told Erik Sherman in his final lengthy interview, for the book *Two Sides of Glory*. "I said, 'Yeah, sure.'"

Buckner noted that he was moving much better than he had in the first two games at Shea but said he would not have protested had McNamara decided for him.

"If McNamara had told me, 'I'm putting in Stapleton,'" he said, "I would have been fine with it."

McNamara's gesture was noble, to be sure. Buckner had sacrificed so much to put the Red Sox in position to win the World Series.

But McNamara put an individual ahead of the team and ignored his own well-reasoned strategy. His failure to replace Buckner, then, is far more egregious than Ron Washington's decision to leave Nelson Cruz in right field for the Rangers in 2011, with a title on the line in St. Louis in Game 6. In 31 previous postseason games, Washington had never lifted Cruz for defense. To do so then would have been out of character.

Of course, that doesn't mean Washington was right to leave him in. While Cruz is a fine athlete—his first love was basketball—Washington had a much better option in Game 6 with a two-run lead in the bottom of the ninth.

Endy Chavez had flied out to right as a pinch hitter to end the top of the inning. He assumed he would stay in for defense and hung around first base, waiting for someone to bring him his glove. Chavez was a renowned defender; five years earlier, on another October night against the Cardinals, he'd famously stolen a homer at Shea Stadium for a catch that still echoes in Mets lore. But here, Chavez was summoned back to the bench.

Had he stayed in the game, Chavez probably would have gone to left or center, with David Murphy switching to right. (Chavez had played only one inning in right field in the previous five months.) In any case it was Cruz in right field, a bit too shallow, backing up timidly and leaping in vain for David Freese's game-tying, two-run triple off Neftali Feliz. A defender like Murphy or Chavez would have had a better shot.

"Listen, Endy Chavez probably should have been in the game; he was on the roster as a defensive replacement," said Jon Daniels, the Rangers' general manager, in 2019. "We probably should have been in no-doubles defense; [Cruz] wasn't playing as deep as he could have. And we also could have won the game 10 other ways, and we could have won Game 7. I don't hang that on Nellie."

It was hardly a routine play; Freese took a 98-mile-an-hour fastball on the outer half and smoked it off the base of the right field wall. Washington had indeed called for a no-doubles defense earlier in the inning, and Cruz was directly in his line of vision from the third base dugout. But with Freese at the plate, Washington froze. He has never forgiven himself.

"The play that Nelson didn't make, it wasn't because Nelson was a bad outfielder—it was because of bad positioning," Washington said in 2021. "If he was playing no doubles, it would have been one of *theeeese* catches."

Nice and easy, he meant. As Washington remembers it, Freese "kept slicing foul balls to right field" in Game 6, although he had only done so once, the inning before. He had not made contact off Feliz until his hit: the sequence went ball, called strike, swinging strike, triple.

There is no disputing that Cruz was too shallow. Up in the press box, Tom Verducci of *Sports Illustrated*, seated just to my left, frantically pointed this out before Freese's fateful swing. But the manager didn't see it and didn't check again with his outfield coach, Gary Pettis, to make sure Cruz was in the right spot.

"So it wasn't the fact—well, you replace Nelson and put a better outfielder out there—no, it was just positioning," Washington says. "If he was in the right position, nobody would ever question Nelson Cruz as an outfielder. You see what I'm saying? Now, it all depends on how you want to look at it. If somebody is [nit]picking, they'll say I shouldn't have had him out there. If somebody is looking at the game for real, they'll say, 'Well, why wasn't he in no doubles?' I could live with the outcome, and I gotta take the blame for the outcome because I make the decisions—and I didn't fully get on that. I did, earlier. But I missed it one time. I should have just kept asking. I should have just kept pounding."

It was the fourth time the Cardinals had erased a Rangers lead that night, and for Cruz, the sting of the moment, and of losing another lead in the tenth, will always linger. Eight years later, after he'd become the sport's premier designated hitter, Cruz said that Freese's hit had left a scar.

"I mean, it's there," he said, in the Minnesota Twins' dugout before batting practice one day in 2019. "You cannot erase that from your mind. It's something that, as a player, you know that you're that close to winning something that important and you weren't able to do it—and not only one time, it was two times.

"It was like, 'Are you kidding me, what is this?' It's a shame, you know? But you cannot be with that weight on top of your shoulders for long. You have to let it go."

Washington said he slept peacefully that night, confident the Rangers would win Game 7. He rallied the team with a raucously profane pregame speech that included a helpful tip for his hitters: forget about driving up the pitch count of Chris Carpenter, who would be working on short rest for the Cardinals—just attack.

And so they did, building a 2–0 lead after only 13 pitches, with Adrian Beltre and Cruz up next. But Carpenter retired them both, the Rangers never scored again, and hours later, when the finality of the loss set in, Cruz and Beltre sought out Washington in his office to apologize. Washington wasn't having it.

"For what?" he said. "Don't apologize to me. If it wasn't for you two guys, we wouldn't have been here. I take the blame. I should have made sure you was in no-doubles and we wouldn't have to worry about this."

Washington lasted a few more seasons in Texas, then resumed his career as an infield whisperer, coaching for Oakland and Atlanta, showing up early every day with a fungo bat, a ball bag, and a pancake practice glove for his fielders. It is a great life, to be sure, but he still yearns for another chance to be the decider, to crouch on the top step of the dugout on a chilly night in late October, one strike from glory.

"It wouldn't matter what team I got," he says. "You give me a team and we're gonna win. We will get together and move in the direction that we want to move in, and I'll be back in the World Series. I have no doubt about that."

A few months later, as a third base coach for the Braves, Washington earned his first championship ring.

In 1985, when the Kansas City Royals won the World Series, Dick Howser made only six pitching changes in seven games: four with his closer, Dan Quisenberry, and once apiece for Joe Beckwith and Bud Black. In the celebration after Game 7, Howser sought out starter Mark Gubicza, who had won an elimination game in the ALCS but never appeared in the World Series.*

----

* It wasn't the first World Series Gubicza had witnessed, however. In 1980, at age 18, he'd seen his hometown Phillies clinch against the Royals in Game 6 at Veterans Stadium.

"Hey, Mark, I really apologize for not getting you in," Howser said. "What do I care?" Gubicza replied. "We won the World Series!"

"OK," Howser said. "That's why I love you."

Gubicza told me this story a while back, and I was glad to hear it. When I was a kid, I would study the cumulative World Series box scores in the old *Baseball Encyclopedia,* and re-create the matchups in a homemade dice game. I loved all the random names who shared the stat sheet with the stars, and I tried to use everyone. Even now, around Game 3 or 4, I'll find myself scanning the rosters and circling the guys who haven't played. How awful it must feel, I reasoned, to be eligible for the World Series but not get to play.

So I've never forgotten what Tony La Russa did at the end of the 1988 season. I was 13, staying up late to watch the Dodgers finish off La Russa's Athletics. In the final game, with two outs and the bases empty and the Dodgers batting in the top of the ninth, La Russa called for Todd Burns, a rookie who had not pitched in the series. He retired his only batter. As the years went by, La Russa earned a reputation as a master tactician, a calculating mind seeking every edge. But I never forgot the humanity he showed that night in Oakland, to give up a small sliver of a game for a sentimental cause.

Before the 2011 World Series in St. Louis, I tracked down Burns by phone in Alabama, where he was running an instructional baseball school. He remembered every detail of his World Series debut and still cherished the respect La Russa showed him as the last man in the bullpen. "He didn't have to do what he did," Burns said. "Getting that last out for us, it meant a ton."

La Russa smiled knowingly when I mentioned it. Yes, he said, he does always try to find at least one game for every player on his World Series rosters. It is a way to show the players that he cares, to make them feel more invested in the concept of a team as a family. Token appearances show up all over La Russa's six World Series: one at-bat apiece for Ken Phelps in 1989, Doug Jennings in 1990, Hector Luna in 2004, and John Rodriguez in 2006. Joe Klink faced one batter in 1990; Brad Thompson faced two in 2006. It was all by design.

"It's a simple thing," La Russa said. "You could show a box score and say, 'I was there, you know,' to your friends, your kids."

Jack McKeon did this as Marlins manager in 2003. In the bottom of the eighth inning of a lopsided loss at Yankee Stadium, McKeon removed star catcher Ivan Rodriguez for a longtime backup, Mike Redmond, just so Redmond could say that he played in the World Series.

Redmond, who flied out, would go on to manage the Marlins himself. Years later, as a coach for the Rockies, he teared up recalling McKeon's gesture. Three years before that World Series, Redmond had promised his father, Pat, who was dying of cancer, that he would someday win a championship. McKeon did not know the story until after the World Series but instinctively grasped the importance of a single appearance.

"I don't wear the ring a lot because it's so big and gaudy," Redmond says, "but I see it in my safe and it always makes me smile, that I got into the game."

World Series managers have that power; they are bouncers for the ultimate baseball celebration. At the very start, though, they also played. A manager actually came to bat in the first inning of the first World Series game, in 1903—Pittsburgh's Fred Clarke, who managed the Pirates and played left field, fouled out to the catcher off Boston's Cy Young.

Player-managers appeared in more than half of all World Series through 1938, but only once since then, in 1948, when Lou Boudreau guided the Indians to their last championship. Boudreau, a shortstop, earned the AL Most Valuable Player award that year and doubled home the Tribe's first run in their clinching victory at Braves Field in Boston.

Boudreau managed nine more seasons for several teams without another pennant, and the 1948 victory would have to sustain Cleveland for generations; the franchise wouldn't even win another series game for 47 years. Maybe the franchise—now known as the Guardians—should try a player-manager again someday, since its only other title, in 1920, also came with a player in charge. Center fielder Tris Speaker, who batted .388 that season, had the good sense to use spitballer Stan Coveleski for three complete-game wins against Brooklyn.

In all, 13 player-managers won World Series titles. Jimmy Collins did it first, which is fitting, because he helped save the event before it began. Collins was first baseman and manager of the 1903 Boston Americans, whose contracts expired at the end of September. The Pirates' owner, Barney Dreyfuss, had signed an agreement with Boston owner Henry Killilea that month to establish the event, which would end before the Pirate players' contracts ran out on October 15. Killilea's players had leverage, then, and rejected their boss's proposal to split the gate profits evenly. Killilea—a Milwaukee lawyer who had helped found the American League—wired Collins his reply on September 24: the series was off.

"There is not a chance in a hundred of the games being played," Collins glumly reported, and the Giants' John McGraw sensed an opportunity. McGraw—who loathed AL president Ban Johnson—offered to face the Pirates in a postseason series to decide the NL champ, thus undermining the upstart AL. Dreyfuss persisted and Johnson implored Killilea to change his mind.

Intervention from Collins brokered the deal. Collins had the team's business manager call Killilea, who offered new terms that Collins eagerly accepted. The players would get more money—reportedly 75 percent of the gate—and could not be accused of ducking the Pirates, the three-time reigning champs of the Senior Circuit.

After signing off on the deal to play, Collins did not have much else to do. For eight games, he wrote the same eight players in the same eight spots of the batting order, including himself at number two. As for the pitchers, Collins used Cy Young or Bill Dinneen for all but two innings of a five-games-to-three victory.

The World Series took a hiatus in 1904 when McGraw—backed by the Giants' owner, John Brush—refused to play the Red Sox, an outgrowth of his feud with Johnson.* It was back on for 1905, with McGraw's players eager for a chance at the bonus money denied to them the year before. This matchup would be a showdown of managerial royalty: McGraw and his Giants versus Connie Mack and his

---

* McGraw had managed the Baltimore Orioles in Johnson's AL but jumped to the Giants after Johnson suspended him; he had exasperated Johnson with his interest in club ownership and by frequently clashing with umpires.

Philadelphia Athletics. Biographers often cast them as opposites; Leonard Koppett used the word "humanistic" to describe Mack, praising his innate empathy, while excoriating McGraw for humiliating players, demanding they play through injury and hectoring them into obedience.

"I understood why [Mack] was so different from McGraw yet equally masterful in handling men," Branch Rickey said, as quoted by Norman L. Macht. "He was a pedagogue, a kindly instructor. It was his desire that his players should learn from him and then think for themselves on the field of play."

McGraw, meanwhile, told players to let him do the thinking. "He was the game," Mathewson put it, in *Pitching in a Pinch,* and McGraw presided over every detail, including new uniforms for the 1905 opener in Philadelphia: black jerseys and black pants, a jarring combination about a century ahead of its time.

To McGraw, the uniforms conveyed a sense of purpose to his team for an event he had dismissed a year before. McGraw remembered an example from his playing career—an 1894 postseason exhibition known as the Temple Cup, when his cocky, first-place Orioles had lost four in a row to the Giants. He would not be embarrassed again.

Mathewson was the greatest weapon of all, taking over the 1905 Series with a record three shutouts in a five-game whitewash. Future World Series would not come so easily for McGraw. He lost six of the nine he managed, oddly bedeviled twice by foul balls in the final inning of the final game.

In 1912, Mathewson took a one-run lead into the bottom of the tenth at Fenway Park. With two on and one out, Boston's Tris Speaker lofted a foul pop on the first base side that fell untouched after Mathewson called for the catcher, Chief Meyers, to take it instead of second baseman Fred Merkle, who was closer.

"Well, Matty, you just called for the wrong man—now it's gonna cost you the ballgame," Speaker said, and he was right. He singled to tie the game, and after an intentional walk, Larry Gardner won the World Series with a sacrifice fly.

A dozen years later, in Washington, McGraw's Giants headed to the bottom of the twelfth in a tied Game 7. With one out, the

Senators' Muddy Ruel popped a foul behind the plate, and catcher Hank Gowdy tripped over his mask in pursuit. Like Speaker, Ruel took advantage of his new life, this time with a double. Two batters later Earl McNeely chopped a bad-hop double, bringing home Ruel with the championship.

McNeely's double skipped over the head of third baseman Freddie Lindstrom, who'd been vexed by the same kind of hop on a game-tying single by Bucky Harris in the eighth. It took two well-placed pebbles, then—and the error by poor Gowdy—to ruin McGraw's last chance in the World Series.

McGraw did take some credit for the Giants' next title, in 1933, his first full season out of the game. In a series of articles for *Liberty* magazine published just after his death in 1934, McGraw praised his successor, the Hall of Famer Bill Terry, for using "old baseball strategies that I had helped to invent" to beat the Senators in '33. Terry, who was also the Giants' first baseman, called for a pivotal hit-and-run in Game 1 and a squeeze bunt in Game 2, helping the Giants win both on their way to a five-game victory.

"It was like a picture out of the past to me," wrote McGraw, who considered the offensive surge of the '30s an affront to dugout tacticians. "'Master-minding' has gone out of style."

McGraw paints himself and Mack as like-minded leaders whose championships "were the result of our dominating the strategy of our ball clubs." The 1911 A's, who beat the Giants in six games, apparently foreshadowed the extreme defensive shifts of today. McGraw explained that Mack upended "all previous principles of so-called good baseball by pitching to the strength of opposing batsmen instead of to their weakness; then they'd move their entire defensive cast over to cover every possible sector to which the batter would hit such a pitch."

McGraw and Mathewson also believed that Mack had ordered the dirt to be watered down at Shibe Park before Game 2 of that series, which had begun in New York with a Giants win. The Giants had led the majors in stolen bases, the thinking went, and a muddy track could slow them down. Mathewson said the ploy "reminded me of the bushes"—but it may have worked.

With the score tied, 1–1, in the sixth inning, the Giants' Fred Snodgrass slipped while rounding first as he tried for a double. The A's threw him out easily at second, and soon took the lead and won the game. Years later, McGraw seemed more proud of the trickery than annoyed by it; the technique, he wrote, was "another little artifice that we had carried to a high state of perfection with the old Baltimore Orioles."

Mack wound up with more championships than McGraw, five to three, breaking their tie in 1929 with a five-game win over the Cubs. It was Mack's masterpiece.

After finishing second to the Babe Ruth/Lou Gehrig Yankees in 1927 and 1928, the A's rolled to 104 victories, the most they'd ever had. They led the majors in homers and ERA, and Lefty Grove was probably the league's best pitcher.

Yet Mack did not start him in the World Series. The Cubs' right-leaning offense had led the majors in runs, and Mack started only righties against them. Grove being Grove, he handled the Cubs just fine, closing out Games 2 and 4. But Mack's choice for the opener was Howard Ehmke, a 35-year-old junkballer who made good on the most audacious hunch of Mack's career.

Late that summer, Mack told Ehmke to stay behind on an A's road trip. Ehmke was a forgotten man on the staff—he made just 11 appearances all season—and he pleaded with Mack not to cut him from a team running away with the AL flag.

"Mr. Mack," he protested, "there is one great game left in this old arm."

Mack thought so, too, and described his assignment for Ehmke: with the Cubs arriving in town to play the Phillies, he wanted Ehmke to study their hitters for a start in the World Series. Ehmke's slow stuff would fluster the slugging Cubs, just as Mack suspected, in a 3–1 win at Wrigley Field with a then-record 13 strikeouts.

It was one of a few indelible moments for the A's that October. They wiped out an 8–0 deficit with a record 10-run inning in Game 4, and won the series on a double by Bing Miller to end Game 5.

Four days later, the city held a victory celebration at the Penn Athletic Club; each player got a wristwatch, and Mack was given a radio.

In his speech, Mack credited the players for meeting a challenge he had issued through the press.

"During the spring I left our training camp and came back to Philadelphia and gave out an interview in which I stated that I did not think we had more than a fighting chance to win and that if we did win, it would be because we were better fighters rather than the better team," he said, as quoted by Macht. "I made that statement deliberately with the idea of keeping my men from being overconfident. It worked. They fought every inch of the way as if to show me, as I had thought they would do, that they were fighters."

The A's didn't stop there; they split the next two World Series with the Cardinals, missing a three-peat by losing the seventh game in 1931.

Mack stayed on through 1950, mostly with terrible teams, as the Yankees again ruled the game. Four Yankee managers won titles in Mack's era—Miller Huggins, Joe McCarthy, Bucky Harris, and Casey Stengel—and Mack was partial to McCarthy, citing him late in life as the greatest manager ever.

"Connie was very kind to say that," McCarthy responded, according to a Mack biographer, Ted Davis. "But, let's not kid each other. There is one man who is baseball's greatest manager and no one else can be spoken of in the same breath. And his name is Connie Mack."

———

Reflecting on his biggest thrill to *The Sporting News* in 1956, McCarthy cited his first championship. Fired in 1930 by the Cubs—who elevated his aging second baseman, Rogers Hornsby, to manager—McCarthy got revenge two years later by sweeping the Cubs for the Yankees.

That World Series was a showcase for Lou Gehrig, who hit .529 with three homers. ("I didn't manage Ruth at his peak," McCarthy said, "but how could anyone be greater than Gehrig?") Those Yankees were a terror, with six Hall of Famers in the lineup and three in the rotation, including the team's oldest player, 38-year-old lefty Herb Pennock. McCarthy said he "had one big move to make in the series," when he summoned Pennock to save Game 3—the famous Called Shot Game—at Wrigley Field.

"One of the most famous of World Series heroes, the ancient Herb

Pennock," as the *Brooklyn Times Union* called him, entered the game with no outs in the ninth and Mark Koenig coming up as the tying run. Koenig struggled against left-handers, so Cubs manager Charlie Grimm, who had replaced the combustible Hornsby in August, countered with Rollie Hemsley, who struck out. Two ground outs preserved the win, but between them was a curious move that would have been unthinkable today: with two outs, Billy Jurges stole third.

Think about that: Jurges was already in scoring position with the Cubs losing by two runs and down to their last out. Why take such a risk for 90 extra feet that were meaningless without another base runner? Understandably, on a day with so much else going on, an inconsequential steal drew no attention. But it underscores how certain strategies of the old days went largely unchallenged, yet would be roasted now.

The Yankees' 1932 victory came at the midpoint of a stretch of 14 pennants under Huggins or McCarthy from 1921 to 1943. They combined for 10 championships, all before the TV age, so have largely avoided historical scrutiny, positive or negative, for standout moves in those World Series.

Huggins's legacy is tightly tied to Ruth. He recommended the Yankees trade for Ruth, earning everlasting gratitude—and a job for life—from owner Col. Jacob Ruppert.

"He planned on a big scale," Ruppert said of Huggins to *The Saturday Evening Post,* in 1931. "I doubt if anybody except Huggins had the foreknowledge of just how predominant Ruth could become in the baseball world."

Perhaps only Huggins, too, could find the delicate balance between tolerating Ruth's excesses while maintaining respect from both his star and his team. The Mighty Mite—he was 5 foot 6—would become the first manager to make six World Series appearances in an eight-year span, a feat matched by three Yankee successors: McCarthy, Stengel, and Joe Torre. While his most famous team, in 1927, breezed to a sweep of the Pirates, Huggins was too nervous to watch the end. He gripped the leg of a bench player, Mike Gazella, who narrated the final few plays until Earle Combs scored the winning run on a wild pitch.

"Huggins never saw a single pitch," Gazella said, as quoted by Jane

Leavy in *The Big Fella,* her engrossing Ruth biography. "All that excitement could have killed him."

Huggins, in fact, would be dead within two years, felled at 51 by a bacterial infection in September 1929. The Yankees dedicated their first monument to him in 1932, and for years it stood in center field—in play—flanked by Gehrig on the left and Ruth on the right. (This configuration would confuse generations of young Yankees fans: "I thought Babe Ruth was buried out there," Billy Crystal said, in the *When It Was a Game* series on HBO. "They were like these big tombstones.")

Had he lived longer, Huggins perhaps would own all the major World Series records for managers. As it stands, McCarthy and Stengel are tied for the most championships, with seven, and Stengel managed in the most World Series, with 10 in a 12-year span starting in 1949.

Stengel had already made a mark in World Series history by then; in 1923, as the Giants' center fielder, he had hit the first World Series homer at Yankee Stadium, an inside-the-parker to win Game 1. He also had much in common with Huggins, McCarthy, and, later, Torre—no titles in multiple seasons as a manager elsewhere, and then a bounty in the Bronx.

Like Sparky Anderson with the Big Red Machine a generation later, Stengel guided a dynasty with hallowed sluggers and a rotating cast of pitchers. Among the 34 pitchers Stengel deployed in the World Series, only Whitey Ford reached the Hall of Fame. His rosters demanded that Stengel recognize hot hands and know how to use them, and for that, he had the vision to hire Jim Turner as pitching coach on his first day as manager in October 1948.

Turner had pitched for Stengel with the Braves and managed against him in the Pacific Coast League, where he had helped turn a struggling Vic Raschi into a mainstay for the Yankees. Stengel courted the press with his clowning and double-talk, but his hiring of Turner was a shrewd background move that made a big difference.

"There was a major change in baseball when the pitching coach for the Yankees, Jim Turner, was hired—he was actually a former pitcher," says Carl Erskine, a Dodger pitcher who faced Stengel's Yankees in five World Series. "I had four pitching coaches in my 12 seasons in the big leagues, and guess what? They were all catchers. In those days, the pitching coach that the manager depended on was a catcher. Of course, the old macho theory was that the catcher is handling the pitcher, so he knows what he's got."

While Dave Duncan, a former catcher, would serve many successful years as a pitching coach for Tony La Russa, Turner's hiring soon flipped the norm: former pitchers, not catchers, got that job. As stalwarts like Raschi, Allie Reynolds, and Eddie Lopat aged, Turner used his understanding of mechanics to help newcomers like Don Larsen and Bob Turley, acquired from Baltimore after the 1954 season.

"Way back before my time, the pitcher actually did a windmill windup," Erskine explains. "Then it got modified and by my era it was just a pump; the pitcher did one pump to get the momentum going. But then when the Yankees acquired Turley and Larsen, Jim Turner cut out all of the extraneous motions and had them pitch from the belt."

Larsen famously used his no-windup motion for his perfect game against Brooklyn in the 1956 World Series. Two years later, against Milwaukee, Larsen got the Yankees their first World Series victory and Turley took care of the rest, shutting out the Braves in Game 5, saving Game 6, and rescuing Larsen to work the final six and two-thirds innings of Game 7, wrapping Stengel's last title.

Stengel had Johnny Kucks warming in the bullpen as soon as Larsen took the mound that day, with Turley soon joining him. Larsen had lost Game 7 to the Braves the year before, chased by Eddie Mathews's two-run double in the third inning. A year later, Stengel would not give Mathews the chance, ordering intentional walks in his first two trips to the plate.[*]

"If I had to pin down one chief trait, I'd say Casey's success is due to his uncanny knack of thinking of everything down to the last detail," *Daily News* columnist Jimmy Powers wrote. He went on to cite the 1949 finale, when Stengel called for his ace reliever, Joe Page, with a four-run lead in the seventh inning. Page closed out the Dodgers with ease.

"There were to be other heroes, other Pages. Yankee players would

---

[*] The Braves' Fred Haney, meanwhile, let Lew Burdette pitch to the dangerous Elston Howard with two outs and first base open in a tie game in the eighth. With a light-hitting defensive replacement, Andy Carey, on deck, Howard singled in the go-ahead run.

come and go, but old Casey would go on and on, winning pennants, fighting the good fight. Let us hope there is a lot more mileage in the old boy yet."

Alas, for Stengel, there would be just two more seasons with the Yankees, ending with the famous seven-game loss to Pittsburgh in the 1960 World Series, when the Old Perfesser outsmarted himself and lost his job.

Stengel turned 70 years old that summer, and the owners, Dan Topping and Del Webb, told him after the World Series that they wanted a younger leader. ("I'll never make the mistake of being 70 again," Stengel said.) The owners had already started undercutting Stengel, firing Turner when the team fell to third place in 1959. Managing his only World Series without Turner, Stengel made a fatal flaw in his pitching plan for the Pirates: he bypassed Ford for the opener in Pittsburgh, choosing Art Ditmar, who led the staff in victories.

"I figured I'd better pick Ditmar because he sometimes won the first games of important series for me," Stengel told the writers, but Ditmar was shelled in Games 1 and 5.* Ford, meanwhile, blanked the Pirates in Game 3 at home and Game 6 on the road, a schedule that left him unavailable for the raucous 10–9 finale.

The Yankees lost despite outscoring the Pirates by 28 runs, making Stengel's decision the perfect cover for a move the owners wanted all along.

"The reason that supposedly Casey got fired is because he didn't start Whitey Ford in the first game," says Bobby Richardson, the MVP of the 1960 World Series despite the Yankees' loss. "Whitey's like [Bob] Gibson, I compare the two; they were different pitchers, of course, but both of them were captain of the team, so to speak. They're the ones you pitch against the tough opponents. Stengel's excuse was it's a small ballpark in Pittsburgh, but Whitey pitched his two shutouts, and had he been able to go three, I'm sure it would have been a different ballgame."

---

* Ditmar did not, however, allow the series-winning homer to Bill Mazeroski, as Chuck Thompson mistakenly said on his NBC radio call. (Ralph Terry did.) When Thompson's call was used in a Budweiser commercial in 1985, Ditmar sued the brewery and the ad agency for libel. The suit was thrown out in U.S. district court.

Mickey Mantle said as much in his book, *The Mick*, written with Herb Gluck in 1986: "I never second-guessed Casey in my life, but I believe the whole Series revolved around that decision."

The immediate failure of the Ditmar decision gave the series a backdrop of dread for Stengel, whose future was already an open question. Down 3–1 in the opener, he made a panic move, pinch hitting for third baseman Clete Boyer with two on and nobody out—in the second inning. ("I was ready to crawl all the way home," Boyer told author Marty Appel. "I was never so shocked in my life.")

With the team trailing 3–2 in the series heading into Game 6, Stengel's job was in such jeopardy that 37 sportswriters signed a petition to retain him. It did no good, of course; the resentment was real after the Game 7 loss, at least to the player most impacted by Stengel's blunder.

"I was so annoyed at Casey, I wouldn't talk to him on the plane ride back to New York," Ford wrote in his memoir. "But in the end, Casey suffered more than I did."

Indeed, Ford thrived under new management, with Ralph Houk and pitching coach Johnny Sain using him regularly on three days' rest. He earned his only Cy Young Award in 1961, and then beat the Reds twice in the World Series to win MVP. Stengel's successors avoided the mistake that haunted his final October: the Yankees reached the World Series four years in a row after Stengel's dismissal, and Ford started Game 1 every time.

———————

Stengel resurfaced in the dugout with the 1962 Mets as the ideal ringleader for a comically hapless expansion team. In the 1970s, another manager came along with a similarly colorful presence: not a clown, exactly, but a showman with a boundless appetite for his sport, his team, and his own celebrity. Tommy Lasorda played a wizard on Saturday-morning TV (*The Baseball Bunch*, with host Johnny Bench), pitched for Ultra Slim-Fast, and brawled with the Phillie Phanatic. But in the Dodgers clubhouse, especially, he knew how to inspire his players.

Lasorda led the Dodgers to three World Series in his first five full seasons as replacement for Walter Alston. Like Lasorda, who pitched in the majors but never won a game, Alston had played in the majors but never gotten a hit; he struck out in his only plate appearance for the 1936 Cardinals. But while the Pennsylvania-born Lasorda adored the spotlight, the Ohio-born Alston ignored it. He was a stern, self-effacing advocate of the Dodger Way, the kind of small-ball believer who would bunt with his 3-4 hitters, Duke Snider and Roy Campanella, in the sixth inning of Game 7 of a World Series. (This happened in 1955, when Alston played for one run and got it, and won 2–0.)

Alston won four titles from 1954 to 1976, and like Lasorda, his second was something of a miracle. The 1959 Dodgers won only 88 games; writing nearly 40 years later, Bill James called it the weakest championship team of all time.

Lasorda's 1988 bunch could challenge that claim, especially the version he used for Game 4 in Oakland. The Dodgers had taken the first two games behind Kirk Gibson's seismic homer in Game 1 and an Orel Hershiser shutout in Game 2. But the A's had won Game 3 on a walk-off homer by Mark McGwire, and would now ask their ace, Dave Stewart, to even things up. With injuries to both Gibson and Mike Marshall, Lasorda's sickly lineup had combined for only 36 regular-season home runs, fewer than Oakland's Jose Canseco had hit by himself.

On the NBC pregame show, Bob Costas put it bluntly: "The A's lineup was stronger than the Dodgers' to begin with, but without Gibson and Marshall—in fairness, pitching aside, and Dodger pitching is excellent—this Dodger lineup has to be one of the weakest ever to take the field for a World Series game."

Unwittingly, Costas had given Lasorda a rallying cry. Even if the unstoppable Hershiser were to win Game 5, Lasorda knew he would somehow have to steal another game to take the series. Gibson was not coming back, nor was his third starter, John Tudor, who had shredded his elbow the night before. Lasorda would need every trick he could find to have a chance in Game 4, so after hearing Costas's commentary, he rattled the clubhouse walls with a fusillade of profane grievances.

"You hear what Costas said? He said you're the worst offensive team ever!" said Mickey Hatcher, the super-sub batting third, recalling Lasorda's tirade. "Oh, man, he was stirring it up. And of course when we were out in the dugout, the players were yelling and Costas didn't know what the heck was going on. But Tommy kept feeding everybody."

Costas finished the pregame show from his spot on the first base side of the grass, by the visitors' dugout. He stayed on the field for the national anthem, having no idea Lasorda had seen his analysis, let alone used it to motivate the Dodgers.

"I'm standing next to Hershiser, who's at the end of the line with his cap over his heart during the anthem," Costas says. "And he looks down over his shoulder and out of the corner of his mouth he goes, 'Boy, Tommy's really got the guys going over what you said.' And I'm startled, like, 'What the hell is he talking about?'

"And then they won, and Lasorda makes a big deal about it afterwards on TV with Marv Albert—and the whole time he's winking at me! I had to go into La Russa's office before Game 5, because the way he understood it, Tommy and I were in cahoots. I sat with him for 20 minutes and convinced him that wasn't the case."

La Russa had never managed against Lasorda but respected his success in the minors, his role on Alston's staff, and his reputation for being "very adventuresome," as La Russa put it, with his offense. So it was in Game 4, a master class in a team taking its cue from the manager with aggression at the plate and on the bases.

Hatcher set up the first run with a textbook hit-and-run single through the right side. The Dodgers scored on a passed ball, an error, and two ground outs, and never struck out in three trips through the order against Stewart. They were caught stealing three times but thoroughly seized the tempo. And when it was time for Lasorda to match his players' urgency, he did, using Jay Howell for a seven-out save one night after he'd been beaten by McGwire.

The Dodgers had no business winning that game. Deep down, they knew Lasorda was full of it and Costas was correct. But Lasorda helped them fool themselves for nine inspired innings. He made them believe that for three hours, they could be better than they really were.

"Oh, Costas was totally right in everything he said," Hatcher says. "I think everybody knows that. That's a World Series lineup? But that's just how Tommy was. He got guys not thinking about the game, just thinking about fighting and getting pissed off."

For an underdog, it helps to not be scared of the opponent. For the favorite, though, a little fear can be useful. The A's were heavy favorites in their three consecutive World Series under La Russa but won just the middle one, a four-game sweep of the Giants in 1989. In processing it all, decades later, La Russa blames himself for failing to mentally prepare the players for the Dodgers in '88 and the Reds in 1990.

Both years, the A's won more than 100 games in the regular season and then swept the Red Sox in the ALCS. Both years, they expected to cruise through the World Series. In 1988, Oakland's Don Baylor said that the A's would rather face the NL's best team, meaning the Mets. Canseco spoke of his team's "overpowering advantage" and said he hoped to "get this thing over in five games"—which it was, but not how he expected.

La Russa said the right things publicly, but his team missed the message. They had played with a purpose all season, and La Russa thought their swagger fueled that drive. He let them believe they could not possibly lose.

"I could have done a better job of scaring them," he says. "There's always that question, when you see a challenge, do you choose the side of confidence that things are gonna work out OK, or do you splash some cold water on their faces and say, 'Hey, this thing could get away'? That was one of my misses. . . . The fact that that series doesn't go six or seven, with the talent we had, is inexcusable."

The A's had been idle for five days after clinching the pennant, and La Russa had considered holding competitive workouts to stay sharp. But the players doubted they could truly bear down against their teammates, so while the Dodgers fought the Mets for seven games, the A's eased up and lost an edge. A year later, with another long layoff before Game 1, the A's did the opposite, carrying over their spirited practices into the first two games of the World Series and stomping the overmatched Giants.

The Loma Prieta earthquake struck just before Game 3, delaying the World Series for 10 days. La Russa had read about Pat Riley's tactic of taking his Laker teams on a retreat before the playoffs, for a mental reset. With rain in the forecast anyway, La Russa thought, why not move workouts to the A's spring training site in Phoenix?

As the team flew over Municipal Stadium on the approach to Sky

Harbor Airport, La Russa noticed cars lining up outside the ballpark, waiting to see his team practice. He knew he'd made the right call.

"After leaving the Bay Area with all the negativity—it was just so sad—as soon as we walked out of that clubhouse, people were cheering and yelling: 'Hey Rickey! Hey Hendu!'" La Russa says. "And the guys all of a sudden just said, 'Wow!' and they started smiling. I hadn't seen them smile for eight or nine days."

The A's overwhelmed the Giants in the last two games to finish their sweep, but a year later they lost just as emphatically to Cincinnati. Again, La Russa blames himself for sensing a problem but failing to address it. In batting practice before Game 1 at Riverfront Stadium, he says, the Reds seemed much more focused than the A's. He thought about saying something but held off, fearful of spooking a roomful of champions.

"We go out there and lose four in a fucking row," he says. "And I'm haunted because I smelled it and I wasn't smart enough to figure out how to hit that button—for years and years and years."

By the time he got the answer, La Russa had retired from his next job, with the Cardinals. In 2012, at an event in Las Vegas, he found himself at a table with Willie Davis and Jerry Kramer, who had starred for Vince Lombardi's Green Bay Packers in the 1960s.

That was a green-and-gold team that did win three titles in a row: the NFL championship game in January 1966, and then the first two Super Bowls. La Russa peppered Davis and Kramer with questions about how Lombardi kept them motivated.

"What he told them was: 'We have a chance to be historic in the history of the NFL,'" La Russa said. "And I'm sitting there thinking: You stupid son of a bitch. If I had told those guys that by winning the World Series two years in a row, and getting into three, they would be remembered in a historic way in baseball for as long as the game is played, I know in my heart that they would have responded to that, because that would have touched their ego. That would have touched everything about their legacy."

Maybe the Reds would have won anyway, La Russa admits. But just like in 1988, he believes that a better mind-set would have at least pushed the series to six or seven games. As it happened, La Russa would not manage a World Series that long until his sixth appearance, in 2011 with the Cardinals, who forced a Game 7 with Texas after one of the most stirring victories in history.

That in itself gave La Russa something to ponder. How could he harness the emotions of Game 6 to shape his team's vision for Game 7? The Cardinals had survived not once, but twice, when down to their final strike. Celebrating later at Mike Shannon's steak house, with highlights on every TV, La Russa could tell the game would live forever. But its true meaning would depend on also winning Game 7.

It reminded La Russa of the time he met Mike Eruzione, the captain of the 1980 United States Olympic hockey team, and asked what coach Herb Brooks had told the players before their gold-medal game with Finland. They had just done the impossible by beating the mighty Soviets, and the euphoria had not worn off. Brooks knew this and warned that a loss to Finland would shadow them for the rest of their lives.

With that memory, La Russa had his message. He slept for less than five hours, waking up at 8 a.m. and calling his coaches to share the story. He gave Albert Pujols an extra hour, rousing him at 9 and telling him to report directly to his office when he arrived at Busch Stadium.

"So as soon as I got the guys together, we came up with this one thing: 'Look, we're gonna put a little box on our shoulder, and anytime something reminds you of Game 6, you put it in that box and slap yourself on the shoulder—shut that box,'" La Russa says. "Now, I don't know if they were jerking me around or not, but I'm walking around the locker room, they're playing all the highlights, and guys start tapping their shoulders.

"But I knew they paid attention, and I'll tell you why. We came out and the fans are going on and on about last night. So I watched us taking BP, and we were just like the Cincinnati Reds prior to Game 1 in 1990: our guys were taking a concentrated practice. They were really serious about everything."

The Cardinals won the game, as we know, but results always shape the narrative. One wayward pitch at the wrong time, and the lessons from a story or a strategy disappear. Managers accept that not all moves will work, and that they often must prepare for situations that never arise. They also have a challenge that their peers in football, basketball, and hockey do not: with no reentry rule in baseball, decisions are cloaked in finality. Every player is Burt Lancaster stepping across the foul line in *Field of Dreams*—once you leave the game, you cannot come back. Even if the team needs you.

Consider the final innings of Game 7 of the 2016 World Series between the Cubs and Indians in Cleveland: top of the ninth, 6–6 tie, one out, man on first. The Cubs' runner, Jason Heyward, took off to steal second, and scrambled to third when catcher Yan Gomes's throw skipped away for an error. Now a fly ball could give the Cubs the lead—and the pitcher, Bryan Shaw, was a cutter specialist whose best pitch moved away from Javy Báez, a right-handed hitter. Indians manager Terry Francona pictured Báez punching a fly to right field and knew he could reduce the chance of Heyward scoring if he had a stronger arm there.

On the bench was Michael Martinez, whose weak bat didn't matter at the moment. Martinez had a much better throwing arm than Coco Crisp, who was 4 for 12 in the series and had homered twice in the postseason. Francona knew he had to make the move. Into right field went Martinez ("basically a designated thrower," Joe Buck said on the Fox telecast), over to left went Brandon Guyer, and out of the game went Crisp—forever, as it turned out. A 15-year veteran, he never played in the majors again.

The count was full on Báez, but Cubs manager Joe Maddon called for a squeeze bunt, which failed when Báez fouled the next pitch at Gomes's feet. Just like that, the whole reason for bringing in Martinez was gone. But Francona would do it all over again.

"If I wouldn't have inserted him when we did, I would have had a hard time explaining that to myself," he says. "We put him into right field because they had a runner on third with less than two outs and we had Coco in the game, who couldn't throw. I always try to tell myself, 'Hey, if I can't explain this, it's wrong.'"

To Francona, it would have been managerial malpractice to leave a better arm on the bench in that scenario, a flagrant violation of the most important rule of his job: again, to put the team in the best position to win. Yet there would be a brutal cost when Crisp's spot in the order came around again, trailing 8–7 with two outs and a runner on in the bottom of the tenth. For the most dramatic of all baseball moments—winning run at the plate, down to the final out of Game 7, the dream scenario for untold millions—the Indians sent Martinez to the plate with nobody left on the bench.

It was checkmate. Martinez was a preposterously bad hitter; of all the position players in the last quarter century with as many plate appearances as Martinez, none had a lower OPS—on-base plus slugging percentage—than his .507. Maddon called for Mike Montgomery, a lefty with a killer curveball that Martinez had no chance of hitting hard. He grounded out meekly to end the season.

Maddon had made some puzzling moves in the World Series, especially using closer Aroldis Chapman for parts of three innings with a big lead in Game 6, leaving Chapman exhausted the next night. But in the end he did what so many Cub predecessors could not, notably Charlie Grimm, the Cubs' winningest manager of the twentieth century. Grimm led the Cubs to three World Series, but in 1935, when his best team faced elimination in Game 6 at Detroit, his conservative approach failed.

With a 3–3 tie in the top of the ninth at Navin Field, the Cubs' Stan Hack led off with a triple off the Tigers' Tommy Bridges. Even after Billy Jurges struck out, the Cubs still had two chances to bring in the go-ahead run from third. But Grimm let starter Larry French bat for himself, playing more for the bottom of the inning than the top, and French tapped a harmless ground out.

"A pinch batter? I considered it," Grimm wrote in his memoir, *Jolly Cholly's Story,* in 1968. "But Larry was pitching very well. Lefty hitters would be coming up for the Tigers. I decided to keep Larry in the game."

The Cubs stranded the runner, and in the bottom of the ninth, those three lefty hitters delivered. In Grimm's defense, the hitters were all future Hall of Famers—Mickey Cochrane, Charlie Gehringer, and Goose Goslin, who had the game-winning single—and the Cubs' best relief option, Lon Warneke, had hurt his arm in Game 5.

"And besides this," wrote a *Sporting News* columnist, Irving Vaughan, "with Bridges bearing down as he was at the time, almost anybody Grimm used as a pinch hitter, for either Jurges or French or both, probably would have been played for a sucker."

Possibly so, and it's also worth noting that Grimm was less likely

Yogi Berra, baseball's lord of the rings, won 10 championships from 1947 through 1962. His favorite ring was from 1953, he would say, because it signified the only team to win five World Series in a row.

Umpire Don Denkinger positioned himself too close to first base to see both Todd Worrell's glove and Jorge Orta's foot in the ninth inning of Game 6 in 1985. He called Orta safe, the Cardinals self-destructed, and the Royals took the title in Game 7.

President Bush takes the mound at Yankee Stadium before Game 3 in 2001, seven weeks after the terrorist attacks on the World Trade Center. To Todd Greene, who caught his first pitch, Bush personified the patriotism of the moment: "Here I am, not only am I coming out here, I'm throwing a dot right down the middle.'"

A statue of Cy Young on the campus of Northeastern University marks the site of the first pitch of the modern World Series, in 1903, at the old Huntington Avenue Grounds.

The Mets' Terry Collins takes some solace from the cheering diehards after the Royals clinched the 2015 title at Citi Field. Collins blamed himself for sticking too long with Matt Harvey in the fateful Game 5.

Mike Schmidt was so confident in 1980 that he choreographed his celebration, leaping onto Tug McGraw—just as they'd planned it—after the last out of Game 6 for the Phillies' first championship. Schmidt hit .381, driving in two runs, to win MVP against Kansas City . . .

. . . but three years later, consumed by a fear of failure, Schmidt was humbled by Baltimore, managing only this broken-bat single as the Phillies fell quietly in five games.

"I woke up at 4 a.m. and walked around the hotel, just to kill time," Steve Blass says, recalling the morning of Game 7 in Baltimore in 1971. By late afternoon, he was flying high as he celebrated the Pirates' title with catcher Manny Sanguillén.

Roberto Clemente and Dick Groat converge on Hal Smith at home plate after Smith's two-out, three-run homer gave the Pirates the lead in the eighth inning of Game 7 against the Yankees in 1960. "Clemente just took me underneath my arm and lifted me up in the air," Smith recalled some 60 years later. "That's how strong he was."

He was irascible, cheap, and vindictive, but A's owner Charlie O. Finley—waving a pennant beside Rock Hudson at the 1974 World Series—was savvy enough to build a dynasty with a bounty of homegrown talent.

David Ortiz slings Koji Uehara over his shoulder after a victory in St. Louis in 2013. Ortiz hit .688 to win MVP for Boston, while Uehara—who flopped so badly in the 2011 playoffs that the Rangers dropped him from their World Series roster—pitched flawlessly under pressure.

Soaking in the cheers at Fenway Park—with a salute from Tedy Bruschi, John Havlicek, and other Boston champions—Bill Buckner tears up before his first pitch on opening day in 2008.

No play since 1960 shifted championship odds as much as Tony Womack's game-tying double for Arizona in the ninth inning of Game 7 in 2001. "We've got 'em by the throat," Womack recalls thinking. "Step on 'em now." Minutes later, the Yankees' dynasty was over.

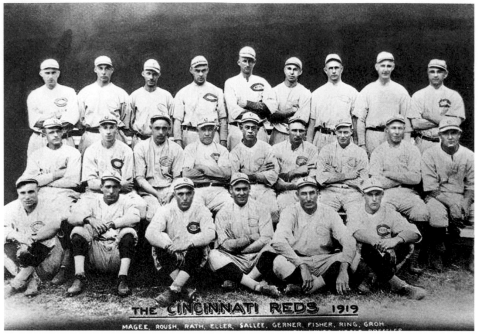

THE CINCINNATI REDS 1919

MAGEE, ROUSH, RATH, ELLER, SALLEE, GERNER, FISHER, RING, GROH

The 1919 Reds had a .686 winning percentage, better than any of the celebrated Big Red Machine teams of the 1970s. They were primed to beat the White Sox in that notorious World Series, even without the help of gamblers.

Only Casey Stengel, perhaps, could coax a wide smile from a manager he'd just beaten in Game 7. Here, Stengel rejoices after the Yankees' fourth championship in a row, over Chuck Dressen's Dodgers, in 1952.

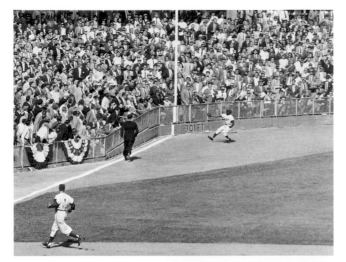

Just after taking Don Zimmer's spot in the lineup in Game 7 in 1955, Sandy Amoros saves the day for Brooklyn with a streaking catch in the left field corner to start a double play. "If he didn't catch that ball," said the Yankees' Eddie Robinson, "we win the World Series."

Sparky Anderson basks in the clubhouse spotlight after Game 7 at Fenway Park in 1975. In the same room the night before, Anderson had chastised the team for blowing the epic sixth game—to the amusement of his stars. "We started laughing," Tony Perez said.

Babe Ruth gets a hand from Lou Gehrig after his "called shot" homer off Charlie Root at Wrigley Field in 1932. Ruth and Gehrig combined to hit .354 with 25 homers for the Yankees in the World Series.

The Yankees' Jorge Posada waits for the Mets' Timo Perez at the plate in Game 1 of the 2000 World Series. Perez failed to run hard all the way, costing the Mets a critical run on their way to a wrenching 12-inning loss.

Facing elimination in 2020, the Rays' Blake Snell can't believe it: his manager, Kevin Cash, is pulling him in the sixth inning of a Game 6 shutout. The Dodgers quickly took the lead and the title.

than most to be criticized. Eternally upbeat and extremely popular, he would sing and play banjo for fans before games and had his ashes scattered across Wrigley Field when he died. And he did, at least, let his best available pitcher decide things in 1935—which is more than the Yankees' Bob Lemon could say in 1981.

Lemon, the Hall of Fame pitcher, had already experienced World Series glory, winning twice for the Indians in 1948 and guiding the Yankees to a six-game triumph over the Dodgers in 1978. Three years later, he met the Dodgers again under much different circumstances: George Steinbrenner had fired him and three other managers since the last World Series, and had stolen headlines after Game 5 in L.A. by breaking his hand in a mysterious—and possibly fictional—elevator fight with hecklers at the Hyatt Wilshire Hotel. Back in the Bronx for Game 6, with Steinbrenner raging and his team on the brink, Lemon pinch hit for starter Tommy John with two runners on in the fourth inning. Bobby Murcer flied out to deep right, and the Dodgers pounded the Yankees' bullpen for seven runs in the next two innings, running away with the clincher.

"Bob Lemon fucked it up," John said nearly 40 years later. "George's edict was: 'Lem, get a lead and then go to the bullpen and win it out of the bullpen.' So I give up my first run in 13 innings, and the game is tied 1–1, and they pinch hit for me. When he told me, I said, 'What, Lem?' He said, 'Don't tell me how to manage.'"

John was incredulous. If Lemon had planned to use Goose Gossage, John said, he might have understood—that move would have matched the urgency of going to his bench so soon. Instead, Lemon called for his ragged middle man, George Frazier, and then for Ron Davis, who was similarly spent.

"Your starting pitcher is your best pitcher that day—if he wasn't, he wouldn't be starting," John says, echoing the wisdom of the time. "I said, 'Bring Gossage in, because what you're saying is it's the eighth inning, not the fourth inning, and you want to get a lead. [Otherwise], it doesn't make any sense!' But George had his meeting, and Lemon, being the good soldier, followed what the Boss wanted."

Lemon was fired two weeks into the next season, and Steinbrenner would continue to churn through managers for the rest of the decade. In 1990 he was banned from baseball for paying a gambler for damaging information on Dave Winfield, and suffered another indignity when Lou Piniella, whom he'd fired twice, won the World Series for the Reds. (Steinbrenner actually hosted NBC's *Saturday Night Live* minutes after the last out, opening his monologue by announcing he'd just bought the Reds.)

Piniella made his mark in that series with an inspired pinch hitting choice in the tenth inning of Game 2. With one out and Dennis Eckersley on the mound, Piniella called for Billy Bates to hit for the pitcher. Bates was 0-for-5 in his Reds career and would never play in the majors again. But he was just the man Piniella wanted, so fast that he had raced a cheetah before a game that summer—and won. (Bates's cap fell off and distracted the cheetah, but facts are facts.)

"Because we're on Astroturf, I knew he could put the ball in play and I knew he could run really well," Piniella says. "And if you brought in a big right-hand hitter, or a big left-hand hitter, Eckersley could throw the ball by 'em. But with Bates, you're gonna make contact. Plus if I'd have brought somebody else in there, I was gonna have to use another player to pinch run for him. If Bates is on, he's fast."

The hitting coach, Tony Perez, told Bates to put the ball in play and run like hell. He did just that, chopping an 0–2 pitch into the hard dirt cutout that acted like a trampoline. The ball never made it out of the infield but bounced so high that Bates dashed to first without a throw. Two batters later, Joe Oliver singled him home with the winning run, sending the series to Oakland. The Reds would return with a trophy.

———

The A's had played in Cincinnati with a star designated hitter, Harold Baines, on the bench. Baines had been a luxury, though, a late-August addition to a team already headed for October. What happens when a manager has more essential bats than spots in the lineup?

This happened most famously in 1968, when the Tigers won the AL pennant despite losing the great right fielder Al Kaline to a broken arm in May. In five weeks without Kaline—who'd been an All-Star 13 years in a row—the Tigers took a commanding lead in the standings with Willie Horton, Mickey Stanley, and Jim Northrup patrolling the outfield.

Kaline returned and played well, but with the DH rule still five years away, it took a clever move by manager Mayo Smith to get all four outfielders into the same lineup. Smith's primary shortstop, Ray Oyler, was good in the field but historically woeful at the plate, his .135 average ranking as the lowest since 1912 among players with at least 200 plate appearances in a season. Perhaps, Smith thought, the athletic Stanley could play there instead.

Stanley had spent four seasons in the majors but never played shortstop before a brief trial in late August. On September 23, Smith tried him there again for a game against the Orioles, and Stanley made two errors. Undeterred, Smith left Stanley at short for the final five games of the regular season, and announced him as his starter for the World Series against the Cardinals.

"This is not a sentimental gesture to get Al Kaline [in] the lineup," Smith insisted. "We're out to win this thing, and by putting an extra bat in the lineup, we think we can do it."

In the *Detroit Free Press,* sports editor Joe Falls wrote that no man had ever put more of a target on himself than Smith, adding, in bold type: "It can blow up on him like no other strategy in all the history of the series." But then Falls pivoted, praising Smith for his courage. The Tigers hadn't won a pennant in 23 years, and maybe they were so charmed that a novice at a demanding position could somehow hold his own.

"It defies all form of logic and I can't intelligently document my reasons why I think it will work," Falls wrote. "But I just feel that Mayo is going to get away with it."

Stanley hit safely in all four of the Tigers' wins, with two harmless errors at short. Meanwhile, Kaline rapped out 11 hits, Horton batted .304, and Northrup broke a scoreless tie in Game 7 with a two-out, two-run triple off Bob Gibson. (Curt Flood slipped in center field but wouldn't have caught the ball anyway.)

Smith, indeed, got away with it, just as he did with his decision to let pitcher Mickey Lolich bat for himself in the seventh inning of Game 5, eight outs from elimination. Lolich singled to start the go-ahead rally, and the Tigers never trailed again in the series.

Lolich and Gibson also homered in that World Series, and the Orioles' Dave McNally did so in 1969 and 1970; the latter was a grand slam. But by 1976, the designated hitter had arrived in the World Series, alternating for a decade—the DH was used in even years, but not in odd years—and adding a wrinkle to managerial strategy.

In 1996, the Yankees' Joe Torre used his DH, Cecil Fielder, at first base for all three games in Atlanta. This was not much of a stretch—Fielder often played in the field that season—but it seemed odd in Game 5 against John Smoltz, a dominant right-hander at his peak, because a slugging lefty-hitting first baseman, Tino Martinez, stayed on the bench. Then again, Torre also kept a lefty hitter with five batting crowns, third baseman Wade Boggs, out of the lineup in favor of Charlie Hayes.

Torre reasoned that by starting Andy Pettitte, a lefty whose cutters often led to grounders to the left side, he needed Hayes at third for his glove. Across the diamond is where he needed offense, and Torre followed his eyes over the platoon advantage. "Big Daddy was swinging really well, and Tino wasn't," he says.

Torre also planned to sit Paul O'Neill that night so a nimbler defender could play right field. But when bench coach Don Zimmer reminded him that O'Neill had essentially been playing on one leg for months, Torre reconsidered. He was not rewarding O'Neill for valor, he said, but because it was not a new injury, he figured O'Neill would be no more compromised than usual.

The moves all worked: Fielder doubled in Hayes with the only run of the game, and O'Neill preserved the win by chasing down a deep drive by Luis Polonia with two outs and two on in the bottom of the ninth. He pounded the wall in celebration, closing down Fulton County Stadium (which would be demolished in 1997) and setting up the Game 6 clincher in the Bronx.

The next season was the first with interleague play, meaning that designated hitters often got to play a few games in the field during the regular season.* This would help Red Sox managers Francona and John Farrell in the new century when they used David Ortiz at first

---

* Fun fact: In years in which only the AL used the DH in the regular season, NL designated hitters batted .255 with 16 home runs, while AL designated hitters batted .243 with 15 home runs.

base for World Series games at NL parks. The Red Sox went 6–1 in those games, and Ortiz made 45 plays without an error.

Gaston, too, prioritized the value of a silver bat over the risk of a rusty glove against the Phillies in 1993. Paul Molitor had played 23 games at first base that season, so he was reasonably comfortable there for Game 3 at Veterans Stadium. But that alignment sent Olerud and his smooth lefty swing to the bench, a strange place to find the reigning batting champion, even with a lefty on the mound.

"That's what I felt we should do to try to win—we wanted to put the best team on the field," Gaston said. "John hit .363 [in the regular season] and everyone thought I was crazy for taking him out of the ballgame, but Molitor—if Molly had not been on the DL so much in his career, he'd probably have 4,000 hits, that's what a great hitter he was. And, of course, I didn't just write him out of the lineup, I talked to those guys before those things happened."

Molitor played all three games in the field—one at first and two at third, where he hadn't played in three years and never would again. The Phillies' lineup leaned left, reducing the chances of grounders to third, and Molitor got only two chances there, handling both with ease. More importantly, he delivered for a Blue Jays team that relied on its offense, going 6 for 12 at the Vet with a double, a triple, a homer, and five runs scored.

Back in Toronto for Game 6, Molitor ripped three more hits, scoring the series-winning run on Carter's clinching homer. He won the MVP with a .500 average and soon appeared with the Phillies' Lenny Dykstra on *Late Show with David Letterman*.

"If there's one thing I learned in this World Series," Dykstra told Letterman, "it's that Paul Molitor can hit."

And Cito Gaston was wise enough to let him.

———

The year before, in Atlanta for another Game 6, Gaston had skillfully woven seven pitchers through 11 innings to clinch Toronto's first championship. Deciding who pitches, and when, is the most visible and hotly debated part of a manager's job, and few did it better than

Gaston that night. He deployed starters as relievers, neutralized his Hall of Fame counterpart, the Braves' Bobby Cox, and leaned on the trust he had built with a veteran to get the final out.

The first six innings went to David Cone, whose arrival in an August trade had bumped David Wells to the bullpen and Todd Stottlemyre out of the postseason rotation. Gaston used both to handle the seventh inning, swapping out the righty Stottlemyre for the lefty Wells and banking on a countermove by Cox.

"Deion Sanders was absolutely killing us and I couldn't wait to get him out of that ballgame," Gaston says. "He was on fire. And when I brought in a left-hander, Bobby took him out of the game, and that was great for us."

The lefty-hitting Sanders batted .533 in the series, and while Cox replaced him with an All-Star righty slugger—Ron Gant—Gaston was happy with the trade. After closer Tom Henke lost the lead on an Otis Nixon single with two outs and two strikes in the ninth, it was Gant, not Sanders, who followed him in the order. Henke, with the right-on-right matchup advantage, retired Gant on a fly out.

Gaston replaced Henke with a lefty starter, Jimmy Key, for the last two outs of the tenth. After Dave Winfield's double put Toronto ahead in the eleventh, the pesky Nixon came up again with two outs and the tying run on third. Gaston met with Key on the mound.

"One thing about Jimmy Key is he's honest with you when he tells you how he's doing," Gaston says. "So that night I walked to the mound and said, 'Jimmy, you OK?' And he said, 'I tell you what, I don't pitch well against this guy, he's kind of got my number a little bit.' And as soon as he said that to me, if a pitcher has any doubt in his mind, I'm gonna go get someone else.

"So I brought Mike Timlin in, and as I was leaving the mound, Joe Carter was playing first base and Joe says, 'Hey, look out for the bunt'—and I turned around and said, 'That's right, look out for the bunt!'"

After swinging away and fouling the first pitch, Nixon indeed bunted, dragging a bouncer between the mound and first. Timlin gathered it and calmly tossed it to Carter, ending the series and finishing an unprecedented bullpen relay—no team before the Blue Jays had used seven pitchers in a clinching World Series game.

In 1975, though, Sparky Anderson had tried. He used seven pitchers in the fabled sixth game at Fenway Park that ended with Carlton Fisk's home run. Three rainouts had given all of the pitchers plenty of rest, and Anderson lived up to his nickname.

"When you're a pitcher, you don't want a manager named Captain Hook," says Jack Billingham, who started once and relieved twice in the series. "But Sparky was before his time."

Anderson felt enormous pressure to deliver a title. He had lost his first two World Series, to Earl Weaver's Orioles in 1970 and Dick Williams's Athletics in 1972, when six of the seven games were decided by one run. Anderson blamed himself for '72, because at a critical point in Game 4, he'd gone against the advice of scout Ray Shore. Needing just two outs to tie the series, Anderson had allowed shortstop Dave Concepcion to play in the hole against pinch hitter Gonzalo Marquez, whom Concepcion knew well from their native Venezuela. Shore's report had said to play Marquez up the middle, and that's where Marquez singled to start a game-winning rally.

Anderson called that a "stupid mistake," and said he made another in 1975 with a three-run lead in the eighth inning of Game 6. Rawly Eastwick was pitching to Bernie Carbo with two on and two out in the eighth. Eastwick was a righty, Carbo was a lefty, and Anderson had a left-hander, Will McEnaney, in the bullpen. Anderson had managed Carbo and thought he'd be vulnerable to McEnaney's curveball. But he wanted to wait until Eastwick had gotten two strikes, and then make the move.

"I took one step up the dugout steps," Anderson wrote in his memoir, *Sparky!*, with Dan Ewald in 1990. "Then for a reason I simply do not know, I changed my mind. I stopped, spun around, and got back in the dugout."

Carbo slammed an Eastwick fastball into the center field bleachers—near a 15-year-old Sox fan named Ron Darling, who would pitch for the Mets in the next World Series at Fenway. It tied the game, and when Fisk won it in the twelfth, Anderson called it a low point of his life. His players were energized by having played in an instant classic, but Anderson was despondent.

"After the game we were sitting around—Pete, myself, Joe, Bench, all the guys—we were sitting around talking about the game and saying it was a great game," says Tony Perez. "Sparky went by and said, 'What are you guys talking about? We just lost, and you guys say it was a great game?' And we said, 'Yeah, it was a great game to be in. Don't worry about it, Sparky, we're tied, we haven't lost yet. We've got another chance.' But Sparky was worried. He was saying we're supposed to be the Big Red Machine, and if we lose this series, too, we're going to be the Big Red Shame Machine, something like that. We started laughing."

Back at the hotel, Anderson couldn't sleep. He was sure he'd be fired if he lost Game 7, forever remembered as the jockey with the best horses who couldn't win the race. He called Shore to his room and dissected the game for hours.

Anderson slept only briefly, but this time he took Shore's advice. Yes, he dreaded what people would think if he lost—but what if he confronted his fears? The reporters would be downstairs at breakfast, Shore knew, and Anderson, a naturally jovial man, should meet with them. It was quite a way to unwind before a Game 7, but it worked.

"I stayed in that press room all morning and afternoon till it was time to go to the park," Anderson wrote. "I told story after story and we were all laughing. When I got to the park, I was the most relaxed man in the world."

By the sixth inning, though, he was nervous again, scratching his head and muttering to himself in the tunnel by the bat rack in the third base dugout. Bill Lee was shutting out the Reds, 3–0, and when Perez went to get his bat, he reassured his downcast manager.

"Don't worry, Sparky," he said. "If somebody gets on, I'm gonna hit one."

And he did, recognizing Lee's eephus curveball—which he had already seen twice that night—as soon as it left his hand. Perez waited, waited, waited, and hammered the blooper over the Green Monster, sparking the Cincinnati comeback. They took a much easier path in 1976, sweeping the NLCS and World Series to repeat as champions.

Anderson was the second manager to win consecutive titles in the '70s. The first was Williams, who guided Oakland in 1972 and 1973, when the A's were outscored in both World Series but won anyway. Williams made his mark with two pitching strategies in the first series, both involving Rollie Fingers.

In the eighth inning of Game 3, with two on and first base open after a two-strike stolen base, Williams met with Fingers on the mound at the Coliseum. He had a surprise planned for the hitter, Johnny Bench: a phantom intentional walk. Williams even pointed to the on-deck circle and first base, to sell the Reds on the move.

"It surprised the hell out of me, because I never thought about doing that," Fingers said, but he executed to perfection. Catcher Gene Tenace stood to signal the intentional walk, then ducked into a crouch to frame a perfect slider on the outside corner for strike three.

Bench said he was simply fooled by a great pitch; the runner at third, Joe Morgan, had alerted him to Tenace's shift. The Reds won that game, anyway, and in Game 7 at Riverfront Stadium, they brought the potential winning run to the plate with two outs in the ninth inning. It was Pete Rose, the future hit king but hardly a power threat. Williams had a plan for Fingers.

"Stay away, stay away, stay away," he told him. "I don't want anything middle of the plate in."

That sounded fine to Fingers, who would not repeat Catfish Hunter's mistake from Game 5 in Oakland. The switch-hitting Rose had homered on the first pitch of that game, turning on an inside fastball and belting it over the wall in right center. Batting left-handed again at the end of Game 7, he would not get the same chance.

"I threw him a fastball tailing away, and it was up a little bit," Fingers said. "I know he likes the ball up, but I knew he wasn't gonna hit it out to left field. And he hit it towards the end of the bat, just a nice little old lazy fly ball to Joe Rudi in left. It made my day."

––––––––

Forty-four years later, well into retirement at age 70, Fingers watched the Cubs-Indians World Series from his home in Las Vegas. With only three healthy starters, Francona, Cleveland's manager, thought the Indians had a narrow path to victory: lean heavily on their bullpen and finish off the Cubs quickly. That gave Francona the urgency to use his best reliever, Andrew Miller, in a way no team had done since the A's of the Fingers era.

Francona made a deal with Miller: if I warm you up, I'll bring you in. The starters understood this, so there would be no confusion if, say, Francona pulled them in the fifth inning of a shutout, which happened to Josh Tomlin in Game 3. Not only that, but it also happened to the Cubs' Kyle Hendricks in the same game. No score, fifth inning, and two healthy pitchers were gone from the game. It felt like a watershed moment, and Fingers loved it.

"Anything can happen in a short series," he said when I called him that night from the Wrigley Field press box. "In a situation where it could be the turning point in the game, with as many arms as they have in the bullpen now—they don't have any junkballers—bring in your best guy in the fifth or sixth to get out of a jam."

It worked for the Indians, who won that night, 1–0, and nearly took the series before the staff finally wore down in Game 7. Miller was usually not the closer that postseason—Cody Allen, who was flawless in 10 outings, filled the role—but as a multi-inning fireman, he was even more valuable.

Fingers didn't always finish games, either. He appeared in Game 1 in each of his three World Series, arriving at high-pressure spots in the middle innings but always giving way to a different pitcher for the save.

"The first game in '74, the phone was ringing in the fourth inning," Fingers said. "I had to turn to the scoreboard to make sure what inning we were in. I'd gotten up before and started throwing, but I don't remember ever going into a game in the fifth. But we needed to win the ballgame, and they figured that might have been the turning point, so why not bring in your closer?"

In the era just before Fingers, starters were often their own closers: in 1957 (Lew Burdette), 1965 (Sandy Koufax), and 1968 (Mickey Lolich), managers got nine innings from their Game 5 starter, brought him back on two days' rest for Game 7—and got another complete game victory.

A generation later, the Braves' Hall of Fame rotation should have given them a distinct edge in the World Series, but it didn't work out that way. Tom Glavine, Greg Maddux, and John Smoltz made 21 World Series starts, but only two that lasted nine innings. The trio combined for a 2.25 ERA, but the Braves went 9–12 in their starts, largely because Cox had few relievers he could consistently trust.

Wohlers secured the 1995 title but allowed the catastrophic Jim

Leyritz homer that turned the '96 series toward the Yankees. In the Braves' four losing World Series in the decade, go-ahead runs scored in the eighth inning or later off Alejandro Peña, Jeff Reardon, John Rocker, Mike Remlinger, Steve Avery, and Charlie Leibrandt.

The Braves' two best regular-season teams of the '90s didn't even reach the World Series. Both times, they lost the NLCS opener in extra innings—Greg McMichael to the Phillies in 1993, and Kerry Ligtenberg to the Padres in 1998—and went on to drop the series in six.

With a better endgame, the Braves almost surely would have won two or three championships in the 1990s. They were a far deeper team, for a much longer time, than the Giants of the 2010s. But the Giants' bullpen was nearly flawless for Bruce Bochy in the World Series, and that is the biggest reason he won three titles.

"It allowed us to win the games we were supposed to win," says Brian Sabean, the Giants' general manager then. "I don't remember many times the bullpen faltered."

There's a good reason for that: it never did. In each of his three World Series with San Francisco, Bochy had Jeremy Affeldt, Santiago Casilla, Javier Lopez, and Sergio Romo in his bullpen. Each time, they got an assist from a more famous guest star: Brian Wilson in 2010, Tim Lincecum in 2012, Madison Bumgarner in 2014. Those seven pitchers—Bochy's go-to World Series relievers—combined for 31 relief appearances for the Giants in the World Series, and 30 were scoreless. *Thirty of 31!* The group's combined World Series ERA, in relief, was 0.28.

Bochy was a catcher, like many managers, and as a career backup he spent years warming up pitchers in the bullpen. That gave him a strong sense of which reliever fit which spot, and with the Giants, no two options were the same.

"Jeremy Affeldt was a four-seam, sinker, big curveball guy from over the top, and then I'm coming from the side," Lopez says. "And then you have Santiago Casilla kind of doing the same thing from the right side—power righty with a power sinker, good breaking stuff—and then you had Sergio Romo with the sidearm delivery. So I think that's probably what Bochy enjoyed more than anything is that you weren't throwing the same type of guy at a hitter all series."

Bochy's players saw him as a master strategist, and that assurance built trust. In the 2010 clincher at Texas, he asked Aubrey Huff to drop a sacrifice bunt with two on and no outs, late in a scoreless game. Huff was the team leader in homers and runs batted in, a headstrong player who had come to bat more than 6,000 times in the majors without a sacrifice bunt. But he got it down, and both runners scored on Edgar Renteria's three-run homer.

Bochy had started his managing career in the Padres' farm system, winning championships with Spokane, High Desert, and Wichita. He learned then that managing in the postseason demanded an urgency and creativity—like asking Huff to bunt, or using Affeldt in every inning from the second to the tenth, as he did in October 2014.

"When I hear, 'Well, this is how we did it during the season, it's how we're gonna do it now,' I've never agreed with that, because to me, you've got to try to win every game you can, pretty much at all costs, and worry about tomorrow tomorrow," Bochy says. "So you can't be afraid to pull the trigger a lot earlier than normal. You've gotta be willing to take risks."

Bochy, like Torre, had a knack for recognizing his players' limitations yet emphasizing the things they did well. By 2012, Lincecum's star had fallen; the two-time Cy Young Award winner led the league in losses, earned runs, and wild pitches. But he had a deceptive delivery and a loose, wiry frame that allowed him to warm up quickly. And while his fastball had lost its old zip, Lincecum still threw harder than Barry Zito, who started Game 1 against the Tigers.

So with three strong relief appearances and one poor start in the playoffs, Lincecum joined the bullpen for the World Series—and even with all of his experienced relievers, Bochy used him first after Zito in the opener. Lincecum fired two and a third scoreless, hitless innings, then repeated the feat in Game 3 at Detroit.

It was a macro version of the way Torre had used his own faded Cy Young winner in 2000. David Cone had endured the worst season of his proud career, morphing from standout starter to bullpen after-thought. Yet in the fifth inning of Game 4 of the World Series, with two outs, the bases empty, and a 3–2 lead, Torre summoned Cone to relieve a stunned Denny Neagle.

The reason was obvious to everyone but Neagle: the batter, Mike Piazza, had slugged a two-run homer off Neagle in his last at-bat, and pulled another long drive just foul. Piazza was the Mets' most fearsome hitter, on his way to Cooperstown with a .379 career average off Neagle. Torre would not give him another shot.

"Denny Neagle was a two-pitch pitcher," Torre explains. "He either threw a changeup or a fastball, so you're giving Mike Piazza a 50/50 chance. You give a guy like him a 50/50 chance, if he hits the ball, it's gonna be a home run. I knew David Cone wasn't the David Cone we all fell in love with, but he had a belly full of guts and he'd dipsy doodle you, because he had a lot of different things that you had to look for."

Cone baited Piazza with sliders off the plate, then jammed him with an 85-mile-an-hour fastball for an infield pop out. Cone never threw another pitch for the Yankees, but Torre knew just when to squeeze the last drop.

The last time the Mets had played a World Series Game 4, the opposing manager showed little of Torre's urgency to grab a three-games-to-one lead. After winning the first two games in 1986, Boston's John McNamara announced Al Nipper as his starter for Game 4, figuring that even if Nipper lost, he would come back with his best starters, Bruce Hurst and Roger Clemens, on full rest for Games 5 and 6.*

Nipper was a historically poor option: he had not worked in more than two weeks, and his 5.38 regular-season ERA was the highest for a World Series starter since Brooklyn's Hal Gregg in 1947. But McNamara believed he could afford to lose that game—and he did, 6–2. The funny thing was, he'd managed differently against the Angels in the ALCS, bypassing Nipper for Game 4 because the Red Sox were down. Now that they were up, the World Series demanded less urgency, just because of the score in games?

"We've got it set up the way we want it," McNamara told reporters

---

* The Mets had a better fourth starter, Sid Fernandez, but manager Davey Johnson kept him in the bullpen for the World Series. Fernandez became an unsung hero of Game 7, with scoreless relief in the middle innings. Johnson's other key strategy, to skip the traditional off-day workout at Fenway Park after two home losses, was similarly inspired; his relaxed team responded with a lopsided win in Game 3.

after Nipper lost Game 4. "They're gonna see our best in the next two games, Hurst and Clemens, with a full complement of rest. We'll have no excuses."

After Hurst won Game 5, a travel day gave Clemens extra rest for his chance to close out the Mets and cap a dream season. Ever since a cool Thursday night in April, when he struck out 20 Mariners before a sparse Fenway crowd, Clemens had owned 1986. He started the All-Star Game and won MVP. He finished 24–4, good for the Cy Young and MVP awards. He finished off the Angels in the seventh game of the ALCS and carried the Sox to the brink of a championship at Shea Stadium.

Clemens gave up two runs in seven innings on 134 pitches. In the top of the eighth, the Red Sox held a 3–2 lead with one out and a runner on second. NBC flashed a graphic showing that the last time the Red Sox won the World Series, in 1918, the average cost of a loaf of bread was 9.8 cents. With Clemens due up, McNamara removed him for a pinch hitter, the rookie Mike Greenwell. Clemens calmly switched out his helmet for his cap, and Greenwell struck out on three pitches. (The Red Sox left 14 runners on base in Game 6, then a World Series record.)

Those are the facts. The confusion over McNamara's motives followed him to the grave. Though Game 6 will always be most remembered for the Mets' two-out comeback in the tenth inning—three singles off Calvin Schiraldi, a wild pitch by Bob Stanley, and Mookie Wilson's grounder through Bill Buckner's legs—it might never have come to that if McNamara had stayed with Clemens, who had retired the side in order in the seventh.

"My pitcher asked out of the game," McNamara insisted later, and when he died in 2020, his widow, Ellen, called Dan Shaughnessy of *The Boston Globe* to reiterate the point.

"I just want to say one thing: my husband did not take Roger Clemens out of that game," she told Shaughnessy. "Roger asked out of the game. He said he had a little cut or something. It tore John up that the press believed Clemens. John would not make something like that up. When Roger told him he wanted to come out, John said, 'You've got to be [expletive] me!' That's what happened. When the chips were down, Roger spit the bit."

Clemens respectfully disagreed, naturally, just as he had when I asked him about it in 2003 for a career retrospective as he approached his 300th win. Yes, Clemens said, he did have a blister on his right middle finger. But it didn't matter.

"The only pitch it was bothering me on was my slider, and I had only given up four hits and they were all on sliders, so it was a good thing," Clemens said. "I was going to stick with curveball-fastball."

McNamara knew about the blister, and might have simply prioritized the chance to pad the lead over sticking with a compromised ace. But if Clemens had really asked out after the seventh, why would he have put on his helmet in the top of the eighth? Rich Gedman, the catcher, told me that Clemens was not in position to question McNamara, who'd been managing in the pros before Clemens was even born.

"If he had been in the big leagues for eight years and the manager said, 'You're out,' then maybe he would look at him and say, 'You're not going to take me out,'" Gedman said. "He was a young guy. He did what they told him."

Clemens, 24, looked strong enough to throw 200 pitches that night, Gedman said. But instead he was done—not just for the night, but for the series. In fact, years later, what bothered Clemens most was not his removal from Game 6, but his absence from Game 7. Rain had pushed the game back a day, and Clemens swore he could have pitched in relief. He watched helplessly from the bullpen with his spikes on.

"Every time that phone rang my heart was jumping through my skin, just hoping it was my call," Clemens said. "I just kept getting more and more mad that they weren't bringing me in."

Hurst started Game 7—a rainout had given him three days of rest—and a more modern plan would have been to summon Clemens after four or five innings. In the 2010s, top starters like C. J. Wilson, Madison Bumgarner, Jon Lester, Trevor Bauer, Charlie Morton, Clayton Kershaw, and Patrick Corbin all worked in relief in Game 7s. In 1986, though, McNamara used Schiraldi, Joe Sambito, Stanley, Nipper, and Steve Crawford in relief but never turned to the best pitcher in baseball.* The Mets scored eight runs in their final three at-bats for a comeback 8–5 victory.

McNamara never managed in another World Series, and Clemens wouldn't make it back until 1999, as a Yankee, when Torre kept him in for the eighth inning of the clincher. Clemens got two more outs, Mariano Rivera got the last four, and the Yankees finished off their sweep of the Braves.

Rivera was such an overpowering force for Torre that in six World Series as Yankees manager, his pitchers never threw a complete game.† But the idea of an ace doing it all by himself, willing his team to victory with the trust of a knowing manager, is an enduring October theme.

Think of Cardinals manager Johnny Keane in 1964, when the Yankees hit two homers off Bob Gibson in the ninth inning of Game 7. Gibson was pitching on two days' rest, coming off a 10-inning complete game, with the tying run on deck and two outs. Asked later why he left Gibson in to finish it, Keane explained: "I had a commitment to his heart."

Three years later, in 1967, Gibson won another Game 7 under a different Cardinal manager, Red Schoendienst, closing out the Red Sox by going all the way in Game 7. Gibson worked on three days' rest. Boston manager Dick Williams started his ace, Jim Lonborg, on two. Lonborg was shelled for seven runs and 10 hits in six innings, and years later, a Red Sox reliever, Dan Osinski, said Williams should have tried a futuristic strategy instead.

"Lonborg couldn't break a pane of glass in the bullpen when he was warming up," Osinski, who died in 2013, said in his SABR biography. "We all knew that, and [Williams] still started him. You know he could have pitched the bullpen an inning apiece, or something."

The 1967 World Series was part of a stretch of 10—from 1962 through 1971—that ended with a complete-game victory: by Ralph Terry, Sandy Koufax, Gibson, Koufax again, Dave McNally, Gibson

---

* McNamara couldn't use Oil Can Boyd in relief because Boyd, who had started and lost Game 3, had gone on a cocaine bender after learning he'd been bypassed for Game 7.
† In fairness, Andy Pettitte would have shut out the Marlins in Game 2 of the 2003 World Series, but Aaron Boone made a two-out error in the ninth, and Jose Contreras got the final out.

again, Mickey Lolich, Jerry Koosman, Mike Cuellar, and Steve Blass. In '71, the Pirates' Danny Murtaugh was so sure of Blass that he let him face the Orioles' top two power hitters, Boog Powell and Frank Robinson, in the ninth inning of Game 7.

"Not one trip to the mound, how about that, in a 2–1 seventh game?" Blass says. "I loved him."

Facing the same hitters for the fourth time in Game 7, Blass retired the side in order to deliver the championship. Murtaugh's closer, Dave Giusti, had led the league in saves and sparkled in October. Yet the game belonged to Blass, just as it did to Jack Morris at the Metrodome 20 years later.

Like Murtaugh, the Twins' Tom Kelly had a strong closer, Rick Aguilera, as an option for the end of Game 7. Morris had fired nine scoreless innings against the Braves, but the Twins had not scored, either. Kelly's instinct was to give the ball to Aguilera for the tenth, because Morris had done his job.

"You say to yourself, 'The guy's pitched nine innings for you. Nine innings. How much is he gonna pitch?'" Kelly says. "Of course there's no other game, I get that, but this is the third time he's pitched in, what, nine days? How much do you want? How much is he supposed to give you?

"There's versions of this story, but I'm gonna tell you what it was. I said, 'Jack, I think that's enough, Jesus Christ.' And I had Aguilera down there—he's pretty good, he's rested and ready to go; it's not like I don't have anybody. But [pitching coach] Dick Such came over to me and said, 'You know, he's OK.' And I looked back at Jack, I was only three feet away from him, and he looks at me with the puppy dog eyes and says, 'I'm OK, I can go.' I said, 'OK, go get 'em. Just a game.' That was the end of it. Maybe I felt like I had to hear it from him, I guess, I don't know. But I was just more than concerned about how much is he supposed to give you? You don't want him to lose; Jesus Christ, he's pitched his ass off. But those guys don't care about that, they just want to get out there and pitch. These big-time pitchers, they just want to be there in that spot. And after the tenth inning I didn't even say anything to him. Actually, the tenth inning was maybe the easiest inning he had. I didn't even think about moving him out after that."

He didn't have to, because the Twins won in their half of the tenth.

Since then, only one pitcher has gone the distance in the World Series clincher: the Marlins' Josh Beckett against the Yankees in 2003. That, too, took some guts from the manager, Jack McKeon, because Beckett was pitching on three days' rest.

McKeon, though, had gone into the postseason determined to ride only his best pitchers. At 72, he was the oldest manager in World Series history, arriving there after aggressively deploying his four best pitchers—Josh Beckett, Carl Pavano, Brad Penny, and Dontrelle Willis—as both starters and relievers against the Cubs in the NLCS. He moved Willis exclusively to the bullpen for the World Series, and after seeing the Yankees maul a soft-tossing lefty, Mark Redman, in Game 2, he sat Redman for the rest of the series. The Yankees had a far more decorated staff, with Clemens, Rivera, Mike Mussina, Andy Pettitte, and David Wells, but McKeon stretched the Marlins' group to make it even deeper.

"They had a better pitching staff than I had, but we used it better, that's all," McKeon says. "We had basically three guys in the bullpen, that's it. Beckett, Pavano, Penny, Willis, all those guys came in in relief. Go to the Yankees series, same thing. We won because I used my best pitchers in a short series. They could rest all November."

Beckett had pitched well in a Game 3 loss, and after the Marlins tied the series the next night, McKeon plotted ahead. Starting Redman in Game 6 would be foolish, he thought, but what about Beckett? He'd never worked more than four innings on three days' rest, but when he did, in Game 7 against the Cubs, he'd looked sharp.

"I'm thinking about pitching you with three days' rest," McKeon said he told Beckett. "What do you think? You all right?"

"Let me throw a bullpen," Beckett said, and once he did, he told McKeon what he wanted to hear: "I'm your guy."

When the Marlins won Game 5, McKeon liked his plan even more. He'd grown up a Yankees fan in South Amboy, New Jersey, and respected the majesty of the pinstripes. The Yankees had gotten to the World Series with a Game 7 comeback for the ages over Boston in the ALCS. If they forced another, McKeon feared they'd have an overwhelming edge.

"I knew about the Yankee mystique from my own visits to Yankee

Stadium—something happens if you let them go to seven," McKeon says. "I'm gonna *make* 'em go to seven, I ain't gonna *give* 'em seven."

Thirty years earlier, the Mets' Yogi Berra had tried the same strategy. He could have used George Stone, a nondescript lefty who'd had a career year, to try to clinch Game 6 in Oakland, knowing he'd have a fully rested Tom Seaver for Game 7. Instead, Berra went for the knockout punch with Seaver, who pitched well but lost, forcing Jon Matlack to start Game 7, also on short rest. The A's battered Matlack early and won.

McKeon's choice for Game 7, Pavano, would also be working on short rest—but it never came to that. Beckett silenced the Yankees with the last clinching shutout in World Series history, validating the instincts of a manager who asked his associates for their opinion, just to be polite, and then went on his own.

"Nobody gave me an answer, nobody would agree," McKeon says with a laugh. "And then when we won? 'I was with you all the way!'"

———

In 2019, McKeon won another championship ring as a senior advisor for the Washington Nationals. That World Series, Nats vs. Astros, was billed as a throwback to the heyday of starting pitchers. Six veterans—Max Scherzer, Stephen Strasburg, and Patrick Corbin for Washington; Justin Verlander, Gerrit Cole, and Zack Greinke for Houston—boasted multiple 200-inning seasons and All-Star selections. And while some of those pitchers were dazzling, especially Strasburg, the ending highlighted the biggest quandary facing World Series managers today.

In an age awash with data, which do you trust—your game plan or your eyes—to answer that timeless question: Take him out or leave him in? If a starter is rolling, should you let him go until he stumbles or yank him before he does?

For most of Game 7, Greinke was the story. He threw 67 pitches in six innings, allowing a single and a walk and making several stylish plays on the mound. Whether he liked it or not, the quirky, cerebral Greinke—a guy so indifferent to history that he once said he'd rather not throw a no-hitter than deal with the "bunch of nonsense" that comes with it—was etching his name in World Series lore.

And then—after a ground out, a homer, and a walk—he was gone. The Astros still led, 2–1, with Howie Kendrick due up. The easy move, the move nearly every manager would have made for the first 110 or so World Series, was no move at all: when a likely Hall of Famer is going strong in Game 7, you let him keep going. But A. J. Hinch, the Astros' manager, considered many more factors, and pulled Greinke for Will Harris.*

Asdrubal Cabrera was up after Kendrick, and Hinch had made up his mind that Greinke would not face him a third time; Cabrera was 2-for-4 off Greinke in the World Series and 18-for-41 (.439) lifetime. The question then became who should face Kendrick. Harris had struck him out in a tight spot in Game 4, and while Greinke is famously unpredictable, the savvy Kendrick—whose career embodied the phrase "professional hitter"—had faced him off and on for a decade. He'd never faced Harris until the World Series.

In theory, Hinch could have turned to Gerrit Cole, who was also getting loose in the bullpen. Cole had beaten the Nats in Game 5 and had two days' rest. Ideally, Hinch hoped to give Cole plenty of time to warm up, and then unleash him to start the ninth inning, as Boston's Alex Cora had done with Chris Sale to close out the 2018 World Series in Los Angeles.

But Hinch was also leery of asking Cole to do something new; Dallas Keuchel and Justin Verlander had struggled for Hinch in past October relief outings, and he wasn't sure what he would get. Harris offered predictability; he'd given up a homer the night before but had otherwise been nearly flawless in October.

Harris got Kendrick to swing and miss at a first-pitch curveball. Then he used his best pitch, the cutter, and put it right where he wanted: the bottom left corner of the zone, the farthest strike from the hitter's eyes. If Kendrick made contact, he'd probably hit it foul.

But that's not what happened. Kendrick smoked a line drive toward

---

* The Nats thought so highly of Harris that they would sign him that winter to a three-year, $24 million contract.

the right field corner. Most balls in that direction will hook foul, and this one, indeed, was headed for the pole, tackily decorated with an ad for Chick-fil-A. BURGERZ R FOUL, read the slogan on the pole—but baseballs that strike it are fair, and Kendrick's clanged off the attached metal screen with a gong that sounded the end for the Astros.

"Let's be honest, in today's world, right or wrong, I'm always going to be questioned," Hinch told Jake Kaplan of *The Athletic*. "If Greinke had given up the homer, then I overextended him. If Cole had come in and not been sharp, it was because he didn't have rest. That's what makes managing both beautiful and agonizing."

It was only the second time in World Series history—after the Yankees in 1960, when Jim Coates gave up a homer to Hal Smith in Pittsburgh—that a team had gone from winning to losing on a single pitch in the seventh inning or later of Game 7. But if Hinch's move caused a tremor of controversy, another manager's decision, one year later, would trigger an earthquake.

————————

What was your best decision last year? What was your worst? Chances are, you're thinking of your best or worst result. The mind does not easily separate decisions from results; life is not a Choose Your Own Adventure novel, so we never know the outcome of choices not made. A decision is only a guess, an attempt to influence a desired result.

"You could have your best hitter pinch hit with the bases loaded, and he could hit into a double play," Joe Torre says. "It's really not making the wrong moves; it's making moves that don't work."

This is why you almost never hear a manager admit he regrets a decision. To do so would imply that his process was wrong, or he willfully ignored information that would have given the team a better chance to win. On the rare occasion a manager does express regret, he's usually shifting blame to protect his players.

When a player performs almost flawlessly, though, there's no blame to deflect. This is how I unwittingly stumped Kevin Cash in the moments after the Tampa Bay Rays lost the 2020 World Series in Arlington, Texas. His starter, Blake Snell, had been having one of those nights, the kind of transcendent, season-saving effort we'd always remember. His line was nearly unprecedented; only one other pitcher in World Series history had fanned nine without a walk while allowing no more than two hits.

That was Roger Clemens, for the Yankees 20 years earlier, and he lasted eight innings. Snell is a different kind of pitcher, and Cash could not push him to be Clemens. Yes, Snell had thrown only 73 pitches, carving up the Dodgers with fastballs, sliders, and changeups. Yes, the mighty L.A. lineup looked utterly helpless. But Cash sensed danger. He wanted Nick Anderson.

This seemed egregiously unfair to Snell—and, selfishly, to observers like me who love dominant starting pitching. I asked Cash later if there was anything Snell could have done to stay in the game.

"That's a fair question," said Cash, who acknowledged that Snell could not have pitched better. "I don't know if I've got the best answer right now. He did above and beyond what any of us could have asked for."

The last line was telling. In the Rays' best-case scenario, Snell would reach the middle of the game with a lead, and the bullpen would hold it from there. He'd done his job exceptionally well, but that didn't mean he'd keep it up. The number nine hitter, Austin Barnes, had just singled, bringing up the dangerous Mookie Betts. Snell had not pitched beyond the sixth inning in 17 months, and Cash, who knew him better than anyone else, could not imagine him going further.

But the Dodgers sure could.

"He may have pitched a complete game," Betts said. "I don't know exactly what would have happened, but he was rolling."

Betts said Snell looked like the Cy Young winner he'd once been, and that the Dodgers were relieved to see him go. Of course they were: their first three hitters, Betts, Corey Seager, and Justin Turner, had all struck out twice. To the Dodgers, Cash could have called for some unholy combination of Bob Feller and Nolan Ryan. As long as it wasn't Blake Snell, they could relax. The very thing that Cash most wanted—a different look—was exactly what the Dodgers wanted, too.

The sight of Anderson only made them more confident. Anderson was one of baseball's best relievers, averaging an absurd 16 strikeouts per nine innings for the Rays, with elite carry on his fastball. Yet he'd given up runs in his last six outings, with opponents hitting .342. When I asked him later if he felt like the best version of himself, he answered with refreshing candor.

"Definitely no," Anderson said. "Workload, 2020 season, the whole thing is just crazy, honestly. Not having a normal routine, lifting, the season, everything—it's been crazy. I didn't feel as good as I would have liked to, but it's the big leagues; you're not going to feel good every time. I was still confident. It wasn't the situation; it wasn't being in the World Series or anything like that. Not a lot of gas."

Even so, Anderson said, he hadn't told anyone how he felt, because relievers don't do that. Players know the difference between injured and hurt—injured means you're inactive, but everyone is hurting, so suck it up and do your job. Besides, if fatigue had caused a mechanical issue, surely the Rays' video analysts or coaches would have picked it up. In their minds—and his, he insisted—Anderson could still succeed.

Few others shared that opinion as Cash strode to the mound. The limited crowd booed. Snell looked away and winced. He had studied for this moment, he said later, and planned for how to keep the Dodgers down. Instead, his lead was gone within a few pitches, the Rays would not score again, and Snell was through with Tampa Bay. He was traded to the Padres two months later, having pitched 10 seasons in the Rays organization without ever working nine innings in a game.

Beckett hadn't done it, either, before McKeon let him loose in October 2003, before most teams were digging deep for data. The low-budget Rays owed much of their success to synthesizing information and rigidly applying their findings. Calling for Anderson in the sixth inning of a shutout was nothing new; they'd done the same thing in Game 7 of the ALCS, with Morton pitching, and survived.

"Third time through, we value that, we value our process," Cash said that night, and he repeated the logic 10 days later, after the Snell move backfired: "The different look means something."

In both cases, the next batter was a four-time All-Star who hits from the opposite side of the starter; the left-handed Michael Brantley was due to face the right-handed Morton, and the righty Betts was coming up against the lefty Snell. In both cases, the hitter represented the tying or go-ahead run. Bigger leads might have led to different decisions, but baseball offers infinite permutations that no model can fully anticipate. This is why managers and statisticians chafe at the perception that game strategy is predetermined.

"As analysts, we're trying to give base rates to the person who has to make real-time decisions in a context that we can't describe beforehand—that's it, and I think that leads to better decision-making," says Sig Mejdal, a former NASA researcher who helped the Cardinals and Astros win championships before moving on to the Orioles. "Doesn't every other field do that, when you have to make decisions with imperfect information in a probabilistic world? I don't think baseball's immune to that. So that's it: we're not trying to script it, we don't think they're robots. We've noticed that they're human beings and they have emotions."

Five years earlier, in another elimination game, Mets manager Terry Collins gave in to the emotions of his starter, Matt Harvey, who had shut out the Royals through eight innings in Game 5 at Citi Field. Closer Jeurys Familia had worked two nights in a row, and while he'd blown two save chances in the World Series, he'd generally pitched well all month. Collins intended to give him the ninth.

"The game is about putting all these guys in positions to have success, and here was a situation: 'OK, this is your closer's job, that's why he's down there,'" Collins says. "But when Matt walked in and I saw that look on his face, I said, 'Shit, he deserves to be out there, he wants it, go get it.'"

In that moment, Collins said, he was proud of Harvey, the self-styled Dark Knight of Gotham who had made a strong return after Tommy John surgery. Harvey had been almost too good, in fact, exceeding the innings threshold his agent and doctor had deemed safe. In early September, Harvey ignited a controversy by suggesting he should limit his workload, and Collins had no choice but to honor that wish.

One night against the Yankees, at a packed Citi Field in a nationally televised game, Collins lifted Harvey after five overpowering innings— and the bullpen gave up 11 runs. Harvey approached his manager the next day and told him to forget what he'd said. He just wanted to pitch, innings be damned, and now he was desperate to finish a World Series masterpiece.

"I really, truly believe there's a time when you have to listen to your players," Collins says. "So now here's a guy who looks you in the eye and says, 'Give me the damn baseball.' That's exactly what I'd been wanting, that kind of attitude out of this guy. So I let him go back out."

Yet the Royals, perhaps, were too familiar with Harvey by then. Lorenzo Cain worked a walk, Eric Hosmer slashed a double, Familia replaced Harvey, and the Royals tied the game. After losing in extra innings, Collins blamed himself in his postgame press conference. "It was my fault," he said, three times, and continued to blame himself until several accomplished peers—Tony La Russa, Jim Leyland, and Joe Torre—called to reassure him. All said he'd done the right thing.

Collins still stands by his move. And while Cash made the opposite call, he wouldn't change it, either. At least, that's how he felt two weeks after the World Series, when he was named American League Manager of the Year. I asked him that night how he'd been handling the fallout of his fateful trip to the mound.

"I would do it the same way all over again," Cash said. "I would plead for a different outcome, that's for sure."

Then Cash mentioned, unprompted, that my postgame question still vexed him.

"I remember you asked me after the World Series, right after the game you asked a great question: 'What did Blake need to do to stay in the game?'" Cash said. "I still don't know if I have the best answer for you. But I know that that decision was not reflective in my confidence in Blake. It was very reflective in my confidence in Nick, and that's how I felt, at the moment, was the best chance for us to win the game: to get the ball in Nick's hand and then line up the bullpen."

That off-season, Cash's move became a punch line. A sampling:

During the Super Bowl, a college football writer, Brett McMurphy, tweeted, "Only way Tampa Bay loses this championship is if Kevin Cash comes out of the stands and pulls Tom Brady."

On something called "National Roast Day," the Rays' account dared the Wendy's account to roast the team. The fast-food chain's reply: "We're surprised you didn't pull your social media manager in the middle of writing that great tweet."

On Valentine's Day, a popular meme depicted Cash on a card beside the tagline "Did you just throw 73 pitches? Because I'm trying to take you out."

And so on. Cash understood that the Snell decision had instantly become part of his legacy, and Francona, his former boss and mentor, said he was proud of how Cash handled the questions. Francona knew, from the way he'd used his Cleveland bullpen in 2016, that Cash saw his relievers as peacekeepers, not fire extinguishers. He was eager to stay ahead of the damage by controlling the matchups. He trusted in the all-important word across sports today: *process.*

Would Francona have left Snell in? If so, he wasn't saying. When he watches a game, he says, he never tries to manage along. Decades in the dugout have taught Francona that no matter what move he thinks he might make, if it's not his team, he'll never know—and neither will we.

"It's so easy for people that aren't there to say, 'I wouldn't have done that,'" Francona says. "Well, you know what? You didn't earn the right to make that decision. He did."

And we won't live with the weight of our decisions and their impact on baseball history. For better or worse, the manager will.

Game 5

"We Love Tournaments"

The Challenge of Building a
World Series Winner

Alex Anthopoulos was stumped. This was the night before the 2021 World Series, on the Atlanta Braves' bench in Houston, a week or so before his players would bound joyously out of that dugout to celebrate a championship. Anthopoulos, the Braves' general manager, could not explain the formula for getting there.

"I wish I knew," he said. "I've been in baseball since 2000, with 10 years as a GM, and I don't know how you get to a World Series, I really don't. You've got to get in. Get in and hopefully guys step up."

That summer, Anthopoulos had engineered the most impactful series of short-term deals in the history of the trade deadline. Just before the All-Star Game, the Braves lost their best player, outfielder Ronald Acuña Jr., to a torn anterior cruciate ligament on a leap at the warning track in Miami. They already had a losing record, and no team since the 1964 Cardinals had been under .500 at the All-Star break and recovered to win the World Series. Anthopoulos feared that his players might check out, mentally, over the break; he wanted a newcomer in the clubhouse when they returned.

That player was Joc Pederson, an outfielder who had reached three of the last four World Series as a Dodger and was available from the rebuilding Cubs. Later in the month, Anthopoulos traded for three other veteran outfielders: Adam Duvall from Miami, Eddie Rosario from Cleveland, and Jorge Soler from Kansas City. He knew he could not find a do-it-all dynamo like Acuña. But if he bought in bulk and got the best versions of each new player, that might be enough.

And so it was: Duvall led the league in runs batted in, Pederson slugged three critical homers in the playoffs, Rosario was the most valuable player of the NLCS, and Soler the MVP of the World Series. It was the first time ever that a team started four position players acquired at midseason in its World Series–clinching lineup. Said Terry McGuirk, the team chairman, on the field after the final out: "I wouldn't trade Alex Anthopoulos for any executive in baseball."

Anthopoulos had been part of seven consecutive playoff runs as general manager of the Blue Jays and Braves, with a Dodgers assistant role in between. For a model, he says, he often thinks of a famous peer who has never won the big one: Billy Beane of the Oakland Athletics. When general managers evaluate each other, they prioritize sustained success over occasional World Series glory. That's what has made Beane a marvel, and a valued source of guidance for Anthopoulos in a season that was frustrating before it turned enchanted.

"Look, just be .500, or close to .500, at the deadline," Beane told Anthopoulos that July. "Sixty games is a lot of games. A lot of teams are just gonna quit, and that will give you an opportunity."

The Braves had been thwarted in October for decades. Starting in 2000, they had made 12 trips to the playoffs without reaching the World Series, the longest streak in baseball. When they finally broke through in 2021, they transferred that distinction to the A's, who have made 11 fruitless visits to the postseason in the same timeframe.

Beane's famous line in *Moneyball*—"My shit doesn't work in the playoffs"—seemed to be self-fulfilling. He actually meant that the wisdom of his strategy reveals itself over the long haul, like any model based largely on data. The postseason, with its much smaller sample, is harder to forecast.

But here's the funny thing: the very existence of a playoff system should benefit a team like the A's. Beane reflected on this in 2019 when I found him behind the batting cage before the AL Wild Card Game in Oakland.

"It's interesting," he said. "In the Premier League, if Manchester City wins the league, they win the title. Thirty-eight matches, they win, and they don't have a tournament. But we love tournaments. It's like the NCAA. We like the NCAA Tournament because we love the thought that Princeton can knock Georgetown out in the first round—and sometimes they do.

"More often than not, it's going to work in our favor. As a smaller team, us and the Rays would prefer randomness to determine it, because a team like the Dodgers, Astros, or Yankees is usually going to be more powerful. So the more teams you add, the more random it's going to be."

A year earlier, in the Bronx, the Yankees had stomped the A's in the wild-card game. Things seemed more promising in 2019, because 54,000 rowdy fans were jamming into the three-tiered Coliseum and the visiting Rays were the lowest-scoring team in the AL playoff field. The A's (with apologies to countless pizza parlors) were the original Rays, winning big with a small payroll, though only Tampa Bay had won a recent pennant.

"The most amazing thing about 2008 wasn't that they made the World Series, but that they won the Eastern Division," Beane said. "I mean, it was amazing they got to the World Series, but winning the division, with those juggernauts, that was the amazing accomplishment."

That was a logical way to look at things, for sure, but it seemed like a rationalization. Players don't aspire to merely get into the playoffs, and fans don't frame the big picture. Had Beane always revered the long season and dismissed the relevance of October?

"Oh, no," he said. "It just fits my narrative."

Beane laughed; he wasn't serious. He reiterated that baseball's postseason tournament should reward teams like the A's, and the fact that it hadn't was simply bad luck. He would not let the whims of October define him.

"Again, honestly, small-market teams want that randomness," Beane said. "They want that luck to be involved, because more often than not, we're not going to be the favorite going into a postseason."

A few hours later, alas, the green-and-gold dice bounced the wrong way again. The first batter of the game hit a homer for the Rays, and the A's never recovered. They slipped quietly into the winter with a 5–1 loss, while the host of the NL Wild Card Game, the Washington Nationals, stuck around a little longer.

They won the World Series.

In the euphoria of the Nats' clubhouse after Game 7 in Houston, their architect, Mike Rizzo, would not claim a superior strategy. His team had won four division titles in the decade but never advanced in the postseason. Why were the 2019 Nationals, with the worst regular-season record of all of Rizzo's playoff teams, the version that went all the way? Was it luck, he was asked, or something special about the group he'd assembled?

"I think it's a little bit of both," said Rizzo, wiping champagne from his eyes. "Our goal—my job—is to build a team that we believe can win 90 or so games every year. Now, sometimes 90 wins equates to 95 wins, and sometimes it's 82 wins like last year, depending on circumstances.

"But we try to create a playoff-caliber team that plays meaningful games in September and October. We've done it for the last eight years. We couldn't get over the hump the last couple of years, but we had great teams. And this year we got over the hump."

Rizzo mentioned the decisive game of the 2012 division series against St. Louis, when the Cardinals took five pitches from closer Drew Storen, all with two outs in the ninth inning, when any strike would have ended the series. The Nationals lost, but if the umpire had called a close pitch a strike, they would have won.

Then again, Rizzo added, the Nationals got their own break when facing elimination in the same round in 2019. With the bases loaded in the seventh and Max Scherzer on the mound, the Dodgers' Pederson lashed a ball into the right field corner. It could have cleared the bases, but it landed an inch or two foul, and Scherzer escaped the jam.

"So there's a lot of things that happen," Rizzo said. "It not only takes a great team to win a championship, it takes a little good fortune."

For the first 65 years of the World Series, luck was not much of a factor in determining who got to play at the end. Baseball was the last of the four major American sports to institute playoffs before the championship round; prior to 1969, teams advanced directly to the World Series by posting the best record in their league.

But when expansion swelled the majors to 24 teams, the leagues split into divisions and adopted a best-of-five league championship series. That expanded to a best-of-seven series in 1985, and a decade later—after further realignment and expansion—a best-of-five division series was layered on top. In 2012, the leagues began holding wild-card games to start the tournament, and the 2022 collective bargaining agreement expanded the field to six teams per league (three division winners, three wild cards), beginning with a new best-of-three round.

Nobody in baseball—except Beane, perhaps—uses the word "tournament," but that is what the postseason has become. In the first 50 years of the divisional play, the best teams in each league met only 11 times in the World Series. And just three of those meetings—Braves/Indians in 1995, Yankees/Braves in 1999, and Red Sox/Cardinals in 2013—came in the era of the division series.

So does that make it easier or harder now to win the World Series? It is much easier, in one sense, because a team can afford to lose more games during the regular season and still reach the playoffs. (The Nationals started 19–31 before their sprint to a title.) But it is harder for the best teams to be rewarded for their excellence, because getting there is only the start. What matters most is succeeding in small samples, which defies the data-driven nature of today's front offices and makes the game's most recent dynasty stand even taller.

"I remember speaking in real time back then: this is a dynasty, this is like a Secretariat, it doesn't come around very often, so stop and really appreciate it," says Brian Cashman, the Yankees' general manager when they won three titles from 1998 through 2000. "What this franchise did for that window was unprecedented and rare—and I say unprecedented because with the new levels of Wild Cards and extra rounds and playoffs, it was that much harder to navigate. The ability to get knocked out was so much easier, and I think it's been proven time and time again: the best team doesn't win the day, more so than not, because of the randomness."

Consider two eras of the A's. They won the AL pennant in 1972, 1973, and 1974, and each time triumphed in the World Series. No other franchise besides the Yankees has won three championships in a row. Those A's were a dynasty, yet the A's of 1988, 1989, and 1990 averaged 10 more wins per season (102 to 92) and also claimed three consecutive AL pennants. But they lost two of their three World Series, emphatically.

So was the latter version flawed in some way? If the Oakland general manager, Sandy Alderson, had constructed the roster differently, would he be remembered as the man who built a dynasty? Does a legacy really depend on a walk to Mike Davis and a chopper off the Astroturf by Billy Bates?

"You know what, if I spent the last 30 years thinking that way, I'd be a bitter old man," said Alderson, at age 72 in 2020, with a laugh. "That's why I don't recall a lot of the details. It's better for your mental health."

————

The power structure behind baseball's early champions was far different than it is today. The owner or manager often assumed the duties we now associate with the general manager, and many World Series stars joined their teams through methods no longer applicable. The best players on the 1903 Pittsburgh Pirates arrived in what was essentially a merger with the failing Louisville Colonels in 1900. Former Colonels delivered the first hit (Tommy Leach), run batted in (Honus Wagner), and victory (Deacon Phillippe) in World Series play.

Yet the Pirates' owner, Barney Dreyfuss, had acquired those players when he ran the Louisville franchise with the same basic traits of today's top executives: tireless study, relentless curiosity, and a vast network of well-informed friends. For their book *In Pursuit of Pennants*—the authoritative source on the history of the front office—the historians Mark L. Armour and Daniel R. Levitt credit Dreyfuss with "as keen an eye for spotting baseball players as the game has ever seen."

This did not come naturally for Dreyfuss, who emigrated from Germany to Kentucky in 1882, when he was 17, to live with relatives who owned a whiskey distillery. He knew nothing about baseball then, but as he acquired stock in the Colonels and gained responsibility in running the club, Dreyfuss poured himself into learning the game. He would scour *Sporting Life* and other publications, seeking news of far-flung prospects and minor league owners who might be willing to sell them. In 1894, likely working off a one-sentence tip he had read, Dreyfuss traveled to Memphis to watch an outfielder for a team based in Savannah, Georgia. The team was broke, and its manager mentioned that he could not afford train fare back to Georgia. Dreyfuss provided it for $200 in exchange for the outfielder, Fred Clarke, who starred for and managed the Colonels and Pirates on his way to the Hall of Fame.

Dreyfuss understood motivations and leverage; he persuaded Phillippe to sign after a barn on Phillippe's South Dakota farm burned down. A top Dreyfuss lieutenant, a former sportswriter named Harry Pulliam, urged him to sign Honus Wagner from a team in Paterson, New Jersey. In the early '20s, Dreyfuss had the foresight to hire a scout, Joe Devine, to cover the Pacific Coast League in California. Devine found pitcher Ray Kremer, who would win Games 6 and 7 of the 1925 World Series, and the Hall of Fame brothers Lloyd and Paul Waner, who led the Pirates to another pennant two years later.

Dreyfuss was somehow not elected to the Hall of Fame until 2008, more than 75 years after his death and decades after contemporaries like Connie Mack and John McGraw. Mack and McGraw are best known for managing—they rank first and third in career wins, flanking Tony La Russa—but they were also instrumental in constructing their rosters. Half of the first 28 World Series, through 1931, included Mack's Philadelphia A's, McGraw's New York Giants, or both.

The Athletics were generally awful or spectacular. But since Mack owned the team, his rule was absolute, and if he needed to sell off his stars—as he did after the 1914 World Series and again about 20 years later—no one could stop him. The A's finished in last place 17 times, but they also won five championships, still the most by any Philadelphia pro sports franchise.

Mack's first World Series team, in 1905, had three Hall of Fame starters: Chief Bender, Eddie Plank, and the eccentric Rube Waddell, whom Mack had managed in Milwaukee in an earlier iteration of the American League. Waddell challenged Mack's reputation as a disciplinarian, wrote Mack's biographer, Norman L. Macht, but he counted on his veteran players to understand that Waddell would have to be an exception—a talented, well-meaning misfit who could not be corralled. Waddell would lead the league in strikeouts in all six of his years with the A's, though he missed the 1905 World Series with a mysterious September shoulder injury, possibly caused by a fall on a train while lunging to swipe a teammate's straw hat. (It was unfashionable, you see, to wear a straw hat after Labor Day.)

Waddell was gone by 1910, when the A's won their first championship, followed by others in 1911 and 1913. After the Braves upset them the next year, Bender and Plank jumped to the upstart Federal League—and Mack gutted the team. Long before the 1997 Florida Marlins, the A's were the first World Series team to tear itself down.

"There was only one way to get out from under the catastrophe," Mack wrote in his autobiography. "I decided to sell out and start over again. When it became known that my players were for sale, the offers rolled into me. If the players are going to 'cash in' and leave me to hold the bag, there was nothing for me to do but to cash in too. So I sold the great Eddie Collins to the White Sox for $50,000 cash. I sold Home Run Baker to the Yankees. My shortstop, Jack Barry, told me he wanted to go to Boston, so I sold him to the Bostons for a song.

"'Why didn't you hang on to the half of your team that was loyal and start to build up again?' This question has often been asked me. My answer is that when a team starts to disintegrate it is like trying to plug up the hole in the dam to stop the flood. The boys who are left have lost their high spirits, and they want to go where they think the future looks brighter. It is only human for everyone to try to improve his opportunities."

The A's lost prodigiously for years (their .235 winning percentage in 1916 is still the worst since 1900), but as attendance rose in the early 1920s, Mack reinvested in the team. In a 12-month period starting in December 1923, he purchased four future Hall of Famers: Al Simmons, Jimmie Foxx, Lefty Grove, and Mickey Cochrane. Foxx was 16 years old, Cochrane and Simmons 21, and Grove 24, and they would lead the A's to the 1929, 1930, and 1931 World Series, winning the first two. Then, as now, there is no better formula than investing money in premium young talent.

McGraw, the impresario of the New York Giants, was on a similar run of scouting glory at roughly the same time. In some ways he was the game's greatest general manager, even without holding the title. Beyond his acumen in the dugout, McGraw built 10 pennant winners for the Giants between 1904 and 1924, winning the World Series in 1905, 1921, and 1922, with another crown in 1934, after health problems had forced his retirement.

McGraw was confrontational and irascible, a drinker and a brawler who had been a scrappy pest of a player for the old Baltimore Orioles in the 1890s—he rarely struck out, walked a lot, and ran wild on the bases. He started his playing career as a teen and was never shy about using young players with the Giants. Three everyday players on his 1921 champions were future Hall of Famers no older than 25: first baseman High Pockets Kelly, third baseman Frankie Frisch, and right fielder Ross Youngs.

The next year, McGraw signed two amateur teenagers, Travis Jackson and Freddie Lindstrom, who would help the Giants win more pennants on their own paths to the Hall of Fame. But McGraw's greatest coup of 1922 came on the way north to start the season, when Tom Watkins, a friend who owned the minor league Memphis Chicks, urged him to meet Bill Terry, who worked for Standard Oil and starred for their local semipro team. As his biographer, Frank Graham, recounted, McGraw noticed the size of Terry's hands and the strength of his grip, and soon signed him to a minor league deal. By 1924 Terry was hitting .429 in the World Series, and six years later he became the last National Leaguer to hit .400 for a season. Terry succeeded McGraw as manager in 1932 and won three of the next five NL titles.

Besides his eye for talent, McGraw was a master at buying low in trades, willing to take players with character issues—distressed assets, in modern lingo—if they could help the Giants win. His rotation for the 1921 World Series included Fred Toney and Shufflin' Phil Douglas, both acquired despite troubling off-field problems.

McGraw purchased Toney from the Reds in 1918 while he was plagued by scandal: during a trial for dodging the World War I draft, Toney was indicted for transporting a woman across state lines for sex. He served time in prison in 1919 but helped the Giants win the World Series two years later. McGraw then traded Toney to the Braves for another pitcher, Hugh McQuillan, who started for the Giants in each of the next three World Series.

Douglas, meanwhile, was a notorious alcoholic. "I never knew where the hell he was, or whether he was fit to work," said Fred Mitchell, the Cubs' manager, after trading him in 1919. McGraw said he could handle the right-hander, a prediction that blew up in spectacular fashion when Douglas—after a forced stay at a sanatorium—sealed his professional doom over a seething hatred of McGraw.

"I want to leave here but I want some inducement," Douglas wrote in a letter to the Cardinals' Les Mann, a former teammate, in August 1922. "I don't want this guy to win the pennant, and I feel if I stay here I will win it for him. So you see the fellows, and if you want to, send a man over here with the goods and I will leave for home on next train."

Mann turned the letter over to Commissioner Kenesaw Mountain Landis, who banned Douglas for life. For McGraw, though, Douglas had served his purpose: he had beaten the Yankees in Games 4 and 7 of the 1921 World Series.

———

That was the Yankees' first World Series appearance, and the first of three in a row against the Giants. They won the third, in 1923, with a pitching staff they essentially bought from desperate rivals, a tactic they have now used for a century. More than any other franchise, the Yankees have understood and exploited other teams' pressure points, positioning themselves as the one franchise rich enough to solve their problems, though often at a devastating long-term cost.

The December 1919 sale of Babe Ruth, the most seismic transaction in major league history, was just one of many ways that the Red Sox helped launch the Yankees' dynasty. All four pitchers Boston used in the 1918 World Series—Bullet Joe Bush, Sad Sam Jones, Carl Mays, and Ruth—would also pitch for the Yankees' first championship team five years later. The mercurial Mays (best known for fatally beaning Cleveland's Ray Chapman in 1920) quit the Red Sox in 1919 and was traded to the Yankees for two players and $40,000. Sensing a dangerous precedent, AL President Ban Johnson tried to nullify the deal. But the Supreme Court of New York intervened, bringing Mays to the Yankees and establishing an alliance that would flip the teams' fortunes for the rest of the century.

The Ruth sale, for $100,000 and a loan that gave the Yankees the mortgage on Fenway Park, took place over the objection of Red Sox manager Ed Barrow, a canny businessman who wore civilian clothes in the dugout, like Mack in Philadelphia. Barrow had helped build the 1918 champions by urging owner Harry Frazee to pluck the carcass of Mack's roster. When the debt-riddled Frazee then started his own sell-off, Barrow jumped to the Yankees as business manager after the 1920 season, riding the AL's momentum shift.

Barrow preyed on Frazee, offering his old boss a lifeline. In 1923, more than 80 percent of the Yankees' innings were pitched by former Red Sox: Bush, Jones, Mays, Waite Hoyt, Herb Pennock, and George Pipgras. The pitchers had cost the Yankees about $200,000 in cash (plus assorted lesser players) in various deals, and the investment paid off when Pennock won the 1923 clincher, with Jones getting the last six outs.

Behind the scenes, another Red Sox castoff was stocking the Yankees with future stars. Paul Krichell, an old reserve catcher for the St. Louis Browns, had scouted for Barrow with the Red Sox. Barrow brought Krichell to the Yankees, and in April 1923 Krichell brought Lou Gehrig to Barrow. Gehrig, a prodigious slugger for Columbia University, was playing for the Yankees some six weeks later.

Krichell would go on to sign players like Whitey Ford, Tony Lazzeri, Phil Rizzuto, and others who would dominate the World Series for decades. Years after Barrow's retirement in 1946, Krichell served as head of scouts for another Hall of Fame general manager, George Weiss, who invested heavily in his department. Those scouts found still more gems, like Mickey Mantle, who kept up the winning tradition.

"The Yankees generally get the scouts they want," wrote *Newsweek* in 1957. "Their salary scale is the highest anywhere in baseball.... The Yankees found men like Mantle and Berra and signed them without significant competition because they were blanketing the country most thoroughly."

With a deeper inventory of young talent, especially before the draft began in 1965, the Yankees had the pieces they needed to aggressively fine-tune the roster. As Weiss said in that *Newsweek* story, "You have to know exactly what you want and you always have to be willing to give up more than you think that the other fellow is worth. We got Tom Ferrick [in 1950]. He wasn't worth what we gave up, but his relief work won the pennant."

The Yankees had shipped $50,000 and four players—none of major consequence—to the St. Louis Browns for Ferrick at the mid-June trading deadline in 1950. After solid work that summer, he earned the victory in Game 3 of the World Series against the Phillies. The Yankees flipped Ferrick to the Senators the next June for Bob Kuzava, another journeyman who made a small but lasting impact: he pitched just once in the 1951 and 1952 World Series, but notched the final out both times.

Their unmatched depth and financial might kept the Yankees ahead of their rivals. And as they had with the Red Sox in the 1920s, the Yankees had one team they continually plundered: the Kansas City A's, whose owner, Arnold Johnson, was a close friend of Yankees co-owner Dan Topping. Johnson's team lacked cash and prospects, and the Yankees had plenty of both.

From 1955 through 1960, these players and more flowed to the Bronx through the Kansas City pipeline: Roger Maris, Ralph Terry, Ryne Duren, Bobby Shantz, Enos Slaughter, Clete Boyer, Hector Lopez, and Art Ditmar. All of them would play for multiple World Series teams with the Yankees.

In 1961, before his first spring training as the Athletics' new owner, Charles O. Finley declared an end to the farce. He found a white van, arranged for the words "Shuttle Bus to Yankee Stadium" to be painted on the side, and had it set ablaze. Finley and general manager Frank Lane doffed their caps to the bus, waving goodbye for the cameras— but they could not resist one last trade. In June they sent a nondescript pitcher, Bud Daley, to the Yankees for Ditmar and Deron Johnson.

It was the seventeenth deal between the teams since 1955, and another coup for the Yankees: Ditmar went 0–5, Johnson hit .216—and Daley won the clinching game of the 1961 World Series.

The Yankees won 10 World Series and lost five others from 1947 through 1964, the first 18 seasons of the integrated major leagues. They were so deep that they continued to win despite waiting until 1955 to use their first Black player: catcher Elston Howard. He worked out pretty well, winning an MVP award and helping the Yankees reach nine World Series in his first 10 seasons.

When the Yankees were not winning it all, a team with a strong African American presence usually was. Seven future Hall of Famers who had played in the Negro Leagues helped lead teams to titles: Larry Doby and Satchel Paige with the 1948 Indians, Willie Mays and

Monte Irvin with the 1954 Giants, Jackie Robinson and Roy Campanella with the 1955 Dodgers, and Hank Aaron with the 1957 Braves. Apart from the more important impact of erasing baseball's shameful color line, these teams showed the value of being early adapters to a trend and finding an edge where others would not look.

"I wanted to get the best of the available Negro boys while the grabbing was good," Indians owner Bill Veeck told *The New York Times* in July 1947, after signing Doby as the first Black player in the American League. "Why wait? Within ten years Negro players will be in regular service with big league teams."

Branch Rickey caught on to this first with the Dodgers, of course, signing Robinson to play for his minor league team in Montreal in 1946, before Veeck bought the Indians. But Veeck always held that he had tried to make an earlier strike with the Phillies.

"Back in 1942, I suggested that the only reservoir of players still untouched during the war was the Negro Leagues," Veeck wrote in an *Ebony* magazine article in 1960. "As a matter of fact, I wanted to buy the Philadelphia ball club to put in an all-Negro team. It wasn't really aimed at being an all-Negro team, but it would have worked out that way. I was going to add 15 Negro players who were better than anything that Philadelphia had and would have won the pennant by 30 games."

Veeck would embellish the story in his autobiography, claiming that he had an actual deal in place to buy the Phillies but shared his integration plan with Commissioner Kenesaw Mountain Landis, who double-crossed him and thwarted the sale. Whatever the veracity, the idea would have been shrewd, exemplifying every executive's wish to conquer unexplored terrain as a pathway to the pennant.

Rickey was the master of this long before signing Robinson. He created the modern farm system as president of the Cardinals in the 1920s, convincing owner Sam Breadon to purchase minor league teams all over the country. Minor league teams had always been unaffiliated fiefdoms, selling their best players to the highest bidder. Rickey's innovation allowed the Cardinals to sign and develop their own talent—their way, at their price—without having to compete for it with richer rivals.

"When the Cardinals were fighting for their life in the National

League, I found that we were at a disadvantage in obtaining play-ers of merit from the minors," Rickey said, as quoted in his official SABR biography. "Other clubs could outbid. They had money. They had superior scouting machinery. In short, we had to take what was left or nothing at all. . . . I do not feel that the farming system we have established is the result of any inventive genius—it is the result of stark necessity."

Through 1925, the Cardinals had never finished higher than third place. But they would play in nine of the next 21 World Series, winning two pennants in the '20s, three in the '30s, and four in the '40s, when they claimed more than 30 farm teams. Rickey's system produced a steady stream of career Cardinals. The 1942 team won a franchise-record 106 games, then stomped the Yankees in the World Series while using just two players who had ever played elsewhere.

The Cardinals were one of four teams, with the Yankees, Dodg-ers, and Mets, who opposed the creation of the draft at the winter meetings in December 1964. By then, the A's and Finley had already begun strategizing for it, moving aggressively to hoard top amateurs. In the first two weeks of June 1964, Finley signed several teenage prospects, including Catfish Hunter, Blue Moon Odom, and Joe Rudi. His success continued when the draft began, with Rick Monday and Sal Bando in 1965, Reggie Jackson in 1966, and Vida Blue in 1967. Monday was traded for Ken Holtzman, who joined the others as the core of the Oakland dynasty in the '70s.

"Finley was no dummy," Eddie Robinson, then the Athletics' scout-ing director, said in 2021, a few months before he died at age 100. "He was a pretty sharp guy. He would listen to you, but he wouldn't do what you said. He would do what he thought was right, and many times he was right."

Finley was clever and cunning at best, shady and stingy at worst. In Kansas City, he had a mule named "Charlie O." and made it the team's mascot. In Oakland, he took a liking to a local kid named Stanley Burrell, made him an honorary vice president (or clubhouse spy, the players suspected), and gave him the nickname Hammer—yes, *that* Hammer, of hip-hop fame. Finley styled his A's in green-and-gold uniforms, paid them to grow mustaches, and pushed the league to use fluorescent-orange baseballs to improve visibility.

Finley was also rash, vengeful, and extraordinarily cheap, running the team from Chicago, the home base of his insurance company. In the 1973 World Series, after second baseman Mike Andrews made two errors in the twelfth inning of Game 2, Finley ordered Andrews to sign an affidavit insisting he was injured in a dubious attempt to drop him from the roster. He sparred with Commissioner Bowie Kuhn and fellow owners, whose distrust of Finley may have blinded them to his prescient idea at the advent of free agency.

In 1974, Finley failed to pay into an annuity in Hunter's contract, a breach that made Hunter a free agent. Alone in the marketplace, Hunter commanded a record deal from the Yankees—five years, $3.5 million—and Finley understood that scarcity would work to players' benefit as free agents. In late 1975, when the arbitrator Peter Seitz struck down the reserve clause, which bound players to their original teams unless traded or cut, Finley advocated for all players to become free agents. The plan would have flooded the market and, by the laws of supply and demand, diminished individual players' bargaining power. The owners rejected Finley's plan—to the relief of the union leader, Marvin Miller, who was always a step ahead.

Just as he had done with the draft, Finley tried to get in front of the free-agent wave, selling Blue to the Yankees and Rudi and Rollie Fingers to the Red Sox, rather than lose them for nothing on the open market. Kuhn struck down the deals, but Finley knew he was doomed. The A's crumbled because of their inability or refusal to adapt to free agency—just like the next dynastic team of the 1970s, the Cincinnati Reds.

The Reds swept the Phillies and the Yankees in 1976 to win their second title in a row (they remain the only team in the playoff era with a perfect postseason), but soon those teams were poaching Reds players on their way to the top. Don Gullett went 14–4 for the '77 Yankees before injuries curtailed a promising career, and Pete Rose willed the Phillies to victory in 1980. The Reds were soon the worst team in the league and did not sign a free agent until Dave Parker in December 1983.

Bob Howsam had been general manager of the Reds' four World Series teams of the '70s, trading for a pair of all-time greats, Joe Morgan and Tom Seaver, during the decade. The Morgan trade, in November

1971, was a masterstroke—Lee May, Tommy Helms, and Jimmy Stewart to the Astros for Morgan, Cesar Geronimo, Jack Billingham, Denis Menke, and Ed Armbrister—but few understood it at the time. The slugging May was a two-time All-Star and, like Helms, a career Red who was revered in the clubhouse. Writers and fans were aghast.

"If the man on the street owned the Reds," went the lead of a fan-reaction story in *The Cincinnati Enquirer,* "general manager Bob Howsam would probably be traded for a trained seal."

Si Burick, the sports editor of the *Dayton Daily News,* credited Howsam for astute deals in the past, like trading Ray Sadecki for Orlando Cepeda as general manager of the Cardinals in 1966. (Cepeda was the MVP in 1967 and led St. Louis to a championship.) But Burick emphasized the intangibles of May and Helms and feared that their absence would crush the Reds' spirit.

"You can't deal in personalities in baseball," Howsam told Burick. "I must try to think in terms of what can be done to make us a contending club, and that's what I went for—the ultimate result. We traded some nice guys away. We're getting nice people."

Nice guys finished fourth for the Reds in 1971, a year after reaching the World Series. Howsam's reinvention brought balance to the lineup, speed to the bases, and premier defense to the middle of the field. The Reds had just played their first full season at Riverfront Stadium, and now they were better suited for a home with turf. May's departure opened first base for Tony Perez, who had twice led the league in errors at third; Billingham became the Reds' most durable pitcher through their glory years; Geronimo won four Gold Gloves in center field; and Morgan became a transcendent star, a slick-fielding second baseman with power, speed, and a keen eye at the plate, the best player on the best team of the era.

For all his skills as a dealmaker, though, Howsam could not adapt to free agency. He telegraphed his disdain for players' rights in a public statement during the strike that delayed the start of the 1972 season. He railed against Miller and warned that his tactics could ruin the game.

"If he wants to influence and guide the players, let him impress upon them the need for better cooperation in autograph sessions, personal appearances, hospital visits," Howsam said. "Let him help baseball, not hinder it."

It was a losing battle for the old guard. Time after time, free agency helped losing franchises win. The Astros had never made the playoffs until 1980, when Morgan and Nolan Ryan arrived as free agents. The White Sox got a boost from Carlton Fisk in 1981 and soon captured their first division title. The Padres won theirs for the first time in 1984, after Goose Gossage joined Steve Garvey as a free agent import.

The owners agreed not to sign each other's free agents in the mid-'80s, a transparent—and illegal—collusion scheme to depress the market. Soon, though, the impact would be profound again: the 1988 Dodgers (Kirk Gibson), the 1989 A's (Mike Moore), the 1991 Twins (Jack Morris), and the 1992–93 Blue Jays (Morris, Dave Winfield, Paul Molitor) all won the World Series with significant help from free agents. Toronto, a talented team with a soft reputation, found an edge with Morris.

"He was a winner, and that brought a lot to the club," says Pat Gillick, the GM who built the Blue Jays from expansion team to juggernaut. "We also had Dave Winfield on that '92 club. They both had good years on the field, but also from a psychological standpoint, to have those two guys along with Joe Carter, Robbie Alomar, John Olerud, and the rest of 'em, they really provided some extra oomph for us."

Gillick went back to the market that off-season, replacing Winfield with Paul Molitor, another proud veteran still seeking his first championship. When Jimmy Key left as a free agent, Gillick replaced him with Dave Stewart, coaxing one last good season from the battle-tested righty. Gillick also bolstered both teams with major August trades, using his farm system to get David Cone in 1992 and Rickey Henderson in 1993. This was a change for Gillick, once derided as "Stand Pat" for going 534 days without a trade in the late 1980s. He had come to appreciate the ripples from a big splash.

"I think you owe it to the players, you owe it to the fans, you owe it to ownership that if you think you're in a position to win, talent-wise or psychologically, you've got to make that move, because there's not too many times you have an opportunity, and you have to do whatever is reasonable to get there," he says.

"In 1985 [when Toronto first reached the playoffs], I probably should have given us a little bit of a boost, whereas later on we made some acquisitions. Not all of them, from a statistical standpoint, worked out really well, but adding guys like Cone and Henderson got us into the World Series. And I'm not saying that's the reason, but I can recall talking to Molitor after he came over with us before the '93 season and he told me, 'When you got Cone in August, we were chasing you guys and we were just mentally deflated.' So it had a mental effect on the Brewers, too."

The Blue Jays had beaten Atlanta in 1992 and the teams seemed poised for a rematch the next season, when the Braves set a franchise high with 104 victories after adding Greg Maddux in free agency. Their first target, though, had been Barry Bonds. With the Pirates certain to lose Bonds as a free agent, their general managers—Ted Simmons for Pittsburgh, John Schuerholz for Atlanta—had agreed to a trade before the 1992 season: Bonds for pitcher Alejandro Peña, outfielder Keith Mitchell, and a prospect. Schuerholz was sure he could quickly sign Bonds to a long-term deal, adding the best hitter in baseball to a pitching staff with Tom Glavine and John Smoltz.

The trade fell apart when Pirates manager Jim Leyland protested vehemently to team president Carl Barger, who called off the deal. Bonds went on to win another NL Most Valuable Player award and sign with the Giants as a free agent, but Schuerholz and the Braves' president, Stan Kasten, viewed Maddux as an appealing pivot.

"We had this money sitting hot in our hand that we had budgeted for Bonds," Schuerholz says. "Stan and I were talking: 'The best guy out there is not a hitter but a pitcher, Greg Maddux. Let's make a very good pitching staff great.' And we did. Once we added Maddux to the roster, a lot of good things happened psychologically in terms of the spirit of the team."

The tangible impact was also profound: Maddux had just won the Cy Young Award for the Cubs and would claim the next three for Atlanta. Maddux had his moments in October—his 95-pitch, two-hit, no-walk complete game to start the 1995 World Series was a masterpiece of efficiency—but his uneven results highlight the vagaries of the month. Maddux had a 2.81 ERA in 29 postseason games with the Braves. But he was 11–13 for them overall and never won twice in a postseason series.

Sometimes Atlanta's losses defied logic; the Marlins won in the

1997 NLCS despite losing a top starter, Alex Fernandez, to an injury in Game 2. No matter: rookie Livan Hernandez stepped into the rotation, beat Maddux in Game 5, and then topped Cleveland's Orel Hershiser twice in the World Series. The Marlins' ace, Kevin Brown, lost twice at home to Chad Ogea and it didn't even matter.

No general manager could have plotted such an unlikely path to the title. Dave Dombrowski, the GM of those Marlins, also built the 2014 Tigers, who rolled out three Cy Young Award winners—Max Scherzer, Justin Verlander, and David Price—in a division series with Baltimore. Each of those pitchers, plus fellow starters Rick Porcello and Anibal Sanchez, would win rings by the end of the decade. But they could not conquer the Orioles, who started Chris Tillman, Wei-Yin Chen, and Bud Norris—and swept the series. That ended a nine-year stretch in which the Tigers reached the playoffs five times and the World Series twice, losing both times in a rout.

Dombrowski, seemingly, had done everything right: he'd drafted Verlander; traded for Miguel Cabrera, Scherzer, and Price; and used the money from an aging and aggressive owner, Mike Ilitch, to sign stars like Magglio Ordoñez, Ivan Rodriguez, Prince Fielder, and Victor Martinez. Yet the Tigers were never at their best when it mattered most, and their strongest team, in 2013, lost to the Red Sox in a baffling six-game ALCS: Scherzer and Verlander combined for a 2.11 ERA in their three starts in that series, but the Tigers lost them all.

"We had good clubs and we didn't play well, and that's the difference," Dombrowski said. "I mean, just think if we'd have won in '06, '12, and '13. You'd be saying, 'Wow, look at that organization!' That's how close we were, and we didn't get it done."

When I spoke with Dombrowski, the Giants were the reigning champions, having just beaten Kansas City in the World Series with an otherworldly effort from Madison Bumgarner, who'd gone 2–0 with a save and a 0.43 ERA. The other Giants starters, Tim Hudson, Jake Peavy, and Ryan Vogelsong, were 0-3 with a 9.35 ERA. They all got rings.

"I tip my cap to 'em, but somebody asked me at a speaking engagement this year, 'When a club wins a world championship, do you as an organization change your philosophies based upon what they did?'" Dombrowski said. "And I said, 'Well, you're always observant of what other people do; I mean, look at what Kansas City did with their bullpen, of course you'd like to have a great shutdown bullpen like that. But if I told you that the recipe for success, for winning a championship, was to have one great starting pitcher and not have anybody else that was going to pitch well for you—is that how you would want that constructed? No. But it worked, and they rode it.'"

Another power team of that era, the Phillies, won the 2008 World Series and then improved in each of the next three seasons under Ruben Amaro Jr., who succeeded Pat Gillick after the parade. Amaro made a habit of adding ace starters to the roster, but each year the Phillies finished a little worse: they lost the World Series to the Yankees in 2009, then dropped the NLCS to the Giants in 2010 and a division series to the Cardinals in 2011.

"When you're talking about playoff baseball, really it's the team that's playing the best baseball—they're getting the breaks and they're making the breaks," Amaro says. "I don't think we had the best team in 2008. I think Boston had the best team in 2008, but they got beat."

The young Tampa Bay Rays took seven games to beat the Red Sox but lost in five to the Phillies. In an effort to repeat, Amaro added Cliff Lee, the reigning AL Cy Young Award winner, at the 2009 trading deadline. Lee beat the Yankees twice in the World Series but the Phillies won no other games, and while Amaro traded Lee after that season, he entered the 2010 NLCS with Roy Halladay and Roy Oswalt supporting Cole Hamels. The Giants won in six.

The next year, with Lee back, the Phillies set a franchise record for victories with 102, yet dropped a five-game division series to St. Louis. Chris Carpenter beat Halladay in the finale, 1–0, and just like that, the Phillies' window slammed shut. The team instantly decayed around the injured slugger Ryan Howard, and the Phillies would not have another winning season for a decade. A few years into that stretch, Amaro acknowledged that a well-intentioned commitment to homegrown favorites had come with a costly price.

"Fans identify with players like Jimmy Rollins, Chase Utley, and Ryan Howard, who are arguably the best players at their position in the history of our franchise," Amaro said. "It's hard to cut them loose. And yet sometimes you have to have that mentality like, 'You know what, maybe we were a little too loyal, maybe we were thinking that we could squeeze some more blood out of the stone.'"

Amaro had given the fans what he thought they wanted, keeping the Phillies' best players and importing some of the top starters in baseball to go with them. But his most successful regular-season team flopped in October because the Cardinals upended the theory that good pitching should beat good hitting. The Cardinals scored the most runs in the NL in 2011, and the Phillies allowed the fewest. Yet the Cardinals advanced.

Indeed, any supposed truism about the right championship formula can be easily debunked. Experience ought to matter, right? Then what about the 2002 Angels, who started their title run without a single position player who had ever appeared in the postseason? Their first-round opponent, the Yankees, were coming off four consecutive AL pennants, and lined up Roger Clemens, Andy Pettitte, Mike Mussina, and David Wells for the division series. The Angels stomped them all and drubbed Livan Hernandez twice in their World Series with the Giants, never mind his flawless postseason record. The Angels had a middling rotation but hit .320 in October, charging madly around the bases and locking down leads with their bullpen.

The Angels had the fewest strikeouts in the American League in 2002. Two years later, the Red Sox had the most. Both teams won the World Series, proving . . . what, exactly? Theo Epstein, the GM of that Boston team, lent some perspective in 2015. His Cubs were playing the Mets in the NLCS, as the Royals met the Blue Jays in the ALCS. Each team was strikingly different.

"Whatever team wins the World Series, their particular style of play will be completely in vogue and trumpeted from the media all off-season—and in front offices—as the way to win," Epstein said. "So if we win the World Series, it's going to be a necessity for every team to develop their own core of young, homegrown position players. If the Mets win, you'll be required to have four ridiculous young starting pitchers on the same staff. If the Royals win, you'll need to have speed and athleticism and contact up and down your lineup. If the Blue Jays win, you'll need to fill your lineup with right-handed, epic mashers and make huge trades at the deadline. So I think that's the only thing I can say with certainty. This game is too nuanced and too complicated for there to be any one way."

———————

Epstein grew up in Brookline, Massachusetts, so Fenway was his neighborhood ballpark. He was 12 when the World Series came to town in 1986, and the very first batter—the Mets' Lenny Dykstra—hooked a home run a few rows in front of him down the right field line. The Red Sox lost in a rout, but a few days later, back in New York, they came within one out—one strike—of a championship in Game 6. Watching from home, Epstein and his twin brother, Paul, planned to be in midair for the final out. They stood on the edge of the family couch for several agonizing minutes and never got to jump.

Making that leap would become Epstein's mission. He went to Yale and landed summer internships with the Orioles, where Calvin Hill, the former Yale football star, was a vice president. Hill took a liking to Epstein, who impressed the Orioles' president, Larry Lucchino. When Lucchino moved on to the Padres, he hired Epstein, who was studying at the University of San Diego law school. That background intrigued Kevin Towers, the Padres' general manager, who mentored Epstein in baseball operations.

By 2002 Epstein was working for the Red Sox, who had been sold from the Yawkey Family Trust to a group led by John Henry, with Lucchino as president. When Billy Beane turned down the general manager's job that off-season, Epstein got it, at 28 years old. Dan Duquette had left a solid foundation—Pedro Martinez, Manny Ramirez, Johnny Damon, Trot Nixon, Derek Lowe, and Jason Varitek—but collecting stars had never been Boston's problem. The way Epstein saw it, the franchise was preoccupied with the Yankees and the headlines. There was no time for honest self-evaluation, he thought, just reactive bursts of short-term satisfaction. Epstein would bring both humility and hubris.

"We fell on this internal slogan: We don't know shit, because baseball's so hard," Epstein says. "Let's not be afraid to look stupid."

To Epstein and his staff—mostly young, well-educated baseball fanatics like himself—this much seemed sensible: the best way to win the World Series was to give yourself as many chances as possible. With nine or 10 visits to the playoffs, they reasoned, a team was likely to snag at least one title. So, they wondered, which teams got the chance?

The prior six seasons—1996 through 2001—had all featured an eight-team postseason format and a 162-game schedule. In those seasons, the Red Sox found, 24 teams had won at least 95 games, and all but one (the 1999 Reds) had qualified for the playoffs.

The driving force for Epstein, then, would be building a team that could always win 95 games. Their internal computer models would annually simulate 10,000 seasons based on the team's projected roster, factoring in all kinds of variables and trade possibilities. Usually the most common outcome was, indeed, about 95 wins. But the possibilities on the low end of the bell curve were terrifying.

"The extremes drive you nuts, because they're real possible outcomes," Epstein says. "If you dig deeper, what happens in that one season when they only win 78? Well, Pedro gets hurt, Schilling isn't good, you have injuries in your bullpen, your defense sucks—and it's all possible. It could happen. Your real season is just one of those 10,000 possible outcomes, and you live with it forever. The whole city either has this incredible ride through the summer and into the fall, or they fucking hate you because you let them down and deprived them of this awesome daily entertainment and lifetime memories. It can be overwhelming when you think about it that way, and it creates this palpable weight that you feel."

The best way to deal with it, Epstein says, is to minimize those season-killing variables. Whatever concerns you, attack it with redundancy—and maybe you'll get lucky. Maybe you'll sign a player who lands on the farthermost positive outcome of his personal possibilities, like David Ortiz.

There was a lot to like about Ortiz after the 2002 season. He was 27 years old and had just helped the Twins reach the playoffs, with 20 home runs and a good eye at the plate. But he had no speed, rarely even played his only defensive position—first base—and was due a raise through arbitration. Finding no appealing trade offers, the frugal Twins released Ortiz in mid-December, putting him into a vast pool of free agents. He languished on the market for five weeks, haggling over rounding errors.

"We wouldn't give him $1.5 million; we would only give him $1.25 million," Epstein says. "We didn't know he was gonna turn into Big Papi."

They did believe Ortiz could be a force in the middle of a lineup; Epstein said as much in announcing the deal. But the Red Sox paid more ($2 million) for a different lefty hitter with similar skills, Jeremy Giambi, and the same amount for a right-handed version, Kevin Millar. Giambi struggled but Millar and Ortiz delivered, on and off the field. Both could beat back brushfires with bravado and saw the Curse of the Bambino as an opportunity, not a burden.

The Red Sox famously lost the 2003 ALCS to the Yankees on Aaron Boone's Game 7 homer off Tim Wakefield, after manager Grady Little had stuck too long with a tiring Martinez. For the teams' rematch a year later, Epstein strengthened his rotation, bullpen, and defense with three bold moves—and one unanswered prayer.

The 2003 Red Sox were very good but had two weak spots on their pitching staff: the aging John Burkett, who made 30 starts, and the shaky Byung-Hyun Kim, the team leader in saves. If the Red Sox could turn their mediocre innings into elite ones, it might look something like this:

2003, John Burkett and Byung-Hyun Kim: 261 innings,
    4.55 ERA

2004, Curt Schilling and Keith Foulke: 309⅔ innings,
    2.96 ERA

That's how it turned out, and while Foulke's deal was straightforward—a three-year, $21 million free agent contract—trading for Schilling was complicated. Schilling, a former Red Sox farmhand, had starred in the World Series for Philadelphia and Arizona and was seeking to cap a decorated career. The Diamondbacks had arranged to trade him to Boston, but first Schilling had to waive his no-trade clause.

"Exciting?" Schilling said when I reached him by phone before he'd agreed to the deal. "No, it's not exciting. Somewhat stressful? Yes. There's a lot of anxiousness."

Schilling and his wife, Shonda, invited Epstein and his assistant, Jed Hoyer, to their home in Arizona for Thanksgiving dinner and contract talks. The Red Sox had a few advantages: a wealthy owner, John Henry; a new manager, Terry Francona, whom Schilling deeply respected from their time together with the Phillies; and the pioneering statistician Bill James, who helped ease Schilling's initial concern about life as a fly-ball pitcher at Fenway Park.

"We were trying to appeal to his ego, which is a powerful driving force with him, and his mind, which is also a powerful driving force in his personality—and a sense of history," Epstein says. "We had a letter from Bill James articulating a lot of the reasons why we thought his profile would succeed. We had a lot about the stage that he'd be on and the history behind what he would be trying to help us accomplish."

Schilling, who had no agent, agreed to a two-year, $25.5 million contract extension through 2006, plus a $2 million bonus if the Red Sox won the World Series. Hoyer found a copy of *Negotiating For Dummies* on the desk in Schilling's home office, but Schilling might have skipped the section on leverage.

"He told me right after it was done that while we were at his house, Cashman kept calling him—which he didn't bring up at the time but could have, the insinuation being that, 'If we don't get the extension done, I'm gonna use my no-trade clause and I'll be in pinstripes,'" Epstein says, smiling at the memory. "Cashman. He's always trying to disrupt things."

Cashman would land a different Red Sox target that winter in a deal that would win him one ring at the cost of extraordinary aggravation. At the 2003 winter meetings, Epstein had arranged to acquire shortstop Alex Rodriguez from Texas for outfielder Manny Ramirez. That deal would then trigger another: shortstop Nomar Garciaparra to the White Sox for outfielder Magglio Ordoñez. Rodriguez wanted the trade so badly that he restructured his contract to essentially take less money, an action the union rejected.

When that deal fell apart, the Yankees got Rodriguez—with all of his talent and insecurities—in February. Garciaparra stayed in Boston, but with his defense sharply declining and no contract for 2005, he was as good as gone. At the deadline, Epstein shipped him to the Cubs in a four-team deal for Montreal shortstop Orlando Cabrera and Minnesota first baseman Doug Mientkiewicz. Both were hitting .246, while Garciaparra was hitting .321.

Even Theo's twin was confused. Paul Epstein was driving home from Cape Cod after the deal, listening to fans rail against his brother on sports-talk radio. Paul from Brookline called the source himself.

"Why did you trade Nomar for a couple of .230 hitters?" he asked.

Theo assured Paul that Cabrera was a better hitter than that but really shone on defense.

"And then Cabrera makes an error his first game after the trade and costs us a game," Epstein says. "But about 10 days after the trade we go 45–15 the rest of the way, including the playoffs. We just became this monster."

The Red Sox were so hot that nothing made sense anymore. They dropped the first three games of the ALCS to the Yankees, including a 19–8 humiliation in Game 3 on a Saturday night at Fenway. I took a run the next morning and had to laugh at the message board outside the nearby First Baptist Church: "Why Does God Allow Suffering?" it read. I didn't peek inside for the sermon, but I wonder if the pastor offered the banal reassurance to keep the faith because the Lord works in mysterious ways.

At least, that's the retrofitted logic for what happened next: the Red Sox swept the next four games from the Yankees, becoming the first team ever to win three straight—let alone all four!—after losing the first three games of a best-of-seven series. The Red Sox would then make eight errors in the first two games of the World Series against St. Louis, but nobody seemed to notice. They flattened the Cardinals in four.

————

Epstein took a bloodless approach to roster construction. Rather than reward stars like Martinez, Cabrera, and Derek Lowe with new contracts, he let them go as free agents and grabbed five of the top 50 picks in the 2005 draft as compensation. Among the haul were outfielder Jacoby Ellsbury and pitcher Clay Buchholz, who both debuted with the 2007 title team and helped win another championship six years later.

Epstein also authorized many draft bonuses well above the commissioner's recommended slot value, an unenforceable gentleman's agreement that smart teams ignored. The strategy allowed Boston, in 2011, to sign a fifth-round second baseman from a Nashville high school for $750,000—some $600,000 over slot value. That player, Mookie Betts, would win MVP in 2018 and lead the Red Sox to yet another crown.

Epstein moved on to the Cubs a few months after drafting Betts, but he learned quickly that he'd have to change his approach to win their first championship since 1908. A new collective bargaining agreement went into effect in November 2011, a month after Epstein took over, with limits on compensatory draft picks and restrictions on bonuses. The worst teams would have the most money to spend on the amateur market, and the best teams would have the least.

"It was almost designed to screw big-market teams and keep those teams away from young talent," Epstein said. "There were some scary moments: Where were we going to get our impact players? It drove us to be really single-minded about the rebuild and transparent about it with our fans. We didn't go to the levels that Houston did in trying to be as bad as you can possibly be—I thought that crossed a line—but we were open that when our short-term interest collided with our long-term interest, we were gonna err on the side of our long-term interest."

Like Jeff Luhnow, the Astros' new GM, Epstein inherited a last-place team after the 2011 season and endured three losing years in a row. The Astros annually lost more games than the Cubs—310 defeats in all, compared to 286 for the Cubs—but both teams made a point to flood their farm systems.

The Cubs drafted impact position players like Kris Bryant and Kyle Schwarber, reasoning that hitters were more predictable prospects than pitchers. The CBA allowed teams one season in which they could exceed their international spending cap, and the Cubs did this in 2013, mainly to collect trade chips for the good days ahead. They also traded pitchers. Lots and lots of pitchers.

The first to go was Andrew Cashner, a strapping hard thrower from Texas who looked the part of a future ace. He went to San Diego for Anthony Rizzo, who had lost the Padres' first base job by hitting .141 in a three-month cameo. The Red Sox had drafted Rizzo under Epstein, but Epstein hadn't seen him in San Diego. Hoyer had—he'd just left the Padres to reunite with Epstein in Chicago—and the impression left him dubious. He'd been too close.

"Jed, we saw him for three years in Boston," Epstein told Hoyer. "He's going to be the guy he was in Double-A."

Epstein still pictured Rizzo as a franchise cornerstone, and trading Cashner for him established a pattern. Pitchers hold extraordinary trade value because the market is so wide; even the best team can find a way to upgrade its staff. As the Cubs rebuilt, Epstein made sure to begin each spring with veteran arms he could flip to contenders in the summer. Those deals netted shortstop Addison Russell and five pitchers who would appear in the 2016 World Series: Jake Arrieta, Carl Edwards Jr., Justin Grimm, Kyle Hendricks, and Pedro Strop. (Every pitcher on the World Series roster, in fact, was acquired by Epstein from outside the organization.)

In some cases, the Cubs got lucky. They unlocked Arrieta's potential by letting him use his natural, crossfire delivery, but never knew they'd gotten a future Cy Young winner by trading Scott Feldman to Baltimore. Likewise, while they saw enough in Hendricks to choose him off a list of prospects from the Rangers for Ryan Dempster, they had first traded for Atlanta's Randall Delgado (a deal Dempster rejected) and then pursued Allen Webster from the Dodgers. Those pitchers would have nondescript careers, but Hendricks—a slender soft-tosser from Dartmouth College—became the majors' ERA leader in 2016 and started the clinchers of the NLCS and World Series.

To reach that pinnacle—"the Holy Grail of sports," as catcher David Ross called it—Epstein had to make a final push. The Cubs sputtered in July after a fast start, and Epstein engaged his old pal Cashman, who was in the rare position of seller at the deadline. As it happened, Cashman played kingmaker that summer, delivering an ace lefty reliever to the teams that would meet in the World Series: Andrew Miller to the Indians and Aroldis Chapman to the Cubs. The Cubs preferred Miller because he was not facing free agency, as Chapman was, but they needed one of those game-changing arms—and knew whom they'd have to trade.

As part of their spending spree in 2013, the Cubs gave $1.7 million to Gleyber Torres, a 16-year-old shortstop from Venezuela. Three years later, in Class A, he'd become their top-rated prospect. The Yankees wanted more for Miller but eagerly accepted Torres as the centerpiece of a Chapman deal. The Cubs were certain Torres would be a star, and knew that Chapman could always sign right back with the Yankees, which he did. But as Epstein said, in announcing the deal: "If not now, when?" He'd run the numbers, and they demanded the deal.

From a math standpoint—if the goal is to win the World Series—trade-deadline moves are much more critical for the best teams than the borderline teams. For them, a new player may help reach the playoffs, but then a whole new set of probabilities takes over. The best teams, like the 2016 Cubs, don't have to worry about the first part.

"We knew we were going to be in," Epstein explains, "so we spent a lot of time quantifying our chances to win the World Series once we were in. And the data showed that a dominant closer is disproportionately impactful in the postseason, because he's pitching (almost) every game, he's pitching at the most important time of the game, and he's pitching for more than three outs. Normally, in an eight-team playoff, you have a 12.5 percent chance of winning the World Series if all teams are equal, and with a really good team, you can maybe bump it up to 15, 16, 17 percent. A dominant team can maybe get to a 20 percent chance. We looked at the numbers and, as constituted, we had an 18 percent chance of winning the World Series—and acquiring Aroldis Chapman would move us to 23 percent. So one person would improve our chances of winning the World Series by 5 percent. It was like: things are probably never gonna come together as well as they are right now."

From Chapman's first game with the Cubs through the end of the regular season, the team went 44–18, a similar run as the one that propelled Epstein's 2004 Red Sox. When those players seemed buried against the Yankees, they could think of their recent success and still feel confident. So could the 2016 Cubs, especially before Game 5 of the World Series, when Chapman saved the season at Wrigley Field.

"There was such anxiety for Games 3 and 4, but Game 5 felt like the first time it was a real Fall Classic–type atmosphere at the ballpark," Epstein said. "You could feel the fans not wanting it to end."

Chapman had never collected more than seven outs in any of his previous 398 career games. No true closer since Jay Howell in 1988 had earned a save of more than two innings in the World Series. But there was Chapman, following Jon Lester and Carl Edwards Jr., stifling the Indians for the final eight outs while facing elimination, preserving a one-run thriller and restoring the Cubs' edge.

Chapman was not on the mound at the end of Game 7. He'd blown the save in the eighth inning when Rajai Davis choked up and lined a three-run homer into the left field corner. As exhausted and despondent as Chapman was, though, he found his way through a 1-2-3 ninth inning, preserving the tie. After a brief rain delay allowed the Cubs to regroup—encouraged by a speech from Jason Heyward—they took the lead on a double by Ben Zobrist in the tenth.

With Chapman out of the game and the Indians mounting a two-out rally off Edwards, manager Joe Maddon summoned Mike Montgomery, a lefty whose sharp curveball would overwhelm Michael Martinez, a meek hitter but the only option left for the Indians. Martinez tapped to Bryant for the final out.

Nobody could have predicted a finish like that, not even Epstein, the executive whose teams had toppled two of baseball's most celebrated curses. But he had traded for Montgomery from Seattle at the deadline, a low-profile move that gave Maddon another choice when he needed one last reliever at the biggest moment in the history of the franchise. The power of redundancy prevailed again.

———

Midseason trades have impacted World Series teams for many years, of course. The 1964 Cardinals arrived at the then–June 15 trading deadline with a 28–30 record, slouching through their first season without Stan Musial. The defending champion Dodgers had led the majors in steals the year before, and the Cardinals wanted to follow the trend.

Manager Johnny Keane was enamored with the Cubs' Lou Brock, believing he was miscast and undervalued at cozy Wrigley Field. Brock had a .257 career average and a weak outfield arm, but he was not yet 25 and had raw power to go with his legs; he had once smashed a homer over the center field wall at the Polo Grounds, almost 500 feet from the plate.

General manager Bing Devine paid a handsome price for Brock, it seemed, dealing Ernie Broglio as part of a six-player deal with the Cubs. Broglio was only 28 and had gone 18–8 the year before, and Cardinals players were so upset about the trade that Keane had to call a team meeting. He held another when Brock arrived, emphasizing the importance of speed.

"We're not just going to match the Dodgers," Keane said, as recalled by David Halberstam in October 1964, "we're going to pass them."

At that point, Halberstam wrote, a wise-cracking backup catcher spoke up: "OK, Johnny, it's a hard job, but I'll do it. I'll steal those bases for you," Bob Uecker said—but Brock was the obvious man for the job. He stole 33 bases the rest of the way and homered to help beat the Yankees in Game 7 of the World Series. Brock, who hit .391 in three World Series in the 1960s, finished his career as the all-time stolen base leader, with 938.

Other in-season deals sparked championship runs in the 1970s—pitcher Mike Torrez from the A's to the Yankees in 1977, third baseman Bill Madlock from the Giants to the Pirates two years later—but a 1989 deal for Rickey Henderson, the man who would pass Brock on the career stolen base list, would have a similar impact.

The A's had promoted Henderson in 1979, when they were buried in last place and averaging fewer than 4,000 fans per game at the Coliseum. Henderson, a hometown kid from Oakland Technical High School, was an instant sensation—100 stolen bases in 1980, a record 130 in 1982. The A's traded him to the Yankees in December 1984, and while Henderson produced in the Bronx, his flamboyance was always better suited for Oakland. The New York assignment was temporary.

"The way he played the game and thought about the game and talked to people and his body language was not very Steinbrenner-like," Sandy Alderson says. "So we just kind of kept an eye on it."

Alderson had built the A's into a powerhouse with a sensibility honed far afield. A graduate of Harvard Law School, he had started in baseball as general counsel of the A's in 1981, after a partner at his San Francisco firm became team president. Named general manager two years later, Alderson, with his analytical bent, would emphasize on-base percentage and slugging before his protégé, Billy Beane, took it mainstream.

"There were two then-contemporary approaches to the game, one personified by Gene Mauch, the other by Earl Weaver," Alderson says. "One was small ball, the other was get on base and hit it out of the ballpark. I was a subscriber to the latter, because I thought it was a lot more fun—and it was also consistent with these new analytical theories."

Alderson also got lucky with two washed-up starting pitchers. In 1986 he signed Dave Stewart, who had been released by the Phillies, solely because Tigers' GM Bill Lajoie was also interested. If Stewart was good enough for the highly respected Lajoie, Alderson figured, he must be worth a look. Stewart became a perennial 20-game winner, and Dennis Eckersley had a similar revival, morphing into a Hall of Fame closer after the Cubs gave him to Alderson for three minor leaguers.

With Stewart, Eckersley, and a trio of sluggers with high on-base percentages—Jose Canseco, Mark McGwire, and Dave Henderson—the 1988 A's won 104 games, their most since Connie Mack's last pennant winner in 1931. But after falling in the World Series, and then losing Canseco to a wrist injury early in 1989, Alderson reacquired Henderson from the struggling Yankees for a trio of complementary players: outfielder Luis Polonia and relievers Greg Cadaret and Eric Plunk.

"It wasn't like we gave them a bunch of stiffs," Alderson said. "But Rickey came back and just went off."

Henderson helped the A's cruise to another playoff berth and then owned the 1989 postseason, hitting .441 and diving into bases with style, his neon green padded Mizuno batting gloves leading the way. In nine games Henderson had 11 stolen bases, eight extra-base hits, and a .568 on-base percentage. He kept on going right through 1990, when he was the AL MVP and seemed poised to lead Oakland to another championship.

Alderson had helped the cause with two August deals that seemed almost unfair. He traded with the Cardinals for Willie McGee, a former MVP who won the NL batting title that season, and with the Rangers for Harold Baines, a Hall of Fame designated hitter.

"We were going for a home run," Alderson said, but the World

Series was a mismatch, a stunning sweep by the Reds that obscured the greatness of Alderson's teams. The A's could have, and probably should have, won three titles in a row. But instead they triumphed only in 1989, with a morbid assist from the devastating earthquake that struck San Francisco just before Game 3 at the Giants' Candlestick Park. The A's had told umpires that their scheduled starter, Bob Welch, was unlikely to pitch after pulling a hamstring the day before. The A's would have likely used the less-imposing Curt Young to start Game 3, Alderson said, but when the earthquake forced a 10-day break, they came back with their aces, Stewart and Mike Moore, and finished a sweep.

Alderson's teams—the A's and the 2015 Mets—would go 1–3 in the World Series; had the record been reversed, he might now be in the Hall of Fame. The first two of his contemporaries to be enshrined, Gillick and Schuerholz, both won titles with two franchises. Gillick might have had another, but his 2001 Mariners, who tied a major league record with 116 regular-season victories, lost to the Yankees in the ALCS. A midseason move for a left fielder or starting pitcher never happened, and a more aggressive mind-set from ownership might have made the difference.

"I think it's important to send a message to the players that you want to win just as much as they do," Gillick says. "Sometimes if management doesn't send that message, the players say, 'Well, why didn't they do something? Do they want to win or do they just want to make money? What is it?' When you make that move, it sends the message to everybody: 'These guys want to win.' I always thought that was an important message to send, because if you win, you're gonna make a lot more money the next year. You can't look at it short-term. Those mental upticks are important, you know?"

Gillick stressed that he was speaking generally, unwilling to shift the blame to owners who never quite seized the moment when the Mariners had their best chance. But history told the tale. In the two decades that followed that bitter loss in the ALCS, 29 different major league teams would reach the postseason at least once. The Mariners were the only exception, and they remain the only franchise to have never appeared in the World Series.

———————

For the Yankees, the 2001 pennant was their fourth in a row and fifth in six seasons. It also closed the career of Paul O'Neill, the fiery right fielder whose arrival in 1993 helped remake a franchise that had staggered through four losing seasons in a row, its longest stretch of futility since the 1910s.

The pillars of the dynasty—Derek Jeter, Andy Pettitte, Jorge Posada, and Mariano Rivera—were developing in the minors when O'Neill came along, safely protected from the whims of Steinbrenner, who was serving a ban. In the 1980s, Steinbrenner had impulsively traded prospects like Jay Buhner, Doug Drabek, Willie McGee, and Fred McGriff, helping plunge the Yankees into disarray. By the time Steinbrenner returned to the team in 1993, general manager Gene Michael had given him a strong foundation by thoroughly changing the culture.

He kept Bernie Williams, a talented but sensitive young outfielder, and shed Mel Hall, a veteran who mercilessly teased him. With encouragement from manager Buck Showalter, Michael sought serious-minded veterans who could lead by example, not intimidation. He signed Jimmy Key and Wade Boggs as free agents, traded prospects for Jim Abbott, and shipped Roberto Kelly to Cincinnati for O'Neill.

It was a curious move, on its face. Kelly was younger and had just hit .272 to O'Neill's .246. But—as author Bill Pennington noted in *Chumps to Champs,* which chronicles the Yankees' rise—Michael believed in trading a talented player before the industry learns he's overrated. Kelly had tantalizing tools but had already reached his ceiling. The headstrong O'Neill had clashed on hitting philosophy with Reds manager Lou Piniella, but he was a solid defender whose left-handed swing would play well at Yankee Stadium. He also drew many more walks than Kelly and had a better on-base percentage, which appealed to Michael before most of his peers had caught on.

"Stick was ahead on a lot of things," says Brian Cashman, who learned under Michael and became Yankees' GM in 1998. "He understood, without being a mathematician, how the numbers worked."

With Boggs and O'Neill in the lineup, the 1993 Yankees jumped from eighth to second in the AL in on-base percentage. They had the league's best record in the strike-shortened 1994 season, won the first-ever AL Wild Card in 1995, and then started reeling in the championships.

Cashman kept them coming by trading for Roger Clemens at the start of spring training in 1999. This would seem elementary, but it carried enormous risk. The Yankees were coming off their best season ever: 125–50, including a sweep of the Padres in the World Series. They were trading David Wells, a proven winner in New York, for a pitcher the Yankees had loathed as an opponent. But Clemens would be driven to win his first championship, and that hunger could help the team keep its edge.

"He was the premier starting pitcher of that generation, and he'd accomplished everything except that one thing," Cashman says. "He had a reputation as one of the greatest teammates you could ever have, which turned out to be true. He's one of my favorite all-time Yankees, one of the true leaders I've ever come across."

Clemens delivered for the Yankees in the World Series, going 3–0 with a 1.50 ERA in five starts. His Game 2 performance in 2000—when he fired eight shutout innings at the Mets, and one shattered bat near Mike Piazza—completed a 14-game World Series winning streak for the Yankees: the last four games against Atlanta in 1996, sweeps of the Padres and Braves in 1998 and 1999, and the first two games in 2000. The starters had a 2.53 ERA in the streak, with Pettitte taking a turn in each of the four series it comprised.

The Yankees had nearly traded Pettitte before the run began. After his rookie season, in 1995, the Mariners asked for Pettitte as part of a deal for first baseman Tino Martinez and reliever Jeff Nelson. Piniella, by then managing the Mariners, also sought Posada. In the end, Seattle accepted a different package—Sterling Hitchcock and Russ Davis, who were useful big leaguers but never stars—and the trade was a steal. The Yankees' deep well of prospects allowed them to keep the jewels of their farm system while adding impact players around them.

For that, they had Brian Sabean to thank. Sabean was the Yankees' vice president for scouting and player development when they signed or drafted Jeter, Pettitte, Posada, and Rivera. Working from the Yankees' Florida headquarters, he built a powerhouse with Bill Livesey.

"Sabean never got the credit he deserved," Cashman says. "It was split back then, Tampa and New York, so Stick had nothing to do with drafting and developing, nothing to do with Jeter, Posada, Pettitte, Rivera, Bernie Williams. Now, he didn't trade them, but Sabean and Bill Livesey built that entire thing. He was the true architect of that Yankee team."

It took a while, but Sabean finally earned his World Series rings as general manager of the Giants. For years he shaped his roster with veterans to try to win with Barry Bonds, but fell short four times in the postseason. Jeff Kent left as a free agent after the 2002 World Series, and Bonds retired five years later.

"Barry was a force of nature as far as offense, and when he left, that was the first step in knowing that we had to play more to our ballpark than worry about what the offense was capable of," Sabean said. "The first wave was the young starters."

Sabean and his pitching whisperer, the longtime reliever Dick Tidrow, assembled a rotation with three homegrown aces, all chosen in the first round: Madison Bumgarner, Matt Cain, and Tim Lincecum. Working with another first-rounder, catcher Buster Posey, they helped the Giants win titles in 2010, 2012, and 2014, going 7–0 with a 1.15 ERA in the World Series. Homegrown position players—Brandon Belt, Brandon Crawford, Joe Panik, Pablo Sandoval—did their part, as did Hunter Pence, who came from the Phillies for a prospect.

Sabean got lucky, too, claiming Cody Ross on waivers down the stretch in 2010 to block him from the rival Padres. Ross, roughly a league-average player for the Marlins, would win MVP in the NLCS and bat cleanup in the World Series clincher. But mostly it was Sabean's savvy drafting and shrewd bullpen structure that gave the Giants their first titles since Willie Mays roamed the Polo Grounds.

Their current ballpark, bordering McCovey Cove, does not have the outrageous center field expanse that Mays covered for his famous catch in 1954. But it is one of baseball's most spacious fields, and in emphasizing pitching and contact hitting, the Giants found a style of play that suited their home and worked in October. The team they beat in 2014, the Kansas City Royals, followed a similar blueprint.

When the Royals defeated the Mets the next fall, they became, perhaps, the most important champion in modern times. Others snapped longer droughts and celebrated curses, but to the industry, the Royals' triumph refuted the idea that small-market, low-payroll teams could not win it all. They must take a different path, to be sure, and will have fewer chances to break through—but it is possible, and Dayton Moore understood that his efforts would resonate far beyond his hometown.

When the Royals won the World Series in 1985, Moore, then a college student, watched Game 7 from a hillside beyond the outfield off Interstate 70 in Kansas City. The Royals remained competitive for the rest of that decade, which they closed by signing free-agent reliever Mark Davis, who had just won the Cy Young Award for the Padres, to the richest annual salary in the majors: $3.25 million per year for four years.

As salaries rose sharply around the game, it would soon be inconceivable for a team like the Royals to set new standards in free agency. They had one winning record in the 18 seasons after the 1994 strike, and made a habit of trading their homegrown stars—Johnny Damon, Carlos Beltran, Zack Greinke—before losing them as free agents.

That changed in 2013. After seven losing seasons as GM, Moore had gathered enough young talent to envision the kind of team he wanted. By conventional wisdom, the Royals should have modeled themselves after the Twins, who had built a perennial division winner in the AL Central but tended to flop in October. The more appealing model, to Moore, was the 2002 Angels: speed, defense, and contact hitting, an action-oriented style suited to roomy Kauffman Stadium and not dependent on sluggers and ace starters, who would be too expensive, anyway. He promised his anchors—Alex Gordon, Eric Hosmer, Mike Moustakas, Salvador Perez, Lorenzo Cain, and Alcides Escobar—that he would support them with major additions when the time was right.

"We tried to share our heart and our vision of how important it was for our city and fan base and the future of the organization—and not just the future of the organization, but the future of baseball," Moore said. "Because if markets like ours can never win, why do they exist?"

Moore had an enticing trade chip in Wil Myers, the Baseball America Minor League Player of the Year, who reminded his scouts of a young Dale Murphy: a catcher with speed and power and the athleticism to change positions in the majors. He also had two promising starters who had been first-round draft picks in Jake Odorizzi and Mike Montgomery. All three would make an impact in the majors, but Moore could not wait. He felt the tug of responsibility to his players and fans, and raided his carefully built farm system by sending Myers, Odorizzi, and Montgomery to Tampa Bay for James Shields and Wade Davis, pitchers with reasonable contracts who could help win immediately.

The deal was widely panned but became a rousing success. After contending in 2013, the Royals reached consecutive World Series. Shields threw the first pitch in 2014, when they lost, and Davis threw the last pitch in 2015, when they won.

Between those World Series, though, Shields signed a four-year, $75 million deal with the Padres in free agency. As much as Shields had done in the clubhouse and on the mound, Moore replaced him with another veteran who was younger and much cheaper: Edinson Volquez, for two years and $20 million. Midway through spring training, he added another well-traveled righty, Chris Young, for $675,000.

Volquez and Young started three of the Royals' four World Series victories over the Mets. The other was started by Johnny Cueto, a stylish Cincinnati right-hander the Royals had scouted in person for every start that season. The Reds, like the A's, were out of the race and eager to deal. Two days before he traded Sean Manaea to the A's for Ben Zobrist, Moore got Cueto from the Reds for three other promising lefties.

The Royals had the AL's best record at the time of the deal, and keeping four young left-handers could have helped them stay upright after the inevitable free-agent departures of Hosmer, Moustakas, and Cain. But while some small-market teams in that era, notably the Pittsburgh Pirates, held off from making major in-season moves, Moore acted boldly, propelled again by a sense of duty to a core he had nurtured.

"We knew 'em from the time they were babies; they were all performing well, and their hunger to win was at an all-time high," he says. "And so we knew that the time was right to take advantage of this. They were on top of a wave."

Zobrist did what he always had, starting at four positions down the stretch, drawing lots of walks and swinging a reliable bat from both sides of the plate. Cueto was erratic but posted two essential postseason victories, including a complete game to beat the Mets in Game 2 of the World Series.

That was the only easy victory for the Royals. The others reflected Moore's belief in the group and commitment to its style of play. Escobar—a leadoff man with a dismal on-base percentage but an aggressive approach his teammates loved—hacked at the Mets' first pitch in Game 1 and circled the bases on an inside-the-park homer. In the ninth inning of the Game 5 clincher, Hosmer scored the tying run by dashing from third on a one-out grounder to third baseman David Wright, who was gamely playing through a chronic spinal injury. Hosmer knew that Wright made looping, sidearm throws to compensate for the pain, and that lumbering first baseman Lucas Duda had a weak arm and would need a perfect, hurried throw to get him. With instincts nurtured in the Royals' farm system, and refined by coach Rusty Kuntz, Hosmer went for it.

"Oftentimes in the playoffs, games are lost more than won," Moore says. "You miss a cutoff man, you boot a routine ball, it's an errant throw on a double play, something funny happens. But if you have a team that truly believes in one another—that puts everybody else's needs and desires first and goes out and plays for each other—you've got a better chance to get through those high-anxiety moments."

A strong throw to the plate would have nailed Hosmer and sent the World Series back to Kansas City, with Jacob deGrom and Noah Syndergaard lined up to start for the Mets. But Hosmer made the charge, Duda's throw sailed wide, the Royals won in 12 innings—and a few weeks later, Hosmer's dirt-stained jersey was on display in Cooperstown, a lasting testament to well-reasoned risks, on the field and off.

Game 6

"It Wasn't Your Fault, Kid"

The Other Side of World Series Glory

Hollywood could not resist the cinematic pull of the 1926 World Series. A generation after Grover Cleveland Alexander saved Game 7 for the Cardinals, Ronald Reagan played him in a movie called *The Winning Team.* Alexander, an aging ace battling booze, strikes out Tony Lazzeri with the bases loaded at Yankee Stadium to win the championship.

In the immediate aftermath, though, the press focused not on Alexander and Lazzeri—whose famous encounter actually happened in the seventh inning—or even on Babe Ruth, who was caught trying to steal second to end the World Series with the winning run at the plate. The first man mentioned in the next day's New York *Daily News* was Bob Meusel, the Yankees' left fielder, who dropped a fly ball in the fourth inning and allowed the tying run to score.

"The goat, the butt, the poor fellow in pantaloons bit soundly on his trousers with the two-bladed slapstick, was Robert Meusel of California," Paul Gallico wrote. On the front page of *The New York Times,* Meusel was called "the unfortunate lad with the feeble fingers." In St. Louis, a guest columnist for the *Post-Dispatch* asserted that "a world's series has been lost by an outfielder muffing a fly ball," under a headline that referenced "Meusel's Muff." The writer knew a bit about baseball, too: he was John McGraw, the storied manager of the Giants.

For Meusel, though, infamy didn't stick. The Yankees swept the World Series in each of the next two seasons, getting revenge on the Cardinals in 1928, when Meusel homered in the opener. History knows him best as part of Murderers' Row, the fabled lineup of the 1927 Yankees; Meusel usually batted fifth, after Ruth and Lou Gehrig, the other guy in a famous trio, like José Carreras in the Three Tenors.

If anyone should be blamed for the loss in '26, it is Ruth for his stolen base attempt. A year or two later, on a barnstorming tour, Cardinals catcher Bob O'Farrell asked Ruth what he was thinking.

"Ruth said he thought Alex had forgotten he was there," O'Farrell told Lawrence S. Ritter in *The Glory of Their Times*. "Also that the way Alex was pitching they'd never get two hits in a row off him, so he better get in position to score if they got one. Well, maybe that was good thinking and maybe not. In any case, I had him out a mile at second."

The notion of the Babe being caught stealing to end Game 7 always amazes modern players. It may be the least-known of Ruth's many significant feats.

"That might be a little extreme for Game 7," says a modern speedster, Trea Turner. "But if you have a game plan and you're trying to execute it, all right, I can respect that. You at least have a thought. You weren't totally dumb, I guess."

Ruth was a singular force every day, of course, and especially that afternoon, when he homered and drew four walks. Like Mariano Rivera in Arizona many years later, Ruth was so revered that even a Game 7 failure could be forgiven. Perhaps only the Babe and Mo could be both a GOAT (greatest of all time) and a goat.

When Meusel died, in 1977, his error was mentioned in his UPI obituary, though not until the sixteenth paragraph. Even then it was cast in a positive light: Meusel had an overpowering arm, the story explained, and he dropped that fourth-inning fly in his haste to make a throw to the plate.

Had the game been televised, perhaps, video could have damned Meusel and made the error cling to him. Then again, an even worse mistake in 1997 did not haunt the memory of Tony Fernandez.

Fernandez had won four Gold Gloves at shortstop for Toronto in the '80s, but by the 1997 World Series, with the Indians, he had already played his final game there. Fernandez was still a sure-handed infielder at 35, though, and he could really hit—his eleventh-inning homer in Baltimore had given Cleveland a 1–0 victory in the ALCS clincher, and he'd batted .471 against the Marlins in the World Series, singling home the Indians' only two runs in Game 7.

That would have been enough for a 2–1 win, but the Marlins rallied off Jose Mesa to tie it in the ninth. Two innings later, with Bobby Bonilla on first and one out, Craig Counsell bounced a ball to Fernandez's left. Would Fernandez spin and fire to second for a force, or take the sure out at first? It didn't help that Bonilla paused on his way to second, shielding Fernandez's view as the ball skipped along.

"I do think that affected his vision a little bit—not completely—and it was one of those balls where I'm sure Tony had a bunch of potential 'where should I throw?' [scenarios] going through his head," Counsell says. "I think a number of things probably distracted him, because it was a poorly hit ball, that's for sure. It wasn't going to be a double play, but maybe when Bobby kind of paused there, Tony thought, 'Hey, I can still turn and throw to second and get an easy force out there.'"

The ball ticked off Fernandez's glove and trickled into shallow right field, moving the winning run to third. As Charles Nagy intentionally walked the next hitter, NBC's Bob Costas solemnly said: "Tony Fernandez, who has worn hero's laurels throughout the postseason, including earlier in this seventh game of the World Series—now, cruel as it may seem, perhaps being fitted for goat horns."

Incredibly, Fernandez got another try on the very first pitch after the walk. With the infield in, he calmly gathered a grounder and whipped a throw home to force Bonilla. But when Edgar Renteria singled in Counsell to win the World Series, there seemed to be no mistaking it: the Fernandez error would loom large in history.

"A nightmare play . . . a disastrous moment in his career," Vin Scully said on the CBS Radio broadcast, focusing on Fernandez in defeat. "A head-down, obviously emotionally crushed Tony Fernandez, walking the length of the dugout . . ."

In the clubhouse later, Fernandez took a spiritual perspective on the play: "I'm prepared for anything in life. I've been at my highest point. I've been at my lowest point. It's something that we all have to live with. I would not be dealing with this if there was not a reason."

Yet when Fernandez died in 2020, his *New York Times* obituary cited his postseason hitting for the Indians, with no mention of the critical error. Over time, Mesa became the designated villain for failing to hold the lead in the ninth. The Indians removed him as closer the next spring and traded him shortly thereafter. When shortstop Omar Vizquel wrote a memoir in 2002, he slammed Mesa for being scared in Game 7.

"The eyes of the world were focused on every move we made," Vizquel wrote. "Unfortunately, Jose's own eyes were vacant. Completely empty. Nobody home. You could almost see right through him. Not long after I looked into his vacant eyes, he blew the save and the Marlins tied the game."

Mesa was so enraged, he drilled Vizquel in the back the first time he faced him that season. The next time they met, four years later, Mesa did it again. By then, Mesa was deep into a nomadic career that wound through San Francisco, Seattle, Philadelphia, Pittsburgh, Colorado, and Detroit. He wound up with 321 career saves, more than many famous closers—Kent Tekulve, Bruce Sutter, and Jesse Orosco. But they all saved Game 7, and Mesa never got another chance to pitch in the World Series.

————

Dennis Eckersley did. A year after Kirk Gibson swatted his backdoor slider into World Series lore, Eckersley wound up with the final baseball of the 1980s in his glove, making the putout at first base to finish the Athletics' sweep of the Giants. It was yet another on a comprehensive list of achievements for Eckersley, who also threw a no-hitter, had a 20-win season, started an All-Star Game, won a Cy Young Award, won an MVP, and made it to Cooperstown on the first ballot.

It is a symphony of memories, to be sure, yet for Eckersley, the Gibson homer is an off-key note that rings loudest. He knows how much he accomplished; everyone does. But to Eckersley, failure comes first. He has learned to accept that.

"When people tell me all the stuff I've done, the only things that stand out are the stuff that hurts," he says. "It's weird how the good doesn't outweigh the bad. Now, obviously there's a hell of a lot more good than bad. But it's funny how—just being honest—that's the shit that stays with you. It just does. It doesn't ruin my life or anything, but the big ones stay with you. They erase all the awards, they do."

Eckersley was 34 years old in 1988 and had reached the right stage of life to handle on-field failure. He had been through so much: as a young player in Cleveland, his wife had left him for a teammate, Rick Manning, and alcoholism nearly cost him his career before rehabilitation in 1986. Rejuvenated by a trade from the Cubs to his hometown A's, Eckersley was finally a man at peace. Two months after the homer, he told Peter Gammons that he felt good about himself for the first time in his life.

The decades since have given Eckersley perspective. Yes, the home run will always be essential to his story, but it's only one chapter of a voluminous book.

"What if I was just some schmo and that's all I did: I played 10 years and I gave up a big bomb, you know what I mean?" he says. "That's why I feel fortunate to have the kind of career I had."

Most players, alas, are not like Eckersley, Ruth, or Rivera—they will never have enough shining moments to eclipse a dark one in October. Long-ago sportswriters delighted in condemning a player as the goat of a given event, a distinction based more on a series-swinging moment than a series-long struggle. As Ed McAuley, a Cleveland columnist, explained in 1946: "It is not the custom of American sportsmen to award the horns and beard to an athlete simply because he does not live up to expectations in mechanical performance."

In rare cases, a player might claim a trifecta of ignominy: sustained poor performance; a mistake that changed everything; and the indignity of making the last out—twice. In the first decade of the World Series, this happened to a luckless Tigers catcher named Boss Schmidt.

In his first series game, against the Cubs in 1907, Schmidt missed a curveball from Bill Donovan that could have been a game-ending strikeout. It skipped past him, allowing the tying run to score in a game ruled a tie after 12 innings due to darkness. The Cubs won the next four, clinching their first title when Schmidt popped to shortstop in Game 5, capping a shutout by Three Finger Brown.

The next year was a virtual repeat: Cubs over Tigers in five, with Schmidt popping out to end a 2–0 finale. The 1909 World Series went the distance, but the Pirates ran wild with 18 stolen bases—including 15 off Schmidt—and blew out Detroit in the finale. Schmidt went

7-for-44 (.159) in his three World Series, and by 1911 he was out of the majors for good.

That season marked the start of another team's three-year streak of losing the World Series. The Giants fell to the A's in 1911 and 1913, but the series in between, against the Red Sox, was by far the most significant, to the eternal chagrin of a fellow named Fred Snodgrass.

Things turned out just fine for Snodgrass, who lived a rich, long life: born before the invention of the pitcher's mound, he died the same month Hank Aaron broke Babe Ruth's home run record. After baseball, Snodgrass served as the mayor of Oxnard, California, sold home appliances, and farmed lemons and walnuts on his ranches in Ventura County. His moment of World Series infamy was a companion all the while.

"Hardly a day in my life, hardly an hour, [goes by] that in some manner or other the dropping of that fly ball doesn't come up," Snodgrass told a writer, Ward Morehouse, in 1940. "On the street, in my store, at my home, in Oxnard or Ventura, it's all the same. They might choke up before they ask me and they hesitate—but they always ask."

Snodgrass was a favorite of manager John McGraw, who'd noticed him in Los Angeles in 1907. McGraw had taken the Giants there for spring training—drawn by the nearby horse racing tracks—and Snodgrass was catching for St. Vincent's College, the opposing team in an exhibition. McGraw was the umpire and Snodgrass bickered with him all game, enough to make an impression. When McGraw returned the next winter, he asked a friend about the feisty catcher he'd seen the year before. A few months later, at 20, Snodgrass was suiting up for the Giants in New York.

In truth, Snodgrass was a defensive misfit; he preferred to play first base but fit best for the Giants in center field. He found himself there for the fateful Game 8 finale at brand-new Fenway Park in 1912, after the Giants and the Red Sox had split the first seven games (with one tie). Before his infamous blunder, Snodgrass was on deck for a remarkable outfield catch in the fifth inning that kept the Giants from taking a 2–0 lead.

"You always hear about Snodgrass dropping that fly ball, but you never hear about the incredible catch that Harry Hooper made in the fifth inning that saved the game for us," Smoky Joe Wood, the winning pitcher, told Ritter. "That was the thing that really took the heart out of the Giants. Larry Doyle hit a terrific drive to deep right center, and Harry ran back at full speed and dove over the railing and into the crowd and in some way, I'll never figure out quite how, he caught the ball—I think with his bare hand. It was almost impossible to believe even when you saw it."

The Giants did not score again until the tenth, when they took a 2–1 lead on Fred Merkle's single. Wood then knocked down a grounder with his bare hand for the final out of the inning, keeping Merkle from scoring but breaking his thumb in the process. That's why Clyde Engle pinch hit for Wood to lead off the bottom of the inning against the great Christy Mathewson, a move that should have helped the Giants, because Wood was actually a much better hitter. Recognizing the mismatch, Snodgrass shaded the right-handed Engle to right field—but Engle punched a fly to left center.

It hung in the air long enough for Snodgrass to get there easily. He could have let left fielder Red Murray make the play, but the Giants swore by manager John McGraw, who stressed that the center fielder should take every ball he can reach. Murray called it, but Snodgrass waved him off.

"Squeeze it, Snod!" Murray cried, but Snodgrass didn't. It was a thousand-to-one shot, he told Morehouse years later, maybe a million to one—a routine play, nothing special. "Because of overeagerness, or overconfidence, or carelessness, I dropped it," Snodgrass said, and Engle hustled into second.

The baseball gods must have ordered what came next. Just as Tony Fernandez would experience far off in the future, the very next ball in play came to the guy who had just made an error. Hooper connected for a deep drive to center—trouble for Snodgrass, who was playing shallow. He figured Hooper would bunt, and with Mathewson holding Engle close, he wanted to be in position to field an errant pickoff throw. When Hooper swung away instead, Snodgrass sprinted for the ball with his back to the plate, snagging it over his shoulder on a dead run. In retirement, Tris Speaker would call it a magic trick, incomparable to any other catch he'd ever seen.

To truly negate the blunder, though, Snodgrass needed help from Mathewson, who made two crucial mistakes. It's true that Mathewson was working his tenth inning of the game and his 339th of the year, more than any other NL pitcher. But it was stunning to see the greatest control pitcher of his time put the winning run on base with a walk to Steve Yerkes.

"That horrified us," Snodgrass told Morehouse, but what happened next was somehow worse. Mathewson faced Speaker, a Hall of Fame matchup with everything at stake. Speaker could drive in two runs to win the championship, or hit into a double play to lose it. Instead he lifted a lazy pop foul near first base—and nobody touched it.

The ball was Merkle's to catch; as the second baseman, he had the best angle on it. But Mathewson apparently called for the catcher, Chief Meyers, instead. Snodgrass said that Mathewson was wary of Merkle, who had made two errors in the series, and thought Meyers was the safer choice. In his interview with Ritter, though, Meyers cites misdirection from the nearby Red Sox dugout.

"The Boston bench called for Matty to take it, and called for me to take it, and I think that confused Fred," Meyers said. "He was afraid of a collision."

The ball landed in the first base coaching box, giving another chance to one of the greatest hitters of all time. Speaker singled home Engle with the tying run, and after an intentional walk, Larry Gardner scored Yerkes with a sacrifice fly to end it. The dropped fly ball became known as "Snodgrass's Muff," or "The $30,000 Muff," referring to the difference between the overall purse for the winners and the losers.

A week later, back home in California, Snodgrass told reporters that he had been "frozen to the marrow" on the error. "It just dropped out of the glove," he added, "and that was all there was to it." In January, *The New York Times* called Snodgrass "erratic" in a headline, and suggested he might lose his job. His misplay, the paper noted, was "a more colossal error than a thousand others would be."

But Snodgrass was McGraw's guy, his personal discovery, and McGraw never blamed players for physical mistakes. "Often I have been asked what I did to Fred Snodgrass after he dropped that fly ball in the World Series of 1912," McGraw wrote in his book. "I will tell you exactly what I did: I raised his salary $1,000." Snodgrass responded by hitting .291 in 1913 and helping the Giants to another pennant.

Yet echoes of his muff would live on, especially in Boston. In 1914, when the Braves moved a game against the Giants to Fenway Park, Snodgrass cursed out Boston pitcher Lefty Tyler, who had hit him with a pitch. As the crowd hooted at Snodgrass, Tyler stared him down, tossed a ball to himself, and dropped it. The fans roared, and Snodgrass all but incited a riot by thumbing his nose to the stands. As trash rained onto the field, the mayor of Boston, James M. Curley, strode to the umpires to demand they restore order.

A year later, Snodgrass found himself playing for the Braves, who cut him in 1917, ending his major league career. The error always followed him but did not haunt him. He told his grandson, Spencer Garrett, that nobody would have remembered him otherwise.

One hundred years after the infamous drop, Snodgrass's hometown paper, the *Ventura County Star,* tracked down Garrett for a story. Garrett said he'd recently taken a tour of Fenway Park and mentioned to the guide that his grandfather had played there in the 1912 World Series. His name, he added, was Fred Snodgrass.

"I'm sorry," the guide said. "He is the guy who dropped the fly ball."

"You don't need to be sorry," Garrett replied. "He was a wonderful guy."

Sportswriters today might seem tough, but a century ago they were merciless, at least at the end of a World Series. Here's Hall of Fame scribe Fred Lieb—so influential that he would coin the term "The House That Ruth Built" for Yankee Stadium—after the Giants lost the sixth and final game to the White Sox in 1917.

"The goat of the 1917 series is Heinie Zimmerman, the great Zim, and the only native New Yorker playing on the Giants," Lieb wrote in *The New York Sun.* "Zimmerman's falldown in the series was pathetic." Various headlines and captions on the page called Zimmerman "the Snodgrass of the 1917 Series" and the "arch blunderer," castigating him for a "bone play" in a rundown. Hero-takes-the-fall was the irresistible narrative: "Zimmerman's failure to live up to reputation big blow to locals," the *Sun* declared, and the *Times* went even further in decrying his apparent "outburst of stupidity."

"Zim's notorious bonehead play will be known in every corner of the earth," the *Times* wrote. "If Zim lives to be 100 years old, he will never be able to live down that awful footrace."

Zimmerman deserved infamy, but not for the slapstick rundown play in the World Series. He indeed hit poorly—3-for-25—and made a throwing error to put Eddie Collins on base in the fourth inning of Game 6. A teammate's error moved Collins to third, and then pitcher Rube Benson fielded a chopper, trapping Collins between third and home. Collins danced along the baseline, giving time for the runners to advance to second and third before outracing Zimmerman—stretching futilely for the tag—to the plate. The White Sox would score three runs and win the game, 4–2, to clinch the series.

McGraw blamed the first baseman, Walter Holke, for leaving the plate uncovered with catcher Bill Rariden up the line. The pitcher, Benson, wasn't covering, either. "Who was I to throw the ball to? [Bill] Klem?" Zimmerman said later, referring to the plate umpire.

In any case, Zimmerman's much greater sin came two years later, and it cost him his career. In 1919 he became close with Hal Chase, the crooked first baseman whose talent, to McGraw, outweighed his nasty habit of fixing games. McGraw had acquired Chase in a preseason trade with the Reds, hoping he would change his ways. But by September Chase was at it again, and Zimmerman, his new pal, helped him in his effort to bribe fellow Giants to lose.

Their actions made them toxic in the aftermath of the Black Sox scandal that followed, and the new commissioner, Judge Kenesaw Mountain Landis, effectively banned them for life. A decade later Zimmerman was operating a speakeasy with a New York mobster, and he spent his later decades as a plumber and steamfitter. The disgraceful end of his baseball life gave at least the possibility of a sinister cause for his poor play in October 1917.

"It is not possible to know exactly when Zimmerman began throwing games," wrote Bill James in his *Historical Baseball Abstract*, "and thus we can never be certain that, when he lost the 1917 World Series almost single-handedly, he wasn't doing it on purpose."

The Giants' next chance at the series came in 1921, when they beat the Yankees five games to three with Art Nehf twirling a four-hit shutout in the clincher. The only run scored on an error by shortstop Roger Peckinpaugh—and, incredibly, something similar happened four years later. With the Senators in 1925, a Peckinpaugh error set up the go-ahead run for Pittsburgh in Game 7. He committed a record eight errors in that World Series, a bitter ending to an MVP season.*

For the Pirates, the championship was their only one in a span of 50 seasons from 1910 through 1959. They did show up against the mighty Yankees in 1927, like a featherweight in the ring with Gene Tunney. That was the only World Series to end with a wild pitch, but the pitcher who threw it, Johnny Miljus, was just trying to delay the inevitable. Down three games to none in the series, with Game 4 tied in the bottom of the ninth at Yankee Stadium, Miljus intentionally walked Babe Ruth to load the bases ... for Lou Gehrig.

Incredibly, Miljus actually struck out Gehrig and then fanned Bob Meusel. But his second pitch to Tony Lazzeri soared up and away, out of reach for the lunging catcher, Johnny Gooch, and Earle Combs scampered in to win the series. Yes, Miljus threw it away—he never confirmed if the pitch was a spitball—but the Pirates never had a chance, anyway.

"I must give credit to the Yankees as one of the finest clubs in the history of baseball," Pirates manager Donie Bush conceded when it was over. "We were dead on our feet from the start."

As errant pitches go, Miljus's wasn't even the most notorious of the period between the World Wars. That happened in another Game 4 involving the Yankees, also with two outs in the ninth inning. It was the first in an excruciating string of near misses for the Brooklyn Dodgers against their American League neighbors.†

The Dodgers had won only two pennants before 1941 and were one of just three franchises, with the Phillies and St. Louis Browns, that still had no championships. The '41 team was Brooklyn's first 100-game winner in the World Series era, and with two outs and the bases empty in the ninth inning of Game 4, Hugh Casey needed just one strike to Tommy Henrich to even the series at two games apiece.

---

* In Peckinpaugh's defense, Forbes Field was so dark and drenched that gasoline was poured on the diamond in an effort to dry off the infield. Wrote H. I. Phillips in the next day's *Washington Evening Star:* "It was really a marine disaster and not a ball game."
† It was also the first of 11 World Series duels between the franchises, who met at least once each decade from the '40s through the '80s.

One more strike, that is, as long as Mickey Owen caught the ball. Casey got the strike—but Owen let it slip past him. The type of pitch was never truly known; Casey died young, and shortstop Pee Wee Reese called it a "little wet slider" in Peter Golenbock's *Oral History of the Brooklyn Dodgers*. If it really was a spitball, though, Owen never confirmed it.

The problem, he said, was that he had only one signal for Casey's two breaking balls. One was a big, looping curveball, and the other broke sharply, like a slider. Owen's only signs were for fastball or curve; he was confident he could catch whichever variety Casey chose.

"Well, he got two strikes on Henrich with the sharp-breaking curve," Owen told Phil Pepe of *The Daily News* in 1988. "So when I put down the signal for a curveball again, I figured he would throw the same one. But he didn't. He threw the big breaking one and it broke about two feet. Henrich missed it by a mile, and so did I. I was just dumb. I should have been ready for it."

Henrich raced to first, the game continued, and up came the last hitter any pitcher would want to face: Joe DiMaggio.

Owen would say that he should have called time and calmed down Casey, who'd lost Game 3 on a go-ahead hit by DiMaggio. Leo Durocher, the manager, blamed himself for the same oversight. It was bedlam on a roasting day in Flatbush—cops on the field, fans howling in the stands—and the passed ball had rudely and irreversibly shifted the momentum.

"The moment it happened, everybody knew the Yankees would win," Roger Angell said in 2021, recalling his view from the stands; the future Hall of Fame writer attended with his Harvard pals on their way back from a football game at Penn the day before. "It was absolutely inevitable."

DiMaggio singled, Charlie Keller doubled in two, and another double brought in two more. The Yankees won, 7–4, and the Dodgers suddenly had their own Snodgrass.

"I don't mind being the goat, Harold," Owen said later, to Harold Parrott of the *Brooklyn Eagle*. "But the tough part is that it costs these other fellows money. I'm square with myself. I knew I gave it everything I had, although I can't tell you, for the life of me, how that ball got away in the ninth."

The Yankees wrapped it up the next day, and while Owen never played in another World Series, he made three more All-Star teams for Brooklyn. The fans never forgot the error, but they never held it against Owen, either. Decades later, he told *The Saturday Evening Post* that he got thousands of letters from supportive fans. Some offered companionship, accompanied by racy photos; Owen said his wife tore them up.

The irony of Owen's error is that defense was actually his strength. Among the top 100 catchers in Bill James's *Historical Baseball Abstract*, Owen is one of just 10 to derive more than half his value from defense. He would devote many years to baseball instruction, buying nearly 600 acres in the Ozarks for a camp along Route 66 in Miller, Missouri.

"Baseball from start to finish," read the brochure for the Mickey Owen Baseball School in 1960. "The boys eat, sleep and think baseball and the atmosphere is so thick with baseball that even dads and little brothers want to play."

In the 84 days of camp the previous summer, Owen says, he was present for all but eight hours. Over the years, future big leaguers like Joe Girardi, Steve Rogers, and Ricky "Wild Thing" Vaughn—well, Charlie Sheen, anyway—attended the camp. The 1976 class included a teenager from North Carolina who would top out at Double-A for the White Sox: a lanky shortstop and pitcher named Michael Jordan.

By then Owen had sold the camp and become the sheriff of Greene County, Missouri, but he remained an instructor, and the business kept his name. It still operates today as the Sandlot Baseball Complex, leaving Mickey Owen's name affixed only to an error. He knew it would always be that way and accepted his fate.

"I don't get upset about it," Owen told writer Steve Calhoun more than 40 years after the play. "It made me famous."

———

Johnny Pesky didn't need an error to make him famous. He lived to be 93 years old, long enough to see himself immortalized all over Fenway Park. His statue—with Ted Williams, Dom DiMaggio, and Bobby Doerr—stands on the sidewalk at the intersection of Ipswich and Van Ness Streets. The right field foul pole has long been named for Pesky;

at 302 feet from the plate, it's close enough even for a little lefty, like he was, to reach with a long fly ball. And along the right field roof, just above the pole, there's a white circle with Pesky's retired No. 6. Bill Buckner wore it, too.

Pesky's story is a quintessentially American tale. Born as John Michael Paveskovich to immigrants from Croatia, he grew up in Portland, Oregon, entranced by the neighborhood game. The family lived four blocks from Vaughn Street Ballpark, home of the Pacific Coast League's Portland Beavers, and as a teenager Pesky worked as a clubhouse attendant—the very best way to absorb and internalize the values of professional ballplayers.

This would be critical for Pesky in handling the aftermath of the 1946 World Series. An unwritten rule in baseball, as in all team sports, is that you never deflect blame to teammates—even if they deserve it. In modern parlance, you just have to wear it. And so it was that for the last 65 years of his life, Pesky—among other things—would always be the man who held the ball.

Pesky returned from World War II to a Red Sox team brimming with power and pitching and the promise of long-term success. As it turned out, the pitchers got hurt, the Yankees and Indians got better, and those Red Sox reached only one World Series, against the Cardinals of Stan Musial, Enos Slaughter, and two Game 7 heroes straight out of Dr. Seuss: Harry the Cat and Harry the Hat.

Harry Brecheen—the Cat—had started and won twice when he entered Game 7 to protect a two-run lead in the eighth. He got two outs but then allowed a game-tying double to DiMaggio, who blew out a hamstring on his way to second base. The manager, Joe Cronin, called for Leon Culberson to replace him.

Everything changed in that moment. Ted Williams popped out to end the threat, and in the bottom of the eighth, Harry Walker—the Hat—came up with two out and Slaughter on first. Walker was a left-handed slap hitter, a future batting champion who almost never struck out. Slaughter was a heady, hard-charging base runner who'd been held up at third in a one-run loss in the opener; he complained to the rookie manager, Eddie Dyer, who told him to trust his judgment from then on.

Slaughter would have the perfect chance with DiMaggio out of the game. A strong-armed, aggressive center fielder, DiMaggio prided himself on expert positioning. He waved at Culberson from the dugout, expecting Walker to bloop a hit to left center, but Culberson moved only a bit from his straightaway spot. Making things worse, the pitcher—a righty named Bob Klinger who hadn't worked at all in the series—did not hold Slaughter close.

Slaughter was off with the pitch, which Walker indeed lofted to left center. Culberson approached tentatively, perhaps uncomfortable with the choppy terrain in the outfield. He gathered the ball and lobbed a weak throw to Pesky, the shortstop on the outfield grass. He did not expect Slaughter to try for home, and neither did Pesky, whose back was turned to the play. Second baseman Bobby Doerr saw what was happening, but in the din of Sportsman's Park, he could not get Pesky's attention. Slaughter was hell-bent for home.

"I knew I was going to score before I hit second base," he told Bob Broeg, the Hall of Fame St. Louis writer, "because I knew Culberson was in center, not Dom DiMaggio."

By the time the ball came to Pesky, so many factors had conspired against him that a run was inevitable. Slaughter's "mad dash," as it is called on his Hall of Fame plaque, would take its place in baseball lore, and so would Pesky's stunned reaction: he held the ball.

"I'm the goat," he said after the game, as quoted in the next day's *Boston Globe*. "It's my fault. I'm to blame. I had the ball in my hand. I hesitated and gave Slaughter six steps. When I saw him, I couldn't have thrown him out with a .22. I couldn't hear anybody. There was too much yelling. It looked like an ordinary single. I thought he'd hold up at third so late in the game."

The *Globe* story, by Harold Kaese, leads with those quotes but takes pains not to blame Pesky. He's not mentioned in the headline, a subhead reads "Not Pesky's Fault," and Kaese quotes the Cardinals' Marty Marion this way: "We won the Series by stopping Williams." Indeed, Williams managed just five singles in 25 at-bats—a victim, in a way, of Boston's runaway pennant. While the Cardinals settled the NL crown with a playoff against Brooklyn, the Red Sox tried to stay loose with competitive practices against fellow major leaguers. An errant pitch from Washington's Mickey Haefner struck Williams in the elbow, and he played his only World Series in pain.

But for the single, series-defining moment, Slaughter was hailed as the hero and Pesky assailed as the foil, even in his home state: "PESKY IS MADE SERIES GOAT IN FINAL CONTEST," read a headline in the next day's *Medford* (Ore.) *Tribune*. The UPI report said that Slaughter would have been out easily if Pesky had not hesitated.

It was not Pesky's nature to dispute the assessment. Here's how David Halberstam described it in *The Teammates,* his touching 2003 book that inspired the statue at Fenway:

> He never tried to exonerate himself or to explain the play. "You can't argue with people," he says, "about what they thought they saw even if they didn't see it." Over the years his teammates, especially Dom and Bobby, would try to explain to others what happened on the play, that John's role in it had been minimal, but Pesky himself never did. That was something he had learned hanging around the old Portland clubhouse. There were some old-timers there, including a veteran pitcher named Bill Posedel, a man who was 13 years older than John. He had warned John that the worst thing you could ever do in baseball was to try to shift the blame when others placed it on you. It didn't matter if the blame was being apportioned fairly or not; if you tried to run from what people believed, then you only made it worse, and dug yourself in deeper. But if you accepted it, then you ended up a better man, and your teammates would know and so would those few other people who needed to know. "Look, John," Posedel had said many times to Pesky in the clubhouse, "it's not a perfect game. Things go wrong. And when they go wrong, you can't fight it. It's easy to deal with things when they go right. It's dealing with them when they go wrong that determines whether you're a man or not. That's the way you become a man."

Pesky the man treated baseball with the reverence and wonder of a boy. The game was as much a part of Pesky as the long and skinny nose that gave him his nickname—Needle, from Williams—and he treated the game with reverence and wonder. After retirement, Pesky spent many years as a manager and instructor, including a stint as first base coach for the Pirates under Harry Walker, the very man whose double he had held way back when.

The Red Sox were the reigning champions when Pesky was born, in February 1919, and he served as an honorary coach when they won their first title of his lifetime, in 2004. Pesky, a master with a fungo bat, shared a locker at Fenway with a later Red Sox great, Luis Tiant. He cheerily spoke with the press before another World Series with the Cardinals, dutifully recounting his fateful Game 7.

"I didn't hear anything," Pesky said, as quoted by George Vecsey of *The New York Times.* "Everybody was screaming. When I looked, Enos was 10 feet from home. I threw the ball. Maybe if I had a better arm, I would have gotten him."

Yes, Pesky added, the old story of the heckler was true: he indeed took his wife to a football game one rainy day in Oregon, and when the ball kept slipping away from the players, a fan shouted, "Give the ball to Pesky, he knows how to hold on to it!" A good line, for sure, and no reason for being bitter so many years later.

"They treat me like a king," Pesky said. "Lowe, Schilling, Myers, Manny, Ortiz, they all give me hugs, like you only used to get from your family."

Life was good for Pesky in the brotherhood of a baseball clubhouse, the place where it all began, where he learned the code of conduct he would honor till the end.

The Yankees would win the 1947 World Series, and a record five in a row from 1949 through 1953. They eased their grip just a bit after that, with only two more championships in the '50s, then started the 1960s with five consecutive pennants.

The first of those set up that weird and preposterous World Series with the Pirates, when the Yankees trounced Pittsburgh in overall runs but lost on Bill Mazeroski's homer off Ralph Terry in Game 7.*

---

* Bing Crosby, the fabled singer who owned one percent of the Pirates in 1960, was too nervous to watch the World Series and instead took his wife on vacation to Paris. Wanting to see Game 7 when he returned, Crosby hired a company to record NBC's broadcast by kinescope—and 50 years later, the complete footage was found on five reels of 16-millimeter film in Crosby's former home near San Francisco. Because networks rarely kept complete recordings of live events, the broadcast was long believed to be lost

The hitters took 78 turns at bat that day, and nobody struck out. Terry was the fifth Yankee pitcher, and none could keep Pittsburgh from scoring. As Casey Stengel watched his staff crumble in his final game as Yankees manager, he kept Terry ready all day long. At Old-Timers' Day in 2016, Terry told me he warmed up five times and grew conditioned to the small, steep bullpen mound.

"I get in the game and they had a big, flat mound," said Terry, who had never pitched at Forbes Field before. "My front foot would come down early and everything was high. If I'd only warmed up once or twice, I'd have been able to adjust. But I couldn't get the ball down."

His warm-ups were so high that he even tried to bounce a few and couldn't do it. He got a fly out to end the eighth, and when the Yankees tied it in their half, Terry returned to face Mazeroski leading off the bottom of the ninth. The mound was no more comfortable then, and when his first pitch sailed high, catcher Johnny Blanchard hustled out to the mound.

The next pitch was worse—"a high cutter, really," Terry said in 2016, in updated pitching parlance—and Mazeroski blasted it into history. The championship soared above left fielder Yogi Berra and landed in a tree-lined park beyond the redbrick outfield wall.

Terry walked off to the third base dugout. He wasn't much of a drinker but had a Hudepohl beer in the clubhouse. Terry had cried over a game just once, the summer after high school graduation, when he let in the winning run of a playoff game. He didn't cry this time, but Mickey Mantle did, perhaps sensing the end for the only manager he'd ever had.

Terry also saw it coming. He met with Stengel in the manager's office and told him how badly he felt. Stengel asked where he'd tried to pitch Mazeroski, and Terry said low and away. That was fine, Stengel said—he had simply made a physical mistake, and those things happen. "Forget it, kid," Stengel said, and wished him well for the next season.

"Casey was God, you know," Terry said. "He could have hung a guilt trip on me. Never looked back."

Only one other pitcher has given up a homer to end the World

---

to time. Crosby died in 1977, but his careful preservation of the film in a cool, dry wine cellar became his final contribution to the entertainment canon.

Series—the Phillies' Mitch Williams to Toronto's Joe Carter in 1993. Less than six weeks later, the Phillies shipped Williams to Houston in a trade, and he never pitched again in October.

Terry just kept going back, pitching in the next four World Series. He went 16–3 for the 1961 champions and 23–12 the next season, taking the Yankees to the verge of another title by beating the Giants in Game 5 of the World Series.

The series then shifted to Candlestick Park, and after a soggy four-day layoff, Ford lost Game 6. Terry had thrown more than 300 innings since opening day, but with five days off, he felt strong. Two years after Mazeroski, he had another chance at Game 7—and unwound at the team hotel with a walk-off win of his own, against Berra, Elston Howard, Clete Boyer, and Hector Lopez in poker.

"Yogi had a pretty bad-looking hand, he got like a king-high flush, he's running everybody out," Terry said. "I stayed in and called it, and I got an ace of hearts on the last card. I raked in $350, which was a big pot, and I said, 'I'm gone, boys.' Nobody likes you to leave the card table—you stick around, you know—but I told Yogi, 'I'm going to bed.' I slept like a baby."

There was more money at stake the next afternoon, and that consumed Terry more than any ghosts from Pittsburgh. The winner's share was worth about $10,000, the loser's share about $7,000. The difference was significant for Terry. He had house and car payments, plus a wife, a child, and another baby on the way. Terry made about $40,000 in 1962; pitching for that extra three grand, he said, was real pressure.

On the bus to the ballpark, the Yankees listened to a radio show with Joe Garagiola as a guest. The host asked for a prediction from Garagiola, the old catcher who'd begun an enduring second act with a microphone. He picked the Giants.

"Terry's already lost one seventh game," Garagiola said, according to Terry. "The pressure'll be too much for him and he'll choke."

Terry spotted Garagiola around the batting cage before Game 7 and told him he'd been listening. "Well, I had to say something," Garagiola protested, and Terry just stared at him.

"You didn't have to say *that*," he said, and then walked away to dominate. After only a few warm-ups in the bullpen, Terry knew he would be at his best: his fastball was hopping, his breaking stuff dropping.

"What a day to wake up feeling good," he said, still beaming so many years later.

Terry carried a perfect game into the sixth inning, and he never walked a batter. With a 1–0 lead in the ninth he allowed a leadoff single to Matty Alou, meaning every hitter to come would be a potential Mazeroski, capable of ending the World Series with one big swing. He struck out Felipe Alou, who still regrets his failure to get a bunt down, and then fanned Chuck Hiller. Willie Mays doubled to right, putting the tying run on third and the winning run on second.

At this point, Terry had faced two Golden Pitch scenarios, against Hiller and Mays, in which a single pitch could win or lose the World Series. Only two other pitchers had ever been in that spot, according to research by Wade Kapszukiewicz, in the 2016 SABR *Baseball Research Journal:* Christy Mathewson in 1912 and Pete Alexander in 1926. Only five have been there since: Rollie Fingers in 1972, Jose Mesa in 1997, Mariano Rivera in 2001, Madison Bumgarner in 2014, and Mike Montgomery in 2016.

In some of those settings, though, the pitcher needed a double play to end the game, or the batter needed a homer and was not a power hitter. This was the ultimate danger, with one Hall of Fame slugger coming up and another on deck. Terry could have walked Willie McCovey to load the bases for Orlando Cepeda, but decided against it. The Giants had clinched the pennant on a bases-loaded walk, he remembered, and with an NL ump behind the plate, he would not risk a tight strike zone.

McCovey had homered off Terry in Game 2 at Candlestick, when Terry let him extend his long arms. This time he jammed him with a fastball, and McCovey coiled his back just to get his hands through. He managed to pull a line drive, but it was low—"Why couldn't McCovey have hit the ball just three feet higher?" groaned Charlie Brown in a *Peanuts* comic strip that winter—and Bobby Richardson snared it to end the series.

Only then, Terry said, could he truly process the fate he had narrowly avoided. With fortune and fortitude, he'd earned a chance at redemption that most players never get. Imagine if he'd blown it!

"After winning that, then all of a sudden it dawned on me: I'd been carrying it around in the back of my mind," said Terry, who died in

March 2022. "And I said, 'Well, think if I had given up another home run—I'd have had to leave the country and change my name!' But I didn't think about it. You get in the game, you're confronted with problems right there. That commands your full attention."

Terry pitched for five more seasons and made his final career start for the Mets in August 1966—at Forbes Field, of all places, against the Pirates and Mazeroski. That game ended with a home run, too, by Willie Stargell, but it didn't come off Terry. He faced 24 batters that day and kept them all in the park.

––––––

Yankees fans regard 1960 as the soul-crushing World Series loss of that era. For Boston fans, the equivalent is 1975. The Red Sox had fallen in seven games to St. Louis in 1967, but that season was a gift from a baseball Cupid, an arrow that pierced New England's heart and revived its love affair with the Olde Towne Team. They called it the "Impossible Dream," after all, and it was—teams that rise from ninth place to the pennant do not beat Bob Gibson in Game 7.

In 1975, though, it was all right there for the Red Sox. That World Series, against the Cincinnati Reds, ended bitterly: in Game 7, with two outs in the top of the ninth inning, Joe Morgan dumped a go-ahead single to shallow center to break a 3–3 tie. Carl Yastrzemski hit it deeper in the bottom of the ninth, but not far enough: his fly off Will McEnaney dropped into the glove of Cesar Geronimo for the final out.

"I was hoping that he'd hit a ball off the wall, or into the net, because I'd seen him do it before," said Carlton Fisk, who was on deck, when I asked him about it before his first pitch at Fenway on the night the Red Sox won the 2013 World Series. "But it's tough. He hadn't faced a left-hander, and he hit a fly ball. He didn't have a bad swing. He just hit it in the air."

As Geromino squeezed it, McEnaney turned back to Johnny Bench, who screamed: "What do we do? What do we do?" McEnaney grabbed his hat and jumped, wrapping his glove around Bench's neck and his legs around his waist.

"I started out in the center of a big mound scrum, and by the time the whole team got there, I ended up on the outside," said McEnaney, who spent years in retirement as the scoreboard operator for spring training games in Jupiter, Florida. "Next thing I know, someone came by and sucker punched me, popped me in the jaw. A fan. I didn't even feel it. It was all a blur."

That off-season, Peter Gammons, the Red Sox beat writer for *The Boston Globe,* watched a Bruins game at a bar with friends. An old man sat nearby, drinking alone for hours. At the end of the game he turned to Gammons and slurred: "How the hell could he have taken out Willoughby?" Then he passed out.

In Red Sox lore, the removal of Jim Willoughby—who had retired four Reds in a row in the late innings of Game 7—might sting more than the work of the next pitcher, a sympathetic figure named Jim Burton. With two outs and the bases empty in the bottom of the eighth, Boston manager Darrell Johnson removed Willoughby for a pinch hitter, Cecil Cooper, who popped out. Cooper was a very good hitter, but not right then: he was 1-for-19 in the series.

"I pinch hit for Willoughby in the eighth because we were trying to win the game," Johnson said later. "He had gotten out their right-handed batters, but there were a couple of tough left-handers coming up in their lineup."

Johnson had three lefties on the staff but had already used two, Bill Lee and Roger Moret. He still had his closer, the right-handed Dick Drago, but Drago had worked three scoreless innings in Game 6. Johnson said that took him out of the mix, yet a month before, Drago had followed up a three-inning outing with a save the next day.

"I've pitched day after day all year," Drago said after Game 7. "Besides, it's the seventh game of the World Series and I could pitch 20 innings if I had to."

Fatigue was no issue for Burton, but sharpness was; he had faced only two batters in the last 31 days. Burton never expected Johnson to call for him in Game 7, considering how little he had pitched. Facing a savvy lineup with its legacy on the line, Burton was set up to fail.

"I didn't want to go out there," Burton told Doug Hornig for his book, *The Boys of October,* published in 2003. "Warming up, my whole body went numb. It was surreal, like an out-of-body experience. In those days, they sent a golf cart to bring you in, and when it came for me, I knew I couldn't ride in it. I had to trot in from the bullpen just to feel my feet on the ground."

Burton had appeared briefly in Game 3 and walked his first hitter, Ken Griffey. The same thing happened in Game 7. "That was from nervousness," Burton told Hornig, "and lack of activity." He bore down after that, but the walk would haunt him: a bunt, a ground out, and another walk brought up Morgan, soon to be named MVP of the National League.

Burton got ahead, 1–2. He'd led the International League in strike-outs the year before and thrown a no-hitter for Pawtucket in June. But this was a stage for Morgan, an elite contact hitter and the best in the majors at reaching base. Of course he would fight his way back—a foul down the left field line, another down the right field line. Burton went to the slider, maximizing his left-on-left advantage.

"I wound up and threw it exactly where I wanted it, as hard as I could throw one," Burton told Hornig. "My slider wasn't a tight one; it was more like a slurve that started in close to a left-hander and broke a lot, away from him."

Morgan needed every bit of his 34.5-inch Louisville Slugger. He reached out and poked the slider off the end of his bat, and a fast-falling bloop landed in shallow center. Griffey scored the go-ahead run, and these were the first words from the NBC analyst, Tony Kubek: "Jim Burton made a good pitch."

It was almost the last of his career. Burton struggled in Pawtucket the next season, unable to shed the loss, and made just one more appearance in the major leagues. "It hurt me mentally," he told Hornig. "And I became a negative focus for a lot of people after '75. I was the scapegoat." Yet he always maintained that he had no regrets.

A decade after the World Series, well into his next career running a printing business in Charlotte, Burton told *Yankee Magazine* that he was at peace with the pitch. "I never wish I had it back," he said. "It was as good a pitch as I'm capable of throwing."

The pitch that lost the World Series was not a source of shame. Burton, who died in 2013, had done his best. The regret, for fans and teammates, is that there might have been a better option.

"Just a little dinker over second base into short center," pitcher Rick Wise said, ruefully, in 2020. "To put that kid in that situation instead of your veteran go-to guys, Jim Willoughby or Dick Drago, it didn't make sense."

It was much the same way for George Frazier, another young reliever whose luck was so rotten that it spared him the wrath of the most bombastic owner in sports history: George M. Steinbrenner III.

I sat with Frazier in the visitor's dugout at the new Yankee Stadium on a June afternoon in 2011. He was broadcasting for the Colorado Rockies, in town for a rare visit to the Bronx that coincided with Old-Timers' Day. Frazier would be taking part for the first time.

It had been nearly 30 years since the 1981 World Series, when Frazier joined Lefty Williams on a dubious list. "I lost three games in a World Series—and I was the first to do it trying," Frazier told his wife that off-season. Williams was a member of the notorious 1919 White Sox and took a $5,000 bribe to lose.

Frazier had spent most of 1981 in the minors. Promoted in August, after the strike and a trade from St. Louis, the lanky right-hander made a good impression in middle relief and the playoffs. But he lost the third, fourth, and sixth games of the World Series against the Dodgers, sunk by a blizzard of ground-ball singles and broken-bat flares. The Yankees blew a two-games-to-none lead in that series and never made it back in the '80s.

Frazier did. He pitched for the Minnesota Twins in the 1987 World Series and retired the next spring, leaving as a champion. It was more than he ever could have hoped for.

"I'm not entitled to any of this," Frazier said, looking out from the Rockies' dugout at Steinbrenner's gleaming new palace. "I wasn't entitled to pitch in the 1981 World Series. I wasn't entitled to pitch in the 1987 World Series. It was a privilege I had an opportunity to do that, and I still feel that every day."

Steinbrenner had died the year before our conversation, leaving his son Hal in charge. Frazier smiled at the thought; when Hal was 12 or so, Frazier and teammate Ron Davis would stuff him in a trash can for laughs. Others may have feared or loathed the Boss, but not Frazier. At his lowest point, after losing the final game of the World Series, Frazier felt a pat on his back.

"It wasn't your fault, kid," Steinbrenner told him. "You'll be a Yankee next year, don't worry about it."

Frazier took every question from reporters that night; in the playoffs he had spoken after winning, so in the World Series, he thought, it was only right to speak after losing. That winter he was heartened by supportive letters from fans, who appreciated his effort and called him a model of sportsmanship. Back home in Oklahoma that off-season, Frazier spoke at an elementary school where the kids said they still loved him, even after the losses.

Steinbrenner was true to his word. Frazier never returned to the minors, staying two more seasons with the Yankees. He pitched mostly in losses but without complaint, a loyal team man who was paid back in kindness by an owner known more for his temper than his heart.

"In 1983, my dad had a stroke and I couldn't get back," Frazier said. "[Steinbrenner] put me on his private airplane and flew me to Missouri. Paid for everything. Picked my kids up in a limousine and had them up to the airport to meet me with my wife. You'll never hear me say a bad word about George or Hal or anything about the Yankees."

While Frazier set a record for losses in a best-of-seven World Series (Williams's follies came in a best-of-nine), history remembers a different goat: Dave Winfield. It was Winfield's picture on the back page of the next day's *Daily News,* his statistics—"1 for 22 (That's .045)"—in the headline. Steinbrenner issued a statement apologizing to fans.

"It has been a great era, but it's over," he told the writers. "There will be changes made."

Yet George Frazier was not one of them. He wore the losses but not the blame.

———

Winfield stayed, too, for a productive but stormy nine-year tenure in pinstripes. Like Frazier, he got one more shot at the World Series and won, in 1992 with the Toronto Blue Jays. Winfield didn't do much until it mattered most, lugging a .192 average to the plate in the eleventh inning of Game 6 in Atlanta. Then he lashed a two-out, two-run double into the left field corner and etched the final line onto his Hall of Fame plaque.

Charlie Leibrandt gave it up. He could have seen it coming. The memories still linger from an early matchup in 1980, when Leibrandt was a rookie with the Reds and Winfield an established star in San Diego.

"He knew exactly what I was doing," Leibrandt said. "Shoot, he almost killed me once! He hit a line drive back at me, I never saw it, hit me right in the thigh. He hit some balls in the old Jack Murphy Stadium, they had these big concrete walls, had to be 20 feet high, he hit one off the center field fence about a foot from going out and that ball had to be 440, 450 feet.

"I had no business being in that game [in the World Series], but Bobby [Cox] had confidence in me. I'm not gonna say, 'You need to come get me.' I'm gonna go out there, do my best, and hopefully get these guys out. It didn't work out—again."

Leibrandt had plenty of October experience by then, some of it quite good. He'd won the pennant clincher for the Royals in 1985, coming to the rescue after Bret Saberhagen's pitching hand swelled up from deflecting a grounder. After Saberhagen shut out St. Louis to win Game 7 of the World Series, Leibrandt wound up on the cover of *Sports Illustrated*, his upraised arm hovering over the masthead above a throng of joyous teammates.

Fittingly, Leibrandt's jacket hid most of his face in the photo. He'd been overshadowed by fate against the Cardinals, pitching masterfully but leaving both his starts trailing in the eighth or ninth inning. Between 1984 and '85, Leibrandt had become the first pitcher in 50 years—since Schoolboy Rowe of the 1930s Tigers—to lose three postseason starts in which he worked at least eight innings and allowed no more than four earned runs.

The four earned runs obscure how well Leibrandt pitched in Game 2 in 1985, when he shut out the Cardinals through eight and two-thirds innings. But a run-scoring single, a bloop double, and an intentional walk loaded the bases, and Terry Pendleton came to the plate. Pendleton had already gotten a thrill by meeting his hero, Reggie Jackson, who was working the series for ABC. Jackson was Mr. October, of course, the man you wanted in the big spot.

"And I thought about that," Pendleton says. "So it was funny, just going up to the plate thinking, 'OK, this is what you always wanted to do since you were 11 years old. Your teammates are waiting on you. You said you wanted to shoulder it and here it is.'"

In Game 7 of the ALCS, Royals manager Dick Howser had called for his star closer, Dan Quisenberry, when Leibrandt gave up two hits in the ninth. But here, Howser froze. He said later that it was Leibrandt's game to win or lose. But after Pendleton doubled home the runners to give the Cardinals a 4–2 lead, Howser's inaction seemed to defy logic.

The loss felt like a knockout blow; no team had ever recovered to win the World Series after losing the first two games at home. Howser had always trusted Leibrandt, believing in him when his career was going nowhere, and reassured him on the plane the next day: "Don't worry about it, you're gonna get 'em in Game 6," he said.

The gesture meant a lot to Leibrandt, who would shut out the Cardinals into the eighth in that game, before Brian Harper singled to break a scoreless tie. The Royals' miracle comeback—and blowout win in Game 7—earned Leibrandt his ring.

The Royals traded Leibrandt a few years later to Atlanta, where he found another advocate in manager Bobby Cox—and another roster stuffed with dynamic young arms. Leibrandt was a veteran mentor, winning 15 games in 1991 and starting the World Series opener in Minnesota, a 5–2 loss. Back at the Metrodome with a chance to clinch in Game 6, Cox summoned Leibrandt for his first relief appearance as a Brave, asking him to hold a tie in the eleventh inning. He passed over Jim Clancy, Kent Mercker, Randy St. Claire, and Mark Wohlers.

"Why not Charlie?" Cox would say later. "He's a 15-game winner. He handled Puckett the first game."

Indeed he did, striking out Puckett twice, both times on changeups out of the strike zone. As Puckett waited on deck in Game 6, he told the next hitter, Chili Davis, "Hey, I don't hit this guy at all"—at least, that's what Davis told Leibrandt years later. In his autobiography, Puckett wrote that he was actually supremely confident, recalling a game from 1987 when the Twins had battered Leibrandt for three homers in the first inning.

"Puck, here comes your man," teammate Al Newman told Puckett, as Leibrandt trotted in from the bullpen. "Yeah, he is," Puckett said he replied. Davis, he added, told him to hunt for a high pitch and win it with a homer. Leibrandt obliged—his changeup, the pitch he'd learned from the great Mario Soto, the pitch he knew could work against

Puckett, simply wouldn't dive. Puckett belted it over the left field wall, and Jack Buck told CBS viewers he would see them tomorrow night.

"I could not get that thing down in the pen," Leibrandt says. "I couldn't figure out what I was doing. If I was starting, it wouldn't have been a big deal; I'd throw a couple pitches down the middle until I settled in. But I gotta get guys out right away."

Intellectually, Leibrandt knew he'd been put in a role that didn't suit him. But he still felt responsible and lingered on the loss all winter, until the familiar rhythms of another spring training came along. Then the season repeated itself: another 15 victories, another NL pennant, another Game 6, another eleventh inning, another future Hall of Famer at the plate.

Leibrandt hadn't pitched at all in the 1992 World Series before Cox brought him into a 2–2 tie. His other options were limited: David Nied, an untested rookie;* Marvin Freeman, who'd been roughed up in the playoffs; and the veteran Jeff Reardon, who had struggled and lost Cox's confidence. So again it was Leibrandt, and with two on and one out, he retired the dangerous Joe Carter. Needing only Winfield to finish the inning, Leibrandt missed with a full-count changeup, gave up the double, and lived out his nightmare once more.

"If you're losing in the World Series, it's almost like you'd rather not be there," he says. "Because you don't feel like it's second. It's distant. It felt like we were a million miles from being the winning team."

The Braves signed Greg Maddux that December and traded Leibrandt the same day. His son Brandon—a future major league pitcher—was born soon after, and Leibrandt would return to Atlanta in retirement, coaching his sons' high school baseball teams. He thinks about the Game 6 heartbreaks sometimes, but he's satisfied with his career: 14 seasons, 140 wins, that championship ring with the Royals. Fans are kind to him.

"If I've gotta put my name down on a reservation, once in a while they'll say, 'Hey, I watched you, I enjoyed your career,'" Leibrandt says. "They're not busting my chops about the things I didn't do well. People

---

* Nied would be the Colorado Rockies' first pick in the expansion draft a few weeks later, and threw the first pitch in team history in April 1993.

down here are pretty nice. But the great majority of the time, nobody knows who I am or what I did, and I'm OK with that."

————————

Leibrandt was watching from the stands the next time the Braves hosted Game 6 of the World Series, in 1995. That time they won, behind Tom Glavine's 1–0 clinching victory over Cleveland. The run came on a David Justice homer off a lefty reliever, Jim Poole.

Like Leibrandt, Poole also settled in Atlanta after his playing career. Unlike Leibrandt, he does hear about his Game 6 loss. Poole is a certified financial planner and personal wealth advisor; diagnosed with ALS in 2021, he continued to work daily from home. His playing background comes up often in his job, and home run talk quickly follows.

"Living here, I have to be ready for that," Poole said in 2020. "And I'm a Phillies fan all the way, so it makes it even worse."

Poole had pitched an inning of Game 2 in Atlanta, and when the series returned for Game 6, the Braves needed just one win to clinch. Justice, though, had groused about the fans the day before, saying they would probably burn down players' houses if the Braves lost. The team, he declared, would play strictly for itself; to Justice, the fans had grown petulant as they waited for a championship.

"If we get down 1–0 tonight, they'll probably boo us out of the stadium," he said. "You have to do something great to get them out of their seats. Shoot, up in Cleveland, they were down three runs in the ninth inning and they were still on their feet."

This commentary was big news in Atlanta, as Poole learned on the afternoon of Game 6. His alma mater, Georgia Tech, was playing Clemson at Bobby Dodd Stadium, so Poole stopped by for a while. As he left for his own game, he got some advice from a former teammate, Jeff Distasio: "Whatever you do, don't let Justice beat you!"

Famous last words, to be sure—but before Justice had the chance to beat Poole, Fred McGriff took his turn. With two out and two on in the bottom of the fifth, Poole replaced starter Dennis Martinez and fanned McGriff to end the threat. That could have been it for Poole, and maybe it should have been. But with Justice due to lead off the bottom of the sixth, Poole stayed in for the left-on-left matchup. He wanted his 1–1 fastball low and away. It sailed up and in.

"As it was leaving my hand, realizing where it was gonna be, I thought, 'I hope it's in enough,'" he says. "I ended up playing with Justice a few years later, actually in Cleveland, and he was kind enough to tell me: 'It wasn't that bad a pitch, Pooley—I just snatched it.' But I totally missed my spot."

Justice drove Poole's mistake deep into the Georgia night. Tony Peña, the catcher, banged his face mask on his knee and winced. Suddenly Justice was the hero, the guy who challenged fans to get out of their seats and made them do it with one big swing.

The Indians traded Poole the next summer, but it wasn't personal. They would bring him back three more times, including one final chance in the summer of 2000, after two other teams had released him. Poole never got back to the World Series, but never looked back in regret, either. He'd gotten his chance and competed, and that was really all he wanted.

"Every backyard pitch was about pitching in the World Series— and there was nothing disappointing about it, even giving up the home run," Poole says. "The competitor wants to win, but being in that position and performing as well as I could was all I'd ever asked of myself."

The difference, Poole said, was not in the effort, but the execution. A mental mistake would have been so much harder to absorb. That's why, of all the Braves' World Series losses in the 1990s, the play that seems to sting the most is Lonnie Smith's hesitation on the bases in Game 7 against the Twins in 1991. The Braves lost to Jack Morris in 10 innings, 1–0, but could have had a run in the eighth if Smith, breaking from first, had picked up the flight of Terry Pendleton's double.*

---

* Pendleton's double might have been a home run if the stadium fans had been blowing out. A Metrodome superintendent, Dick Ericson, admitted to the *Star Tribune* in 2003 that he would turn the blowers on when the Twins were batting and turn them off when the visitors hit, including in the World Series. Could Pendleton's drive have carried over the fence, if given a hometown boost? "No doubt," Pendleton says. "It wasn't tough to go oppo in that ballpark, trust me. And you have to believe that they were mic'ing more noise in that place, too. It wasn't just those fans making all that noise."

Lonnie Smith—whose baserunning blunder would hurt the Braves in the finale of the greatest World Series ever, in 1991—plows into the Twins' Brian Harper in Game 4. "Boy," said Jack Buck in the CBS booth. "That's hardball."

With the hills of Chavez Ravine as a backdrop, Baltimore's 20-year-old Jim Palmer shuts out the Dodgers in Game 2 of the 1966 World Series. He beats Sandy Koufax, who never pitches again.

The Dodgers' Orel Hershiser greets Mike Davis after a Game 5 homer in Oakland in 1988. Davis, who hit .196 in the regular season, drew a two-out walk before Kirk Gibson's famous home run in the opener, and Hershiser (two complete games) took over from there.

The Dodgers recovered from Don Larsen's 1956 perfect game with a stirring 1–0 victory over the Yankees in Game 6 at Ebbets Field. Clem Labine—normally a reliever—pitched all 10 innings, and Jackie Robinson won it with the final hit of his career.

Ken Phelps, Jose Canseco, and their families leave the field at Candlestick Park after the Loma Prieta earthquake postponed Game 3 of the 1989 World Series. The A's trained in Phoenix during the 10-day break, then finished off the Giants in a sweep.

Manager Cito Gaston congratulates his Blue Jays for outlasting the Phillies in a rollicking Game 4 comeback in 1993. The Veterans Stadium scoreboard tallies 29 runs, a single-game World Series record.

Reggie Jackson takes a cut at Dodger Stadium during his final World Series, in 1981. Jackson—the MVP for Oakland in 1973 and for the Yankees in 1977—slugged .490 in the regular season and .755 in the World Series.

Geoff Blum was dismayed in July 2005 when San Diego traded him to Chicago just after his wife delivered triplets. He was smiling in late October as he lifted his eldest daughter, 22-month-old Mia Lea, to the sky after his homer helped the White Sox sweep the Astros.

Rajai Davis exults after his Game 7 homer off the Cubs' Aroldis Chapman jolted the Indians in 2016. "It was like it was a walk-off," Davis says—but it only tied the game in the eighth inning. The Cubs regrouped during a brief rain delay and recovered to win in the tenth.

The Giants' Madison Bumgarner works on his Game 5 shutout of the Royals in 2014. He is the best World Series pitcher ever: 4–0 with a save and a 0.25 ERA, allowing just one run in 36 innings.

Derek Jeter, flanked by Andy Pettitte (far left), Jorge Posada, and Mariano Rivera, opened the new Yankee Stadium in style with a victory over the Phillies in the 2009 World Series. Fittingly, Jeter, No. 2, had 200 postseason hits, and Rivera, No. 42, had 42 postseason saves.

Theo Epstein, then just 30 years old, celebrates the 2004 World Series title as general manager of his hometown Boston Red Sox. He would build another winner in 2007, then do it again with the Cubs in 2016.

Rival managers, a century apart: the Giants' John McGraw with the Athletics' Connie Mack in 1911, and the Rangers' Ron Washington with the Cardinals' Tony La Russa in 2011. Mack, La Russa, and McGraw rank first, second, and third on the career wins list for managers.

Disaster struck the Dodgers in Game 4 in 1941 when sure-handed catcher Mickey Owen missed a third strike that would have evened the series for Brooklyn. "The moment it happened," said writer Roger Angell, then a college student in the stands, "everybody knew the Yankees would win."

Hall of Famer Don Sutton struggled in a soggy sixth game in 1982, but St. Louis rookie John Stuper went the distance. Sutton sought him out after the Brewers lost in seven: "This never would have happened without you."

Dusty Rhodes hooks a tenth-inning homer down the right field line at the Polo Grounds—just 258 feet from the plate—to win the opener against Cleveland in 1954. Rhodes came off the bench to go 4-for-6 with two homers and seven RBIs in the Giants' sweep.

Fifty-eight years after their seven-game thriller, Red Schoendienst shares a laugh with Johnny Pesky at the 2004 World Series. Pesky took the blame for the Red Sox' loss, but became one of the most beloved figures in franchise history.

Pat Gillick, who built the Blue Jays into two-time champions, hoists another Commissioner's Trophy as Phillies general manager in 2008. Three years later, he was in the Hall of Fame.

The Marlins' Josh Beckett, shown here exploring Monument Park in 2003, won the final World Series game at the original Yankee Stadium with a Game 6 shutout on short rest.

"I was going with the pitch on a delayed steal," Smith said after Game 7, as quoted in *The Philadelphia Inquirer*. "I got about halfway and I heard the sound of the bat. I made the mistake of not looking in when I started running. I just assumed that the ball would be hit on the ground. Before I had a chance to look back, I saw the two infielders trying to glove something."

The Twins' middle infielders, Chuck Knoblauch and Greg Gagne, were pretending to turn a double play. Smith didn't fall for it—if he had, he would have slid into second—but he did stop in his tracks just after rounding the bag. When he finally found the ball, which one-hopped the fence in left center, Smith could only make it to third.

Long saddled with the nickname Skates for his habit of on-field pratfalls, Smith had just made his costliest baserunning gaffe. But the Braves still should have found a way to bring him home.

"When I looked over at third and saw him standing there I was like, 'Oh man!'" Pendleton said. "But I thought to myself, 'We've got second and third and nobody out, we're definitely scoring here. No doubt.'"

The Braves played it cautious, with third base coach Jimy Williams telling Smith to hold at third unless a ball got through the infield or took a high bounce off the turf. So he stayed there on a soft ground out to first, and after an intentional walk loaded the bases, Sid Bream pulled a Morris forkball to first for a 3-2-3 double play, ending the inning. Atlanta never put another runner on base.

A baserunning blunder, though, always seems to hurt worse than routine failure in the batter's box. Consider the riveting but too-short 2000 World Series, when the Yankees held the Mets' offensive engine, Edgardo Alfonzo, to three singles in 21 at-bats. That may have been the biggest factor in the Mets' five-game loss, but much of the blame goes to Timo Perez for a play on the bases in the sixth inning of Game 1.

Perez was on first when Todd Zeile lofted a drive to deep left. Thinking it was a homer, Perez raised his arm to celebrate instead of running hard all the way. But the ball hit the top of the wall, and Derek Jeter nailed Perez at the plate on a relay throw from Justice.

"I was confused by the ball," Perez admitted after the game, a 4–3 loss in 12 innings. "I saw the fans put their hands up and I thought it was a home run. I slowed up a little. If I would've run all the way through, I would've scored. I have no excuses about it."

Another culprit for the Mets' Game 1 loss: the extra rows of seats on the dirt in foul territory at Yankee Stadium. Two outs from victory in the ninth, Armando Benitez walked Paul O'Neill in a 10-pitch duel to spark the Yankees' game-tying rally. One of O'Neill's foul balls twisted just out of reach of Mets third baseman Robin Ventura, who would have caught it easily with just a little more room.

For the Yankees of that era, though, if it hadn't been Perez's base-running or an elusive foul pop, they would have found another break to exploit. Zeile knew this all too well; in each of the Yankees' four postseason championship runs under Joe Torre, they beat a Zeile team along the way. At the pivotal moment, he knew, the Yankees would somehow come through.

"When you play the Yankees," Zeile says, "it's like, 'God, why do they *always* seem to make that kind of play?'"

Zeile is not convinced that if Perez had run hard, the Mets would have won the opener and eventually toppled the Bronx dynasty. Others still rue the run that never was and the lead that slipped away.

"In retrospect, the Timo thing really hurt, because that's another run and runs were at a premium in that World Series," said Al Leiter, who started the first and last games. "You put another run up there, it just changes things. And, listen, when you're winning in the ninth inning with your closer and you lose the lead? It didn't feel like we were down 1–0 [in games]. It felt like we were down 3–0. If I give up five or six early and we lose 6–1—'All right, we had no shot, let's get 'em tomorrow, boys, we're gonna split and go back to Shea.' But when you're winning 3–2 in the ninth against the fucking mighty Yanks who've won three of the last four World Series and you lose it, you walk into the clubhouse, you're trying to be upbeat, but you're like, 'Fuck! Did we just . . . ugh!'"

Yankee Stadium stood for eight more years. For the rest of the ballpark's lifespan, an enlarged photo from Game 1 faced the doors of the press elevator on the loge level. It wasn't a shot of Jose Vizcaino, who got the winning single in the twelfth, or even of O'Neill—George Steinbrenner's beloved "Warrior"—who wore down Benitez in the ninth. It was an image of a shell-shocked Perez, his path to the plate blocked by catcher Jorge Posada, ensuring that all who covered the Yankees would get a final reminder, on their way to the press box, of just which team owned the city.

————

Some two decades later, the general manager of the 2000 Mets, Steve Phillips, was hosting a radio show on SiriusXM Radio with Eduardo Pérez. Each caller got a trivia question based on his or her favorite team. A Red Sox fan was asked to name the pitcher when the ball went through Bill Buckner's legs in the 1986 World Series.

"That would have been, oh man," the caller stammered. "It's either Stanley or Schiraldi."

He guessed Calvin Schiraldi, who gave up three singles with two outs. The answer was Bob Stanley, who allowed a game-tying wild pitch and then the infamous little roller up along first by Mookie Wilson.

There was so much going on, so many shards of madness to remember, that even die-hard fans might scramble the particulars. Here's what happened with two outs, the bases empty, and the Mets down by two in the bottom of the tenth: Single to center by Gary Carter. Single to left by Kevin Mitchell (who remembered that Schiraldi, his former minor league teammate, had once told him he could never handle his slider). Single by Ray Knight to score Carter. Stanley replaces Schiraldi, facing Wilson. Wild pitch gets past catcher Rich Gedman, Mitchell scores, tie game. Error by Buckner, Knight scores, game over, mayhem at Shea Stadium.

There are eight players in that scene, but Buckner is shorthand for all of it. Nobody forgets him. When Buckner died in 2019, columnists wrote that one error should not define a man's life. But we all used it to frame his story. That little ground ball never stopped rolling, following Buckner to the great beyond.

"He handled it amazingly well," said Bobby Valentine, his old minor league roommate. "But it killed him."

Some years after the error, Valentine and Buckner found themselves in a hospitality suite at a postseason event. Valentine introduced his friend to Frank Cashen, the general manager of the 1986 Mets. Cashen reacted like the fans at Shea in Game 7, when they greeted Buckner with a standing ovation.

"You're my favorite all-time Red Sox player!" Cashen exclaimed. Valentine was mortified. Buckner just walked away.

There was plenty to admire about Buckner, who played in four decades and never struck out three times in a game. The error is not his only indelible highlight: when Hank Aaron broke Babe Ruth's home run record against the Dodgers in 1974, the ball cleared the glove of a spry young left fielder scaling the wall in Atlanta. That was Buckner at his athletic peak: he was 24 that season and hit .315, with more steals (31) than strikeouts (24). He helped the Dodgers to the NL pennant and homered in the World Series.

Everything changed the next April when Buckner slid awkwardly into second base; he'd been trying to learn a new technique from teammate Davey Lopes but caught his foot under the bag and flipped over it. He needed two surgeries that year, and another in 1976 after a staph infection. When the Dodgers traded Buckner to the Cubs, his new team tried in vain to cancel the deal; the Cubs were not expecting their new first baseman to limp into spring training on a cane.*

What the Cubs didn't know was that Buckner had uncommon perseverance and integrity. He would hit .300 for them and win the 1980 batting title, risking it by playing on the season's final day with a five-point lead on Keith Hernandez. Buckner went hitless but still took the crown.

"Ted Williams told me when I was 19 that I was going to win the batting title," Buckner said that day. "But that was a long time ago, when I could run."

Buckner would come to believe that the injuries robbed him of a chance at 3,000 hits and the Hall of Fame. But he would remain a productive regular through that 1986 season, when he needed nine cortisone shots, like squirts of oil for the Tin Man, to keep going. The Red Sox needed him: he drove in 102 runs in the regular season, and then sparked the rally that saved their season. Three outs from

---

* The Cubs would trade Buckner to the Red Sox for Dennis Eckersley in 1984, and Buckner actually wore a batting glove stamped with a Cubs logo beneath the black MacGregor first baseman's mitt he used in Game 6.

elimination in the ALCS, down by three to the Angels on the road in Game 5, Buckner singled to lead off a four-run ninth.

Two games later, in the clincher at Fenway, he damaged his Achilles tendon by beating out an infield single. Buckner wore high-topped spikes to stay upright for the World Series, and by then he was icing his ankle, Achilles, back, elbow, and shoulder. It all looked a little ridiculous, but Buckner was determined to endure.

"Hey, if you think he runs funny, you ought to watch him walk," Red Sox reliever Joe Sambito told columnist Edwin Pope of the *Miami Herald*. "He walks like all the pieces are working independently of each other. Every step is an adventure."

That was after Game 5 against the Mets, when Buckner scored from second on a single and flopped onto the plate, a symbol of exhausted valor. At his Fenway locker after the win, he showed reporters a bottle of clear liquid sent from a fan—healing water from Egypt, supposedly. "If I die, you know the reason," Buckner cracked, taking a swig. He was a go-to quote for the writers all series, self-deprecating but prideful.

"I'm going to gut it out to the last possible moment," Buckner said. "When I [hurt] the tendon in the playoffs, I figured it wasn't just the World Series in doubt, it was my entire career. I know this: when I go, they're going to have to carry me off."

So Buckner's condition—and the Red Sox' gamble in trusting him—was already a prominent subplot, and Boston's own miracle comeback in Anaheim was still fresh. Those story lines converged at the frenzied finish of Game 6, when the Red Sox felt the same sort of pain they'd inflicted on the Angels, and Buckner—poor, limping Buckner—had been cruelly exposed at last.

The error itself was so easily understood, a routine task so obviously bungled, ending the game *like that*. Most fans can't relate to hesitating on a relay throw from center field. But a slow roller that skips through your legs to lose the game? That's the baseball version of a face-plant just before the finish line. In time, the error would symbolize everything that went wrong in Game 6, a touchstone for decades of Hub heartbreak.

"It's just the way the replay looks," Buckner told *The Boston Globe*, many years later. "You miss a ball, everybody walks off the field."

Wilson never gets enough credit for taking the at-bat of his life: 10 pitches, with any of the first seven representing a chance to end the season. The seventh, after two fouls with two strikes, was really the biggest play of the game—a fastball by Stanley that surprised Gedman by slicing down and in, not down and away. With the game tied, the ballpark all but burst; someone fired a roll of toilet paper from the upper deck, and when it clumped in a messy pile behind the plate, nobody bothered to clear it. Wilson slapped another foul, and another, and then second baseman Marty Barrett rushed to the mound: he'd had Knight picked off second, but Stanley hadn't seen him.

This was critical, as Buckner told *The Boston Globe*'s Stan Grossfeld in 2003:

> I saw Marty move over to second, so I moved way over toward the hole. Normally with Mookie, you would play up with a runner on second base. You play a little deeper because you don't want the ball to go through. So then he dribbled the ball down the first base line. The reason he would've beat it out had nothing to do with Stanley getting over there. It's because I was so far out of position, trying to cover the hole over there. An infield hit still would've had Knight on third base. I had run up a long way, but I don't remember feeling like I was rushed.
>
> I didn't feel any kind of tension to catch the ground ball. Usually, when you miss a ground ball, it's because you look up. I didn't look up. The ball hit . . . I'm pretty sure the ball hit something . . . because the ball didn't go underneath my glove. It went to the right of my glove. It took a little bit of a funny hop, bounced to the right a little bit. It wasn't like, you know, you feel rushed and you look up. It took a funny hop. I mean, it's funny. It's funny. What do I chalk it up to? Fate. That's part of the game.

The moment it happened, naturally, Buckner was mad at himself. But almost instantly, he told Grossfeld, excitement replaced despair:

> The second thought was, "Oh, man, we get to play the seventh game of the World Series." I mean, I was having so much fun. You're trying to win, obviously, but I mean, if we won the game,

it was over with. I'm thinking, "We get to play another game, and we'll win." There was no doubt in my mind we were going to win the last game.

As rain washed away Game 7 the next night, Buckner got a call in his hotel room from Reggie Jackson, then of the Angels, telling him not to let a near-miss defeat the team. That's what had happened to the Angels, Jackson said, and the Red Sox were too good for that. Buckner appreciated the call, and sure enough, after stoically absorbing the mocking cheers, he singled in his first at-bat of Game 7. He singled again in the eighth, after the Red Sox had lost their three-run lead, and was due up next when Jesse Orosco fanned Barrett to end it.

Hard as it is to believe now—when runners-up get roasted on social media for giving out league champion rings, continuing a long tradition—the city of Boston held a parade for the Red Sox after they lost in New York. Buckner was not looking forward to it and expected the worst.

"This whole city hates me," he told his wife, Jody, on his way into the city, as Peter Gammons reported in *Sports Illustrated*. "Is this what I'm going to be remembered for? Is this what I've killed myself for all these years? Is a whole season ruined because of a bad hop?"

Buckner expected a very small crowd that would boo. Instead, some 750,000 fans lined the route from Copley Square to City Hall and cheered wildly for Buckner, who lifted his cap and blew kisses. He was not scheduled to speak, but the fans' reaction so touched and surprised him that he asked to say a few words.

"We needed this," Buckner told the roaring fans, shaking his fists by his sides with gusto. "We're gonna be back next year, believe me!"

It was a winning line on a crisp and sunny New England day, but the 1987 Red Sox never even managed a winning record after mid-April. On their way to a fifth-place finish, they visited Shea Stadium for a charity game in May. McNamara ducked the media, and Schiraldi and Stanley, who were not scheduled to pitch, stayed home. Buckner showed up.

"It was a little like Richard Nixon spending the night at the Watergate apartment complex," Dan Shaughnessy wrote in the next day's

Boston Globe, only Buckner had no reason to be ashamed. He gamely took questions from the press, and made a joke when someone mentioned Mookie: "I asked him to hit me some ground balls," Buckner joked.

When he really did meet with Wilson before a game in 1989—when Buckner was with Kansas City and Wilson with Toronto—Buckner used that very line. He and Wilson would become friends and partners on the card show circuit; Buckner would say that he made enough money signing autographs to put his kids through college.

"My wife wasn't real happy about me signing that photo with Mookie because of how that moment would go on to affect our whole family," Buckner told Erik Sherman in *Two Sides of Glory.* "At first I agreed with her, saying, 'No way; I'm not going to do this.' But then I thought, 'I need to get something back from this torture, man!'"

Buckner finished his playing career with a handful of games for the Red Sox in 1990; the fans gave him a standing ovation on opening day. But a few years later, in Pawtucket, Rhode Island, while signing autographs as a coach for the Syracuse Chiefs, Buckner snapped when a fan made a wisecrack: "Don't give him the ball. He'd just drop it anyway." Buckner grabbed the fan by the collar and pushed him against a wall, and the incident made national news. Soon Buckner moved his family from Andover, Massachusetts, to Idaho, citing the incessant reminders of his error.

That comment fueled a belief that Buckner had literally fled for the hills to escape vengeful fans. In truth, he'd owned a ranch in Boise since the '70s and had always planned to retire there. He bought and sold real estate in the area, invested in auto dealerships bearing his name, hunted elk with a bow and arrow. He coached his son's Little League team and ran a baseball camp.

Buckner had perspective on real tragedy. He was 14 when his father died, and that, he told Grossfeld, was the worst moment in his life. A misplay in the World Series did not compare.

"I like the way things are going," Buckner said. "I don't sit in the woods and think about it. Ever."

Grossfeld had visited Buckner because the Red Sox were on the verge of returning to the World Series. The franchise had lost 13 postseason games in a row starting with Game 6 at Shea, but the swaggering 2003 team seemed different. Though the Yankees would win that year's pennant, the Red Sox went all the way in 2004.

Buckner heard plenty of talk about redemption then, but chafed at the idea; players never apologize for physical mistakes, because they understand the nature of the game. He turned down an invitation to the ring ceremony at Fenway on opening day in 2005 but accepted three years later, after another Red Sox title.

The way Buckner saw it, he didn't need to be forgiven; he had to forgive his antagonizers. On a glorious sunny day, he emerged from the Green Monster to long, heartfelt cheers from the fans, the players, and New England champions like Tedy Bruschi, Bobby Orr, and Bill Russell. He stood tall on the mound in his crisp Red Sox jersey, basking in the applause and wiping away a tear. Then he threw a strike to his old teammate, Dwight Evans.

"I really had to forgive, not the fans of Boston, per se, but I would have to say in my heart I had to forgive the media, for what they put me and my family through," Buckner said later, after an emotional pause in the interview room. "So, you know, I've done that and I'm over that."

———

There was one last frontier for Buckner to cross. The ordeal had given him a measure of celebrity beyond baseball, a kind of cultural resonance few athletes ever achieve. The broad strokes of his story were powerful enough to melt the acerbic old heart of a man not exactly known for compassion: Larry David, a Yankees fan who had rejoiced when the Red Sox blew Game 6.

"I watched it at Kramer's apartment," David says, matter-of-factly. "I never hated the Mets, like most Yankee fans—but I hated the Red Sox, of course. So I was rooting for the Mets, and I loved it."

David is talking about the real Kramer—his buddy Kenny Kramer, the inspiration for the Michael Richards character on *Seinfeld*. David cocreated that show with Jerry Seinfeld, and then devised *Curb Your Enthusiasm* for HBO. David plays a fictionalized version of himself on *Curb*, oblivious to social norms and seemingly incapable of empathy.

At his core he's a good guy, but he's so self-absorbed that he often comes off as a jerk.

The real Larry's a nicer fellow, but when forced to choose between syrupy and bitter, he tends to obey his comic instincts. Sweet isn't funny—which is why, when a writer named Pat McNalley pitched a *Curb* episode casting Buckner as the hero, David almost flipped the script. Where was the humor in Buckner catching a baby falling from a burning building?

"I loved the idea," David explains. "I mean, I always had something in my heart for Buckner. I felt so much sympathy for him for what he went through. I just thought it was awful. I felt sorry for him, to tell you the truth. And so, when I read that, I thought, 'Oh my God, what a fantastic idea.'

"Of course, being the mental defective that I am, my initial reaction was, 'How about if he drops the baby?'"

David laughed at his twisted revision. It was absurdly impractical, and he knew it.

"I had to give it to Buckner to read because we needed him to do the show, and I didn't figure he had that much of a sense of humor that he would be OK with dropping the baby," David says. "Although you gotta admit, it is pretty funny."

Even with Buckner as the hero, the episode, which aired on September 4, 2011, would have to revolve around the error. To set it up, Larry is playing softball in Central Park and lets a ball skip through his legs to lose the championship. ("You Bucknered me!" screams the irate coach.) The error makes Larry feel bonded to Buckner when he meets him at an autograph show, and they become fast friends.

But life's not so easy being Bill Buckner. He's cursed on the street, booted from a Kaddish—"Herman here is from Boston. He's a big Red Sox fan and he can't be in the same room with Bill Buckner"—and berated after dropping a ball with Wilson's autograph out a window.

Buckner projects a casual ease through his scenes, as if years of scorn had created a force field around him. He agreed to appear as part of a deal with David, who cast Buckner's daughter, Brittany, in another episode ("She did a great job," David says, "so that was an easy trade for me"). He also found the ending irresistible.

Strolling through Manhattan, Buckner notices a crowd gathered on the street, gaping at a panicking woman clutching a baby in the fifth-story window of a burning building. Firefighters hold a canvas off the ground and plead with the woman to drop the baby to safety. But when she does, the baby bounces high off the canvas, imperiled again.

As the helpless child hurtles toward the pavement, Buckner springs to action, breaking from the crowd and diving to snatch the baby in midair. Cradling the bundle to his chest, Buckner has saved the day. The gapers around him go wild, lifting him onto their shoulders, and the old ballplayer beams, triumphant at last in New York.

David calls it one of the very best moments in the series. All joking aside, he admits, he desperately wanted to make the episode for a very simple reason.

"Because I did want to redeem him," David says. "I did want him to catch that baby. And I have to tell you, when I was editing that show, every time he caught that baby, and it was in slow motion, I would actually well up. I mean, it was emotional watching it for me, almost every single time.

"It's never happened before, but there was something about that guy that engendered that. I can't explain it. He just made you feel for him, something in his personality. It felt like everything that he'd been through, he was carrying with him. Now, I don't know if he was like that before that World Series error. I don't know what his personality was like, so maybe a lot of this was in my head. But that's how I felt."

Buckner would later tell David that he loved the episode, too. Filming it was fun, he told Sherman, a release from the usual nonsense. Maybe he didn't need to be redeemed, not exactly. But it's always satisfying to win, and it takes a special man to melt the heart of a guy like Larry David.

"It was maybe one of the few times in my life I did do something good," David says. "I felt like, yeah, this might be the nicest thing I've ever done."

Game 7

Potato Chips and a
Glass of Champagne

The Ultimate World Series Lists

Behind the microphone for a close game in the 1980 World Series, Vin Scully could not help himself. "One and two the count," he said, across the CBS Radio airwaves. "Boy, I love this game. I don't mean just this particular game, but this game of baseball is just magnificent."

That kind of enduring, endearing passion is one reason Scully stands as the most widely beloved and longest-serving broadcaster in baseball history. He could surely fill his own book with personal World Series memories—but lucky for me, he shared a few in a pregame conversation in the Dodgers' booth a few years ago.

To begin our chapter of wide-ranging lists and tidbits, pull up a chair and enjoy these three Vin Scully World Series memories, in his words:

Describing why he grew up a Giants fan in the Bronx,
Scully recalled Game 2 of the 1936 World Series,
an 18–4 Yankees victory over the Giants:

"My school was at 175th Street and St. Nicholas Avenue, I guess, and the Polo Grounds was at 155th. I was a member of the Police Athletic League and the Catholic Youth Organization, so I could go to a lot of the games for free. School, in those days, we got out about 2:30, and the games were always 3:15—no night games, of course. So I could walk the 20 blocks from my school to the Polo Grounds and see, oh my gosh, a whole bunch of games. There was an occasional time when I'd see an entire homestand, either free or I would sell my soft drink bottle—you got your deposit back—and I would sit in the bleachers for 55 cents. So that's where I grew up, in the Polo Grounds, and I was growing up a rabid Giants fan. I worshipped Mel Ott.

"What happened was, I was 9 years old, and I was walking home from my grammar school in Washington Heights, and there was a Chinese laundry. And the Chinese laundryman had the line score on a piece of paper on the window of the laundry. I don't know what number game it was, but the Yankees beat the Giants and they scored in double figures. I mean, they just crushed them. And here is this nine-year-old, knowing nothing, and visibly, I can see it, I stopped and looked at the line score and my first thought was, 'Oh, those poor Giants.' And that's why I became a Giant fan."

Describing the Dodgers' celebration after winning
Game 7 at Yankee Stadium in 1955 for their
first and only championship in Brooklyn:

"The one thing I remember, Walter O'Malley and several of the other executives, they took me in a car, so I wasn't on the team bus. And they took me to the Lexington Hotel, and they had a suite and we sat around for a while, and then we scattered because we were having the victory party in Brooklyn at the Bossard Hotel. And I had a date, so I went to pick her up. And it was an interesting feeling, in Manhattan it was the fall and football was in the air, two hours after the baseball game, it was winter, it was football. We drove through the tunnel, and it was like V-J Day and V-E Day all rolled into one in Brooklyn. They were dancing in the streets. It was just one monumental block party. And when we got near the Bossard Hotel, the streets were lined with people. They had sawhorses to restrain them—although the people were very good, they weren't about to do anything—but they took our cars about a block from the hotel, and we had to walk down the street into the hotel, like you were in a parade, with people cheering. I know the girl that I was with, a terrific girl named Joan Ganz—she went on to invent *Sesame Street*—and we walked down the street together into the Bossard Hotel where all hell was breaking loose, and that was amazing."

Describing a much more subdued toast
the next time the Dodgers clinched a
championship at Yankee Stadium, in 1981:

"I remember in '81, I did the game, my wife was with me, and I thought I would celebrate with the team. I guess Peter O'Malley never liked to turn them loose—he was afraid he'd never get them back—so when they won at Yankee Stadium, the team left town. I was doing football in those days as well, so I was leaving the next day to do a game somewhere. And here's my wife and I saying, 'Wow, we don't have anybody to celebrate with.' And we were staying at George Steinbrenner's hotel, the Carlyle, and I remember I went into the bar and I said to the bartender, 'Could I buy a bottle of Champagne?' So the bartender, looking around, he said, 'Yeah, I'd be happy to do it, as long as Mr. Steinbrenner doesn't see me helping you celebrate.' So we went up and ordered potato chips and a glass of Champagne, that was our celebration."

THE THREE HALL OF FAMERS
WHO FELL TO RED OLDHAM

Red Oldham had been a Pittsburgh Pirate for two months when he took the mound for the ninth inning of Game 7 in 1925. He'd spent most of the season with minor league teams in Vernon, California, and Des Moines, Iowa, and had not appeared in the majors in three years. The Pirates promoted him in August, mainly to help with some doubleheaders down the stretch. He faced 233 batters, struck out only 10, and did not appear in the first six games of the World Series.

But Game 7 was wild. The Senators had lost twice to the Pirates' Vic Aldridge, but this time they knocked him out in the first inning. Two relievers settled things down, but the Pirates needed a pinch hitter in their go-ahead rally off Walter Johnson in the bottom of the eighth. Manager Bill McKechnie turned to Oldham to preserve a 9–7 lead in the ninth.

In the span of 12 pitches, Oldham retired three Hall of Famers in order to win the championship. Here's how he recounted those matchups to the *Pittsburgh Post-Gazette* the next spring:

Sam Rice: "Well, old Sam came up and looked at a fast one on the inside for a strike. The next was a fast one between Sam and the plate for a ball. Rice tried to bunt the next one, which was a swifty on the outside. He fouled it. With two strikes and one ball, I thought I would loosen him up a bit, and I wasted one on him, which might have made him a bit nervous. Then I came through the middle with a fast one, and Sam was called out."

Bucky Harris: "Harris wasn't up there very long. We slipped two fast pitches over the plate and he looked at both, so we had Bucky in a hole. The next offering was a fastball and Bucky hit it smartly to [second baseman] Eddie Moore on a line. That left nobody but Goose between us and the victory."

Goose Goslin: "Our first shot to Goslin was a hook on the inside. Goose had a country cut at the ball, but he fouled it. The next pitch also was a slowed-up curve. The ball broke over the plate with Goose looking at it. With the count two strikes and no balls, we broke a curve outside, the sphere being beyond the plate far enough to be a ball. The next was another slow hook that broke across the plate, and the battle was over."

Goslin grumbled at the plate umpire, Barry McCormick, as fans poured from the stands at Forbes Field. It would be 87 years before another pitcher got a called third strike to end the World Series: the Giants' Sergio Romo, who shook off a slider and sneaked a fastball past Miguel Cabrera to finish a sweep in 2012.

THREE STOLEN CAPS OF THE 1960s

For a few years, most notably in the 1960s, a truly bizarre phenomenon sprang up at the end of the World Series: umpires swiping players' hats. Friendly collegiality? Brazen entitlement? You be the judge.

1960: As he rounded second base after slaying the Yankees with a Game 7 homer, the Pirates' Bill Mazeroski clutched his helmet in his right hand and windmilled it in triumph. He switched the helmet to his left hand as he hit third, and clutched it tight as fans and teammates swarmed him on those final joyous steps at Forbes Field.

Everyone wanted a piece of Mazeroski, and the plate umpire, Bill Jackowski, succeeded—he asked Mazeroski for the helmet, and the hero obliged. Jackowski's family donated it to the Hall of Fame in 1989.

1962: Bottom of the ninth, Game 7 at Candlestick Park in San Francisco, the winning run on second base, and up steps Willie McCovey. At this moment of extreme tension, Yankees second baseman Bobby Richardson was startled by an odd request. "I was down in my position, ready," Richardson told me in 2007, "and the NL ump [Al Barlick] said, 'Hey, Rich, can I have your cap for my little cousin?'" Richardson said yes, and then got back to work. After McCovey lashed a foul to right, he decided to shift a bit to his left, positioning himself perfectly to snare a screaming liner to end the series. And the very first thing Richardson did at that moment of glory was dutifully hand a souvenir to Barlick. Only then did he rush—capless—to join his teammates in celebration.

1967: At least Jackowski and Barlick had the courtesy to ask. After Game 7 at Fenway Park in Boston, when St. Louis's Bob Gibson struck out George Scott to win the championship, umpire Augie Donatelli simply reached into a throng of Cardinals and plucked the cap off Julian Javier's head. The thievery surprised Javier, who didn't mind—he could easily get a new one, he figured—but also didn't forget. Javier told Benjamin Hochman of the *St. Louis Post-Dispatch* that he tracked down his hat some 15 years later at a place called El Cap (appropriately enough) in St. Petersburg, Florida: "Augie Donatelli had a bar there, and I said: 'Augie! Where's my hat?' And he said, 'Right there! On top of the bar!' And he got it right down." Javier let Donatelli keep it, and the joint is still in business. But the cap at El Cap, alas, is long gone.

THE BEST FIRST PITCH EVER— AND OTHER NOTABLES

For the fiftieth anniversary of the first World Series, Major League Baseball invited Cy Young to Yankee Stadium to christen the event in 1953. From his spot in the stands along the third base railing—flanked by others from the first Classic, including Fred Clarke and Bill Dinneen—the 86-year-old legend made a stiff lob to Yogi Berra.

According to the next day's Rochester *Democrat and Chronicle,* a veteran scribe was not impressed: "That," Grantland Rice told Red Smith, "is not the motion I knew in 1905."

Even the most elegant writers, it seems, can be a little heartless. But few could question the majesty and accuracy of another first pitch at Yankee Stadium, by President George W. Bush before Game 3 in 2001, which ranks as the most stirring of all time.

Just seven weeks after the destruction of the World Trade Center in lower Manhattan, Bush's visit required intense security: bomb-sniffing dogs in the clubhouse, Secret Service men disguised as umpires, military jets overhead, snipers poised on rooftops. Derek Jeter was hitting in the indoor batting cage when Bush dropped by to say hello. Jeter asked where he planned to make his throw, and Bush said from the base of the mound. Wrong answer, Jeter replied: if you don't do it from the top of the mound, the fans will boo.

Bush agreed, and as Jeter left the batting cage, he gave the president another warning: "Don't bounce it."

That was a distinct possibility. A decade earlier, when he owned the Rangers, Bush had watched his father, President George H. W. Bush, one-hop his first pitch on opening day in Texas. A year later, in Baltimore, the forty-first president did it again to christen Oriole Park at Camden Yards, wincing and throwing his hands up in dismay. No sitting president had ever thrown a first pitch from the field at the World Series—Dwight Eisenhower had done so from the stands, to Roy Campanella, at Ebbets Field in 1956—and, as Bush told the umpires in their dressing room, he had never even *been* to a World Series. Jeter's friendly advice, he said, only added to the pressure.

But with a bulletproof vest under his FDNY jacket, Bush strode from the Yankees dugout to the top of the mound, raising his right arm and signaling to the crowd—and the world—with a thumbs-up. Then he rocked and tossed to Todd Greene, the Yankees' reserve catcher, who was crouched behind the plate. The arcing pitch tailed right over the middle.

"There's been celebrities and politicians, including presidents, who go out there to throw the first pitch, and whether they take it for granted or not, it doesn't look very athletic," Greene says. "President Bush went out and threw a perfect strike. I think it was pretty dynamic, for not just him but as a symbol for our country: 'Here I am, not only am I coming out here, I'm throwing a dot right down the middle.'"

How did Greene, a journeyman who had started the season in the minors, end up catching the most famous first pitch in baseball history? The Yankees had plenty of All-Stars, including their catcher, Jorge Posada. Yet for all of the planning it took to get the president up on that mound, nobody knew who would stand 60 feet, six inches away.

"Jorge was still in the pen, because Rocket [Roger Clemens] was pitching that night and he took forever in the bullpen," Greene says. "So President Bush is getting ready to go out on the field and there's no catcher. It's just natural for the backup, so I grabbed my glove and ran out there. There was no buildup to have any apprehension or anything."

Greene played only a few months for the Yankees, a small slice of an 11-year career. But people still remember him for his cameo that night in 2001, when the president used the World Series stage to reassure an anxious nation.

"I can't remember a time in my life when we were more united as a community of citizens for our country," Greene says. "And to have him walk out on top of the mound and salute the crowd with the thumbs-up and his head held high, it was kind of a symbol of: 'You're not going to intimidate us and make us crawl in a hole. Here we are, and we're going to come back.'"

Other notable first pitches:

First a righty, then a lefty: Lefty Grove

In 1972, after California governor Ronald Reagan tossed the first ball in Oakland before Game 3, Lefty Grove—star of the Athletics' last World Series team, in 1931—got the nod for Game 4. The press was still buzzing about Rollie Fingers fanning Johnny Bench on a fake intentional walk the night before. A *Boston Globe* columnist, Harold Kaese, asked Grove how many of his 2,266 strikeouts had come this way. "None," Grove replied.

Your pitch, Mom: President Jimmy Carter

Jimmy Carter did not throw out a first pitch at the World Series during his administration, but his mother, Lillian, did, before Game 4 in Los Angeles in 1977. Carter finally made first pitches in the 1992 opener and the 1995 clincher, both for his hometown Braves.

Most interesting year: 1985

This was the only instance since 1975 in which no former players threw a first pitch. Among the eclectic group were Coretta Scott King, Missouri senator Thomas Eagleton, astronaut Sally Ride, and longtime Kansas City sportswriter Joe McGuff.

Perfect attendance record: Carl Yastrzemski

He doesn't like to stick around for the games, but whenever the Red Sox host Game 1 of the World Series, they know the great Yaz will be there to toss the first pitch. He did it for the opening games in 2004, 2007, 2013, and 2018—each one a Boston victory.

Longest wait: Joe Oeschger

Oeschger pitched for the Phillies in 1915 but didn't appear in the World Series. He never got there in a 12-year career but finally made it in 1983, at age 91. Oeschger was the last surviving member of the Phillies' first pennant winner, and did the honors before Game 3 at the Vet.

A pitch before the fall: Sammy Sosa, Mark McGwire, Barry Bonds

Before admissions and leaks and grand juries, baseball proudly showed off its steroids-fueled sluggers at the World Series. Bonds threw a first pitch in Arizona in 2001, as McGwire did in San Diego and Sosa in New York, both in 1998. Sosa was actually feted with a ticker tape parade down the Canyon of Heroes in lower Manhattan a few hours before his pitch.

NATIONAL ANTHEMS

When the World Series comes to their hometown, a few rock stars know they'll have a microphone waiting. The Mets have turned to Billy Joel three times (1986, 2000, 2015), and the Red Sox have welcomed James Taylor four times (2004, 2007, 2013, 2018). The Phillies have twice called on Daryl Hall and Patti LaBelle, and often, stars of network shows just happen to stop by—Zooey Deschanel, from Fox's *New Girl,* performed in Texas in 2011 and in Detroit the next year.

Most prolific

Robert Merrill, the baritone star of the Metropolitan Opera, performed it 10 times at the World Series from 1976 through 2000: nine at Yankee Stadium and once in Baltimore.

Greatest longevity

The country music icon Charley Pride stands alone here. If not for a bum elbow, though, he might have been pitching in World Series games, not singing before them.

"If you put my windup right next to Bob Gibson, it's the exact same windup," Pride told me in 2020, six months before he died at age 87.

Pride did pitch in the Negro National League and briefly for a Cincinnati farm team. He was cut from the Angels' first spring training camp in 1961, run by another future Country Music Hall of Famer, the team owner Gene Autry.

"They sent me packing with a tuna fish sandwich and an orange," Pride said. "Mr. Autry was eating a hamburger out there on the porch. I said, 'Mr. Autry, don't let them send me home. My arm will come around!' He said, 'Well, I own the team but I don't run it.' Marv Grissom was the pitching coach. He came to me and said, 'Charley, you ain't got a major league arm.'"

His voice, however, would be plenty good for the big leagues. Pride performed the anthem in four decades and four ballparks: 1976 in Cincinnati, 1980 in Philadelphia, 1991 in Minnesota, and 2010 in Texas, where he was part owner of the Rangers. He'd been practicing the song since his boyhood in Mississippi.

"I remember walking to school four miles there and four miles back, I'd sing for most of that and sing the national anthem," he said, and as for his style, he preferred straightforward.

"I think I do the national anthem probably better than anybody you want to do it," he said. "I always do it a cappella, sometimes I do it in a different key. I just grab it and do it. I don't try to soup it up or put some little curlicues on some notes. The best way to do it is just do it straight."

Most controversial

The slow jazz interpretation of Jose Feliciano, with a guitar accompaniment, was stirring or startling before Game 5 at Tiger Stadium in 1968, depending on your perspective. Feliciano's unique spin on the stodgy standard was front-page news in the next day's *Detroit Free Press,* and outraged fans called it "disgusting," "disgraceful," and "belittling."

Feliciano, then only 23 years old, was invited by legendary Tigers broadcaster Ernie Harwell, who defended Feliciano's right to interpret the song as he pleased. Feliciano, a native of Puerto Rico, felt compelled to defend his love of country.

"America is young now," he explained, "and I thought maybe the anthem could be revived."

The commercial market responded. Released as a single, Feliciano's World Series performance spent five weeks on the Billboard Hot 100 chart, a first for the national anthem.

TEN THINGS WE STILL HAVEN'T SEEN

We've seen players end the World Series with homers. But until Jorge Soler in 2021, nobody had ever started the show by going deep in the top of the first inning of Game 1.

"It's pretty amazing we can come up with all of these things," Adam Duvall, Soler's teammate with the Atlanta Braves, told my colleague

Scott Miller in Houston that night. "Even more amazing is that the game has been played this long and there are still the first players to do something. That's pretty cool. I guess there will be a day when there are no firsts anymore."

Maybe so, Adam, because we've already seen a lot of crazy stuff: an unassisted triple play, a perfect game, even an immaculate inning (by the Royals' Danny Jackson in 1985). But there's still a long list of things that have never been done in the World Series. Here are just 10.

Hit for the cycle: Lou Brock had a double, triple, and homer in 1968 (Game 4), but somehow he didn't manage a single.

Four-homer game: Two players have come to bat after already hitting three home runs in a World Series game—Babe Ruth in 1926 (Game 4) and Pablo Sandoval in 2012 (Game 1). Alas, Ruth walked and Sandoval singled.

Comeback from 0–3 to win: Hard to believe, but no team has even forced a Game 6 after losing the first three games of the World Series. The last team to even force a fifth game was the 1970 Reds, who bowed in five to the Orioles.

Position player pitching in relief: We're talking about a mop-up man scenario. Babe Ruth, of course, was a dazzling starter for the Red Sox in 1916 and 1918. (He also spent two innings as a left fielder in the 1918 World Series.)

Thrown out at the plate to end the World Series: There was, however, an ending like this in Game 5 in 1972. The A's had a chance to clinch the title in Game 5, and pitcher Blue Moon Odom (serving a pinch runner) tried to tie the game by tagging up on a foul pop to Joe Morgan of the Reds. Morgan slipped but regained his balance and nailed Odom on a close play to end the game. "It cost me 500 bucks because I bumped the umpire," Odom told me before an A's spring training game in 2020. "If they had had replays like they have today, it would have come back safe."

Walk-off grand slam or walk-off walk: Incredibly, though, these happened in consecutive games to close out the 1999 NLCS between the Mets and Braves (technically, Robin Ventura's grand slam was ruled a single because Todd Pratt swarmed him on the bases before he could finish his trot).

A Game 7 for the Phillies: Fifteen of the 16 franchises that existed in 1903 have played a World Series Game 7, including the White Sox in a best-of-nine format in 1919. Nine expansion franchises have also reached Game 7, yet somehow the Phillies never have. They've won in six, lost in six, won in five, lost in five, and lost in four. But they've never gotten to a seventh game—not even in the NLCS.

Three home runs in a row: It feels like this should have happened in the homer-happy series of 2002 (Angels vs. Giants) or 2017 (Astros vs. Dodgers), but no.

Comeback from three-run deficit in the ninth inning or later: The 1929 Cubs blew an eight-run lead in the seventh inning of Game 4 to the A's. But every team that has ever led by at least three runs in the ninth inning or later has held on to win.

Game 9: It could have happened when the World Series was a best-of-nine event, in 1903, 1919, 1920, and 1921. But none of those series went the distance, making Game 9 the winner-take-all showdown that never was.

ALL-TIME WORLD SERIES TEAMS

The Yankees throw off this exercise with their 40 pennants, so let's break this into two teams: one with Yankees and one without. Not sure which would win, but I'd love to see them play a best-of-seven series.

(Note: These are intended to be functional, 26-man rosters, with backup infielders, outfielders, and catcher and at least a couple of relief specialists per team to go with starters and swingmen. I limited this to players who appeared in at least two World Series.)

ALL-TIME WORLD SERIES TEAM (no Yankees)

C   Pat Borders—Hit safely in 11 of 12 games and won MVP in 1992.

1B   Jimmie Foxx—Homered and hit .333 or better in all three series he played.

2B   Eddie Collins—Played in six series in the 1910s, batting .400
in three.

SS   Edgar Renteria—Walk-off hit in 1997, MVP in 2010 (also
made the last out in 2004).

3B   Pablo Sandoval—And not just the three-homer game; also
went 12-for-28 (.429) in 2014.

LF   Lou Brock—Hit .391/.424/.655 in three series, tying Collins's
record for steals (14).

CF   George Springer—"I understand the magnitude of the games,"
Springer once told me, "but at the same time, if you can't enjoy
it, I don't know what to tell you." He has seven homers in 14
World Series games.

RF   Roberto Clemente—How divine was Clemente in the 1971
World Series? The organist at Three Rivers Stadium played
"Jesus Christ Superstar" on his way to the plate.

DH   David Ortiz—"I was always concerned about going home
without a trophy; it was something I used to have nightmares
about," Ortiz said in 2022, on the night he was elected to
the Hall of Fame. "It was the ride-or-die type of situation."
In each of his three World Series, Big Papi rode away with a
trophy.

Bench: Hank Aaron, Lance Berkman, Marquis Grissom, Pepper
Martin, Tim McCarver, Paul Molitor

P   Jack Billingham—Did it all for the Big Red Machine: starter,
middleman, closer, 0.36 ERA.

P   Harry Brecheen—The Bumgarner of the 1940s: very good in
the regular season, otherworldly in October.

P   Madison Bumgarner—He's also thrown two shutouts in wild-card games, just for fun.

P   Rollie Fingers—Collected 100 outs across 16 relief outings for Oakland—and his elbow injury in 1982 probably cost the Brewers the championship in a tight World Series with the Cardinals.

P   Bob Gibson—Best big-game pitcher of all time: nine starts, 81 innings, two MVPs.

P   Lefty Grove—Three complete game wins as a starter, three shutout outings in relief.

P   Sandy Koufax—Even in defeat, he was astounding. Four complete game victories: 0.75 ERA. Four appearances in Dodger losses: 1.29 ERA.

P   Jon Lester—Close call over his 2007 Boston teammate, Curt Schilling; both were 4–1 and led two franchises to titles.

P   Christy Mathewson—Three shutouts in 1905, then a lot of tough luck: eight starts, 1.33 ERA, 2–5 record.

P   Babe Ruth—Pitched only for the Red Sox in the World Series; his first start was a 14-inning CG.

P   Duane Ward—Worked in all eight Blue Jays victories and none of their losses.

ALL-TIME WORLD SERIES TEAM (Yankees)

C   Thurman Munson—Hit .373 and also coined a teammate's all-time great nickname: "It was after a game against the Tigers, and Thurman was grumpy and didn't want to talk to the press," Reggie Jackson says. "He said, 'Go down there and talk to

Mr. October.' It was almost October, and I'd hit a home run and driven in my 100th run for that year, and it stuck after that. The nickname really was born on that day."

1B   Lou Gehrig—Won six of his seven series, hitting 10 homers with a .361 average and .483 OBP.

2B   Billy Martin—His 1953 performance was an all-timer: .500/.520/.958, walk-off hit to end the series in Game 6.

SS   Derek Jeter—Batting average in his seven World Series: .250, .353, .353, .409, .148, .346, .407 (and in 2001, the year he hit .148, he had a walk-off home run in Game 4).

3B   Bobby Brown—The future cardiologist and AL president played in four World Series, won them all, and hit .439.

LF   Babe Ruth—Yes, he's on both teams. He's the Babe.

CF   Mickey Mantle—Actually hit better in World Series the Yankees lost (.290) than he did in those they won (.234). But his 18 homers are a record.

RF   Reggie Jackson—So great in 1977 that he actually got two rings; Balfour made him a special one with an extra diamond in the center of the NY logo.

DH   Hideki Matsui—What a way to end his Yankees career: 6 RBI in the 2009 World Series clincher, tying Bobby Richardson's single-game World Series record.

Bench: Yogi Berra, Scott Brosius, Earle Combs, Charlie Keller, Lou Piniella, Bobby Richardson

P   Roger Clemens—The infamous bat toss obscures his brilliance for the Yanks: 3–0, 1.50 ERA in five starts.

P   Whitey Ford—Holds World Series records for wins (10), starts (22), innings (146), and strikeouts (94). Had a 2.03 ERA through his first 18 starts and finished at 2.71.

P   Ron Guidry—Lined up to pitch Game 7 after complete-game wins in '77 and '78, but both times the Yankees won in six. Also starred in the 1981 opener.

P   Waite Hoyt—Worked 27 innings and allowed no earned runs in the Yanks' first World Series (1921).

P   Eddie Lopat, Vic Raschi, Allie Reynolds—How did the Yankees win a record five consecutive championships from 1949 through 1953? These three were the biggest reason, working 70.5 percent of the Yankees' innings in those World Series. The trio combined for 15 of the Yankees' 20 victories and a 2.39 ERA.

P   Jeff Nelson—Made 16 relief appearances (15 scoreless) and never lost a lead.

P   Monte Pearson—Each of the Yankees' victorious World Series from 1936 through '39 included a win by Pearson, who nearly no-hit the Reds in 1939.

P   Mariano Rivera—Pitched more than one inning in 18 of his record 24 appearances.

P   Red Ruffing—Made 10 starts, but this stretch stands out: five complete game wins in a row, with a 1.20 ERA, from 1937 through '41.

SERIES + SLOGANS = SWAG

When I covered the Mariners for the *Seattle Post-Intelligencer*, my colleague Jim Street wore an Oakland A's World Series ring from 1972.

Jim had covered the team as a beat writer for the *San Jose Mercury News*—and for that, the A's eccentric owner, Charles O. Finley, gave him a ring. On its side was a cryptic equation: "S+S=S," which Jim explained was a favorite expression of Finley's, meaning sweat plus sacrifice equals success.

That was the first instance of a team engraving a slogan on its championship ring. A few more would follow in the 1970s: the Reds included their nickname, "Big Red Machine," on their rings in 1975 and 1976, and the Pirates etched "We Are Family" on theirs in 1979, in honor of their theme song by Sister Sledge.

The trend didn't extend to the 1980s, but it's come back in a big way ever since. Here are some of the inscriptions teams have included on their rings over the last few decades.

1990 Reds: "Wire to Wire," commemorating the Reds' season-long stay in first place.

1992 Blue Jays: "4,028,318," the team's home attendance, which was then an all-time major league record.

1994 Expos: "Land Of Opportunity"—alas, this exists only on a poster, commissioned by GM Kevin Malone, of the ring he wanted to make for having baseball's best record in the strike year. Players had no interest, and the ring was never produced.

1995 Braves: "Team of the '90s," a bold but accurate claim if you go by pennants, not championships, in the 1990s.

1997 Marlins: "One Heartbeat"—and owner Wayne Huizenga silenced it by immediately gutting his high-priced roster.

1999 Yankees: "The Century's Team," fitting for the franchise that won 25 titles in the 1900s.

2001 Diamondbacks: "Fastest Ever," referring to their record four-year sprint from expansion team to champions.

2004 Red Sox: "Greatest Comeback In History," for the team that lost the first three games of the ALCS to the Yankees, then roared back to win eight in a row.

2011 Cardinals: "Happy Flight," a rallying cry for a team that won 17 consecutive getaway days (the last game before a flight) on its way to the World Series.

2013 Red Sox: "Bearded Brothers," in honor of the hairy bunch that bonded over the "Boston Strong" slogan (which is also on the ring).

2016 Cubs: "We Never Quit"—and they didn't, winning three elimination games to vanquish a 108-year curse.

2017 Astros: "Earned History," which became truly embarrassing after the revelation that they'd cheated by illegally stealing signs.

2018 Red Sox: "Damage Done," a saying that trolls Yankees' GM Brian Cashman, who claimed during the season that the Yankees were the only team to do damage against Boston.

2019 Nationals: "Go 1–0 Everyday," a mantra of manager Dave Martinez, who also told the team to "stay in the fight" after starting 19–31. "Fight Finished" is engraved on the ring, too.

2021 Braves: "Battle Won" and "For The A," meaning Atlanta, appear on the ring, but there's also a more provocative engraving: "We Are Those . . . ," referring to Joc Pederson's speech at the victory parade: *We are those motherfuckers!*" (Crass, sure, but the fans went wild.)

A few teams went beyond words and featured unofficial mascots on their rings:

The 2011 Cardinals include a "rally squirrel," honoring the varmint that darted across the field during a playoff win.

The 2016 Cubs pay homage to the Curse of the Billy Goat with a goat head on the ring's inner band.

The 2019 Nationals used that space for a smiling cartoon shark, a playful nod to utility man Gerardo Parra's sing-along walk-up music.

TOP 10 RAJAI DAVIS MOMENTS

When Rajai Davis was 13 years old, he watched from home in Connecticut as Joe Carter homered to win the 1993 World Series for the Blue Jays. It made a profound impact on him.

"That's when I really started dreaming about the big leagues," Davis says, "making that moment happen."

He didn't do it, but boy, did Davis come close for Cleveland in 2016. Trailing in Game 7 by two runs with two out in the bottom of the eighth, Davis choked up against the Cubs' Aroldis Chapman and lashed a low fastball just inside the left field foul pole to tie the game. Davis romped joyously around the bases, sticking out his tongue, pointing to the sky, pounding the Indians script across his chest.

"It was like it was a walk-off," Davis says—except it wasn't. The Cubs won in extra innings, making Davis the signature example of a hit that would have meant oh so much, if only his team had won the game. Here are a dozen other examples of high-impact hits for losing teams, with their Win Probability Added scores; that is, the increased likelihood of the player's team winning as a result of their hit.

1912: Fred Merkle's go-ahead single for the Giants in the tenth inning of Game 8 vs. the Red Sox (WPA: 29 percent) When I was 11 years old, I led off from first base in a Little League game as my teammate drove in the winning run with two outs. Seeing the ball go through the infield, I dashed home to join the celebration. Later, an umpire gently informed me that I had never touched second, and if the other team had noticed, they could have forced me out and negated the run. This was the mistake Fred Merkle made in a critical game for the Giants in 1908, when he escaped the field too soon to avoid charging fans after an apparent game-ending hit. It cost the Giants a win—and a pennant—and became known as "Merkle's Boner." Four years later,

Merkle seemed to atone for the blunder with a go-ahead single in the top of the tenth inning of the decisive Game 8 at Fenway Park . . . until the Red Sox recovered to win. Merkle would play in five World Series and lose them all.

1925: Roger Peckinpaugh's go-ahead homer for the Senators in the eighth inning of Game 7 vs. the Pirates (WPA: 25) Poor Roger Peckinpaugh, whose bat couldn't quite make up for his glove. Peckinpaugh, a shortstop, homered off Ray Kremer to put Washington ahead by a run with six outs to go for the great Walter Johnson. But the Pirates tied it in the bottom of the eighth, and Peckinpaugh's two-out error—his record eighth miscue of the series—brought up Hall of Famer Kiki Cuyler, who doubled in the go-ahead run. Improbably, it was Peckinpaugh's second error in a series-clinching game. As a Yankee in 1921, he booted a grounder in Game 8 to bring home the only run in the Giants' 1–0 win.

1946: Dom DiMaggio's game-tying double for the Red Sox in the eighth inning of Game 7 vs. the Cardinals (WPA: 32) For Red Sox fans between the eras of the Babe and Big Papi, it wasn't so much that their team always lost in the end—it was that the Sox would invariably make a spirited comeback and then go splat. The 1946 sequence set up decades of such agony: losing by two runs with four outs to go in Game 7, Dom DiMaggio drove a Harry Brecheen screwball off the right center field wall for a game-tying double. Great news, right? Yes—except DiMaggio blew out his hamstring running to second, and the Cardinals' Enos Slaughter would be the hero.

1953: Carl Furillo's game-tying homer for the Dodgers in the ninth inning of Game 6 vs. the Yankees (WPA: 36) Whitey Ford had spun seven sharp innings. But with a two-run lead and a fifth consecutive title in sight, Yankees manager Casey Stengel pulled his young ace for the stalwart Reynolds, by then a 36-year-old swingman. With one out and one on in the ninth, Furillo—the majors' leading hitter at .344—revived the Dodgers with a game-tying homer. "Had Brooklyn gone on to win," wrote Dan Daniel in *The Sporting News*, "Casey would have been raked over the coals until done to a cinder." Billy Martin saved Stengel that fate with his clinching single in the bottom of the frame.

1962: Willie Mays's double for the Giants in the ninth inning of Game 7 vs. the Yankees (WPA: 14) When Mays stepped in against Ralph Terry, the Giants trailed 1–0 with two out and Matty Alou on first. An out would win the series for New York; a homer would win it for San Francisco. Instead, Mays prolonged the outcome with a line-drive double to right that stuck on the wet outfield grass. Alou might have scored had it reached the wall, but he held at third as Roger Maris fired the ball in. "If it had been me, they would've had to throw me out coming home," Mays said in 2020, when I asked him about it through his biographer, John Shea. "I would've tried for home. Matty slowed down when he got to third. There's no way I would've stayed on third." That's where Alou remained when Willie McCovey lined to second to end it. ("People ask me how I'd like to be remembered," McCovey said in his Hall of Fame speech in 1986. "I tell them I'd like to be remembered as the guy who hit the line drive over Bobby Richardson's head.")

1985: Brian Harper's go-ahead single for the Cardinals in the eighth inning of Game 6 vs. the Royals (WPA: 26) Harper would have a very busy World Series in 1991, hitting .381 for the Twins and surviving a brutal home-plate collision with Atlanta's Lonnie Smith. In 1985, though, he was a little-used backup for the Cardinals. Harper had gone 53 days since his last hit when he broke a scoreless tie with a broken-bat single in the eighth inning of Game 6, putting St. Louis on the verge of a title before the Royals came back.

1986: Dave Henderson's go-ahead homer for the Red Sox in the tenth inning of Game 6 vs. the Mets (WPA: 35) He leaped after the swing and back-pedaled out of the box in delight. The ball, weighted with decades of October heartbreak, clanged off a *Newsday* billboard (IT'S A HIT) above the left field wall. Dave Henderson, who had saved the Red Sox with a homer in the playoffs, had done it again with this go-ahead blast off Rick Aguilera. Henderson seemed destined to be a Boston icon, and in the bottom of the tenth, he actually caught the final out of the game in center field. Problem was, the Mets still had an out to spare—and the Red Sox couldn't get it.

1992: Otis Nixon's game-tying single for the Braves in the ninth inning of Game 6 vs. the Blue Jays (WPA: 47) He'd watched the 1991 World Series in a rehab clinic after a drug suspension. A year later, Nixon came up in Game 6 as the potential last out of the World Series—and slapped an 0–2 pitch for a game-tying single off Tom Henke. Alas, two innings later, with John Smoltz (!) pinch running at third as the tying run, Nixon tried a drag bunt against Mike Timlin, who scooped it up and tossed to first to end the series. Nixon had 17 bunt singles that season but pushed this attempt just a little too hard. "I wanted to be the guy," he said later. "I don't think anyone wanted this as bad as I did."

2001: Alfonso Soriano's go-ahead homer for the Yankees in the eighth inning of Game 7 vs. the Diamondbacks (WPA: 23) The Yankees scored only 14 runs in their seven games against Arizona, and this was the last—a deep drive over the left field wall off a Curt Schilling splitter. The pitch was hardly a hanger; the Diamondbacks' catcher, Damian Miller, had his glove on the dirt as Soriano connected. When Schilling left the game soon after, manager Bob Brenly promised: "That ain't gonna beat us." He was right.

2002: Shawon Dunston's go-ahead homer for the Giants in the fifth inning of Game 6 vs. the Angels (WPA: 22) What a moment—Dunston, a 39-year-old son of Brooklyn, propelling the Giants to their first title since leaving New York. I was all set to write this as my story that night until the Angels, down by five runs, pulled off the biggest comeback ever by a team facing elimination. The homer ended up as the final hit of Dunston's 18-year career.

2003: Ruben Sierra's game-tying triple for the Yankees in the ninth inning of Game 4 vs. the Marlins (WPA: 40) The Yankees traded Sierra on their way to the 1996 World Series, the first of the Joe Torre era. He floated through seven organizations—and the independent Atlantic City Surf—before they brought him back in 2003 for Torre's last World Series run. Down to his last strike against Ugueth Urbina with two outs in Game 4, Sierra lined a two-run triple into the right field corner. The Yankees seemed destined to take a three-games-to-one Series lead, but the Marlins recovered with a walk-off homer by Alex Gonzalez and won it in six.

2011: Josh Hamilton's go-ahead homer for the Rangers in the tenth inning of Game 6 vs. the Cardinals (WPA: 43) It should have been the hit that lifted the Rangers to their first championship. But the Cardinals had already rallied once from the brink of oblivion, and they'd soon do it again.

THE ALL-NEVER-PLAYED-IN-THE-WORLD-SERIES TEAM

C	Joe Mauer	DH	Edgar Martinez
1B	Frank Thomas	SP	Phil Niekro
2B	Nap Lajoie	SP	Roy Halladay
SS	Ernie Banks	SP	Fergie Jenkins
3B	Ron Santo	SP	Gaylord Perry
OF	Ken Griffey Jr.	SP	Ted Lyons
OF	Harry Heilmann	RP	Lee Smith
OF	Andre Dawson	MGR	Gene Mauch

Bench: Luke Appling, Buddy Bell, Rod Carew, Bobby Grich, Rafael Palmeiro, Ryne Sandberg, Sammy Sosa, Ichiro Suzuki, Joe Torre, Billy Wagner, Billy Williams

THE MISSING MVPs

As the advertising director for *Sport* magazine in 1955, Phil Hyland wanted sponsors with money and status. Naturally, then, he wanted a car company—and he asked the editor, Ed Fitzgerald, to devise a promotion to attract one.

"I thought, what better way than to give a car to the most valuable player in the World Series?" Fitzgerald told the *New York Times'* Dave Anderson in 1979. "So Phil took the idea to Chevrolet, and they went for it. We paid for the first Corvette at dealer's price, but we also got a commitment for six ad pages."

The first World Series MVP winner, Johnny Podres of the Brooklyn Dodgers, got a white Corvette with red-leather upholstery and a speedometer that reached 140 miles an hour. Podres giddily drove it home to Witherbee, New York, up in the Adirondack Mountains, and for decades he used "MVP 55" on his license plate. With two complete-game victories, including a shutout in the clincher at Yankee Stadium, Podres deserved the recognition.

Other winners probably didn't (more on them later), thanks largely to the modern, hurried process in which MLB collects ballots from 11 different entities after the seventh inning of the clinching game.* Imperfect though it is, the act of linking a player to every World Series gives us a tangible hint about what happened, and who stood out as the hero.

It's a shame, then, that the first 51 World Series have no player officially attached to their legacies. Henry Ford founded the Ford Motor Company in 1903, just a few months before the first World Series. If only he'd thought to give a Model A to Bill Dinneen that October, he could have started the tradition, which now includes a Chevy truck or sports car for the winner.

Instead, the following list will have to do. Here's who should have won all those missing World Series MVP awards:

1903: Bill Dinneen, Red Sox—Dinneen flung four complete games in the first World Series, including the Game 8 clincher. It's safe to say he held up fine the next year, making 37 starts—and completing them all. Dinneen went on to serve 30 years as an AL umpire and worked the plate for Babe Ruth's 14-inning masterpiece in the 1916 World Series.

---

* Since 2019, these have been the voters for the World Series MVP award (each entity counts as one): Fox Sports broadcasters; ESPN Radio broadcasters; MLB International broadcasters; a fan vote on MLB.com; the official scorer; MLB Network talent; the president of the Baseball Writers' Association of America (if he or she is on site); the BBWAA chapter chairs who have covered the competing teams; the sideline reporters for the teams' regional sports networks (if they are on site); ESPN.com's BBWAA members; an international BBWAA member who has covered the entire World Series.

1905: Christy Mathewson, Giants—How's this for a six-day work week? On Monday, Mathewson shut out the A's in Game 1. On Thursday, he shut them out in Game 3. On Saturday, he shut them out in Game 5 to win the series. Mathewson faced 94 batters and only one got as far as third base—and that was after a wild pitch on a strikeout. It's the greatest performance in World Series history.

1906: George Rohe, White Sox—Within a year, he'd played the last game of a brief career. But Rohe, a third baseman, went 7-for-16 in the White Sox' four wins over the Cubs, and drove in all three runs in Ed Walsh's Game 3 shutout.

1907: Harry Steinfeldt, Cubs—While Detroit's Ty Cobb followed up his first batting title with a meager .200 average, the Cubs' Steinfeldt hit .471 in an easy five-game victory.

1908: Orval Overall, Cubs—What a name, what a series: 2–0 with two complete games, including a two-hit shutout with 10 strikeouts in the finale.

1909: Babe Adams, Pirates—How about the contrast in Adams's two World Series? In 1909, as a rookie, he went 3–0 with three complete games. In 1925, as the oldest player in the NL, he pitched one inning in relief. The Pirates won both times.

1910: Jack Coombs, Athletics—It wasn't as tidy as Mathewson's showing five years earlier, but "Colby Jack" (whose name still graces the baseball field at his alma mater, Colby College in Maine) also won three complete games in six days. He gave up 10 runs and skirted danger (24 hits, 14 walks) to thwart the Cubs.

1911: Frank "Home Run" Baker, Athletics—John McGraw's Giants tried to intimidate Baker by spiking him repeatedly at third base. Baker responded by hitting .375 with two pivotal homers, earning another title and one of baseball's enduring nicknames.

1912: Tris Speaker, Red Sox—Smoky Joe Wood won three times, but his woeful start in Game 7 (one inning, six runs) takes him out of consideration. Speaker hit .300 and tied the decisive Game 8 with a single off Mathewson in the bottom of the tenth, when a double play could have ended the series.

1913: Frank "Home Run" Baker, Athletics—Only one homer this time, but Baker hit .450 and knocked in seven runs. The Giants' lone victory was yet another shutout by Mathewson, who finished his World Series career with a 0.97 ERA—but just a 5–5 record.

1914: Hank Gowdy, Braves—Went 6-for-11 with five extra-base hits in the Miracle Braves' shocking sweep of the A's.

1915: Rube Foster, Red Sox—Game 2 was the first World Series game attended by a president, and Foster treated Woodrow Wilson to quite a show: nine innings on the mound and three hits at the plate, including the go-ahead single in the ninth. He went the distance again to close out the Phillies in Game 5.

1916: Duffy Lewis, Red Sox—The famous left field wall at Fenway Park once rose from a grassy slope known as "Duffy's Cliff," named for Lewis's skill in playing there. He could also hit, with a .353 average in this five-game victory over Brooklyn.

1917: Red Faber, White Sox—Faber pitched 27 of Chicago's 52 innings against the Giants, going 3–1 with a 2.33 ERA and wins in the last two games.

1918: Babe Ruth, Red Sox—Get used to this name. Ruth shut out the Cubs in the opener, then worked eight innings in Game 4, ripping a two-run triple in a one-run win.

1919: Dickey Kerr, White Sox—Kerr fired a shutout in Game 3 and then worked 10 innings to win Game 6, but some of his teammates, of course, conspired to lose. "I still can't understand it," Kerr told *The*

Sporting News in 1937. "They were a swell bunch of fellows." The Reds took the title, but Kerr gets this honor.

1920: Stan Coveleski, Indians—In the last year the spitball was legal across the league, the Tribe and the Dodgers started experts for three games apiece. Burleigh Grimes went 1–2 for Brooklyn and Coveleski won all three starts for Cleveland.

1921: Irish Meusel, Giants—After going hitless while the Yankees won the first two games, Meusel came alive, collecting 10 hits and driving in seven as the Giants won five of the last six games. This was the final time baseball used a best-of-nine format.

1922: Heinie Groh, Giants—Groh used his distinctive bottle bat to hit .474. The third baseman also picked up the Yankees' hitting signs in the opener, he told Lawrence Ritter in *The Glory of Their Times,* so he always knew when they might be bunting.

1923: Babe Ruth, Yankees—Just 2-for-17 against the Giants the year before, Ruth took over this time, hitting .368 with two homers and eight walks to lead the Yankees to their first championship.

1924: Bucky Harris, Senators—Harris, a 27-year-old player-manager, hit safely in all seven games against the Giants, going 3-for-5 in the capper. Harris played a dozen seasons and hit just 11 homers—but two came in this World Series.

1925: Max Carey, Pirates—Walter Johnson is probably the greatest pitcher ever, and Max Carey got four hits off him in Game 7. Carey, a 10-time league leader in stolen bases, swiped three bags in the series and hit .458 overall.

1926: Grover Cleveland Alexander, Cardinals—Ol' Pete, who had the Phillies' only World Series victory until 1980, led the Cardinals to their first title in grand style. Even before his famous relief outing to close out the Yankees, he went the distance to win Games 2 and 6.

1927: Babe Ruth, Yankees—Ruth, who'd been caught stealing to end the '26 World Series, left nothing to chance this time. He slammed the only two homers of the series and hit .400 as the Yankees swept the Pirates.

1928: Babe Ruth and Lou Gehrig, Yankees—This is the most fearsome duo in major league history at the height of its powers. Ruth and Gehrig combined to hit an absurd .593 (16-for-27) with seven home runs in yet another sweep.

1929: Jimmie Foxx, Athletics—The man called Beast hit .350, homered in the first two games, and singled twice in the biggest inning in World Series history: a 10-run explosion in the seventh inning of Game 4 that brought the A's back from an 8–0 hole. They wrapped the title in Game 5 on a series-ending double by Bing Miller—just after an intentional walk to Foxx.

1930: George Earnshaw, Athletics—In Game 6, with one day's rest, Earnshaw held the Cardinals to five hits in a complete-game, 7–1 victory to clinch the championship. He also won Game 2 and had a stretch of 22 consecutive scoreless innings within the series.

1931: Pepper Martin, Cardinals—With a .500 average (12-for-24) and five stolen bases, Martin was critical in ending the A's dynasty. Though hitless in Game 7, he made a racing catch in center, with a man on, to end the series.

1932: Lou Gehrig, Yankees—In a simply overpowering performance, Gehrig hit .529 (9-for-17) with three homers. Only one player in World Series history (David Ortiz in 2013) has hit for a higher average with at least 20 plate appearances.

1933: Carl Hubbell, Giants—King Carl won Games 1 and 4 of a five-game Giants victory over the Senators. He's the last pitcher to allow no earned runs in at least 20 innings in a World Series.

1934: Dizzy and Paul Dean, Cardinals—It took seven games, but only one pitching family, for the Cardinals to outlast the Tigers. Dizzy Dean won the bookend games and his brother Paul took two in between—with no relievers appearing in any of the victories.

1935: Charlie Gehringer, Tigers—The Hall of Fame second baseman had two hits in each of the Tigers' victories over the Cubs, with a .375 average. He batted 90 times in World Series play and struck out once.

1936: Jake Powell, Yankees—An inconvenient hero if there ever was one, Powell was 10-for-22 (.455) against the Giants. Two years later he was suspended for making racist comments—a hypocritical punishment from a league that banned Black players—and in 1948 he was arrested in Washington for writing bad checks. He shot himself to death at the police station.

1937: Lefty Gomez, Yankees—Gomez had a 6–0 World Series record, the most wins without a loss in the history of the Classic. He finished both of his starts against the Giants, winning the opener and the Game 5 clincher while allowing three runs.

1938: Red Ruffing, Yankees—Pretty much the same story, with a different pitcher this time: Ruffing won the first and last games against the Cubs, completing each one while allowing three earned runs in the Yankees' sweep.

1939: Charlie Keller, Yankees—Keller, a rookie left fielder, batted .438 with three home runs against the Reds. Everyone else in this brief and forgettable series combined to hit .190.

1940: Bucky Walters, Reds—With the Yankees mercifully absent for a change, Walters led the Reds to a six-game victory over the Tigers. Pitching to catcher Jimmie Wilson, who was activated from the coaching staff at age 40 following the suicide of Willard Hershberger and an injury to Ernie Lombardi, Walters won Game 2 and then closed out Detroit with a Game 6 shutout, hitting a homer in the process. Wilson, his unlikely batterymate, hit .353.

1941: Joe Gordon, Yankees—In the first of their 11 World Series matchups with the Dodgers, the Yankees got a standout performance from Gordon (7-for-14 with seven walks) to prevail in five.

1942: Johnny Beazley, Cardinals—How'd you like to hear these words from Babe Ruth as you celebrated a championship in the visitor's locker room at Yankee Stadium: "Where's that guy that whooped my Yankees?" Beazley, a 24-year-old rookie, lived that fantasy after his second complete-game victory clinched the title in Game 5.

1943: Spud Chandler, Yankees—Chandler played the Beazley role this year, capping his MVP season by winning the first and last games against the Cardinals, the latter a Game 5 shutout at Sportsman's Park.

1944: George McQuinn, Browns—The Cardinals won for the third time in five years, but McQuinn, a first baseman who went 7-for-16 (.438) with seven walks, was the star of the series. Alas, the rest of the Browns hit .160 in their only World Series appearance before moving to Baltimore.

1945: Hank Greenberg, Tigers—Hal Newhouser beat the Cubs in Games 5 and 7, but his ERA for the series was 6.10. Greenberg, the other Hall of Famer on this Tigers team, hit .304 and led all hitters with two homers and seven runs batted in.

1946: Harry Brecheen, Cardinals—Brecheen (pronounced "brick-EEN") went 3–0 with a 0.45 ERA against Boston. Twenty years later, he was pitching coach for the Orioles when they fired three shutouts while sweeping the Dodgers.

1947: Tommy Henrich, Yankees—Henrich hit safely in all seven games against the Dodgers, leading the teams with 10 hits, including the go-ahead single in the fourth inning of Game 7. Two years later, in Game 1, Henrich would hit the first walk-off homer in World Series history.

1948: Bob Lemon, Indians—One Hall of Fame righty named Bob went 0–2 in this series, but the Tribe had another to spare. While Feller lost twice, Lemon won Games 2 and 6 at Braves Field with a 1.65 ERA. Thirty years later, he earned another ring as manager of the Yankees.

1949: Allie Reynolds, Yankees—After shutting out the Dodgers in the opener, Reynolds worked a spotless 10-out save in Game 4. Superchief, as he was known (Reynolds was part Creek Indian), appeared in six World Series and earned a win in every one.

1950: Joe DiMaggio, Yankees—In the ninth of his 10 World Series, DiMaggio gets the nod for a tenth-inning homer to win Game 2 in Philadelphia and a run-scoring double in the first inning of the clincher. Joltin' Joe hit .308 in the sweep.

1951: Eddie Lopat, Yankees—A quintessential crafty lefty, Lopat beat the Giants twice, allowing one earned run in 18 innings. He was also on the mound for the infamous Willie Mays fly ball in Game 2, when the stately DiMaggio, in center field, called off Mickey Mantle, the fleet rookie charging for the ball from right. Mantle, then just 20, suffered a devastating knee injury when his spikes caught on a drain cover as he stopped short.

1952: Mickey Mantle, Yankees—The injury robbed Mantle of his breathtaking speed, but not of his Hall of Fame career. He wrecked the Dodgers with a .345 average, leading the Yankees to their final two victories with homers in Games 6 and 7 at Ebbets Field.

1953: Billy Martin, Yankees—The year before, he'd raced in from second base to snag a windblown pop-up with the bases loaded in Game 7. This time, Martin hit .500 and capped the finale with a walk-off single to vanquish Brooklyn again.

1954: Dusty Rhodes, Giants—No player in World Series history made a bigger impact with so little playing time. Rhodes didn't start at all, didn't play in the Game 4 clincher, and came to bat only seven times. But he singled twice, walked, drove in seven, and homered off future

Hall of Famers Bob Lemon (a three-run shot to win the opener) and Early Wynn.

THE SNUBBED SEVEN

1956: Who won it? Don Larsen.
Who should have won it? Yogi Berra.

By the time Berra torched Don Newcombe for a pair of two-run homers in a Game 7 rout, Don Larsen had already been awarded the Corvette. The *Sport* magazine editors made the call after his Game 5 perfecto, delighting Larsen—"I shouldn't have any trouble picking up women in this thing," he said—though obscuring the efforts of Berra, who hit .360 and became the first player to drive in 10 runs in a Series.

1960: Who won it? Bobby Richardson.
Who should have won it? Bill Mazeroski.

Yes, Richardson set a record for runs batted in, with 12, while batting .367. But he was 4-for-16 with one RBI in the Yankees' losses, and Mazeroski did more than swat the series-winning homer. He batted .320 overall and hit another important homer, a two-run shot in the Pirates' 6–4 win in the opener.

1982: Who won it? Darrell Porter.
Who should have won it? Joaquin Andujar.

When you think of Joaquin Andujar in the World Series, you probably think of his Game 7 tirade at umpire Don Denkinger in 1985. That's a shame, because Andujar should be remembered for beating the Brewers twice in 1982, with a gutty performance in Game 7 and a 1.35 ERA. (Porter hit .286 with a homer and five RBIs.) "Joaquin Andujar was the toughest competitor I have ever been around—ever," says John Stuper, who won Game 6. "He had this persona of being crazy, but he was one of the nicest people I ever played with in my life."

1997: Who won it? Livan Hernandez.
Who should have won it? Moises Alou.

Hernandez was a feel-good story, a rookie from Cuba who beat Cleveland twice and then, before Game 7, saw his mother for the first time in two years. But he was hardly dominant (a 5.27 ERA, with more walks than strikeouts), and needed a three-run homer from Moises Alou to earn both of his wins. Alou also started the game-tying rally in the ninth inning of Game 7 and hit .321 overall. Later, he picked a telling name for a racehorse he owned in the Dominican Republic: The Real MVP.

2002: Who won it? Troy Glaus.
Who should have won it? Barry Bonds.

Glaus was an understandable choice: he hit .385 with three homers and smoked the go-ahead two-run double off Robb Nen to cap an extraordinary comeback in Game 6. But all of his homers came in losses, and the series was defined by the Angels' efforts to contain Bonds. By this point Bonds had pretty much broken the sport, and the Angels walked him 13 times, seven intentionally. When Bonds did swing, he was lethal: 8-for-17 with four homers and two doubles.

2003: Who won it? Josh Beckett.
Who should have won it? Brad Penny.

Beckett authored a performance for the ages with a Game 6 shutout on short rest to finish off the Yankees on the road. But he lost his other start, while Brad Penny won twice—and had the biggest hit of Game 5 with a two-run single. Beckett pitched better, true—but Penny had a sharp ERA (2.19), and for value to a winning effort, 2–0 is better than 1–1.

2018: Who won it? Steve Pearce.
Who should have won it? David Price.

This should have been an easy call. Steve Pearce had no hits in the World Series until Game 4. By then, David Price had won his Game 2 start and pitched in relief in the ninth inning of Game 3. Pearce was huge in the last two games (4-for-8 with three homers and seven RBIs), but Price won Game 5, lasting into the eighth inning on extremely short rest, and went 2–0 with a 1.98 ERA overall.

ONE-AND-DONE HALL OF FAMERS

I've always been fascinated by players whose major league careers lasted one precious game, barely enough time to sip from their coffee cup. But how many all-time greats had a comparable career in the World Series? These are the six Hall of Famers who made just one appearance on the grandest stage.

Eppa Rixey

Eppa Rixey had one month to enjoy life as a Hall of Famer. Elected by the veterans committee on January 27, 1963, he died of a heart attack on February 28. A durable lefty for the Phillies and Reds, Rixey made his lone World Series appearance in relief against the Red Sox in 1915, taking the loss to eliminate the Phillies in the decisive Game 5. Harry Hooper drove in the go-ahead run in the ninth when his deep drive bounced over the fence and into the center field stands. Now, of course, that's an automatic double. Sadly, for Rixey, it counted as a homer back then.

Dazzy Vance

The strikeout king of the 1920s, Dazzy Vance was hanging on as a reliever for the 1934 Cardinals, who used him for four outs in their 10–4 loss to the Tigers in Game 4. In the end, it was Dizzy, not Dazzy—Dizzy Dean, that is—on the mound when the Cardinals clinched Game 7.

Satchel Paige

In 1948, three of history's greatest pitchers appeared in the seventh inning of Game 5 as Cleveland tried to close out the Boston Braves: Bob Feller, who started the inning, Warren Spahn, who flied out, and Satchel Paige, who made history. Paige, a 42-year-old rookie and a towering figure of the Negro Leagues, became the first Black man to pitch in the AL/NL World Series. Paige got Spahn to fly out, balked a runner to second, and retired Tommy Holmes on a ground out. The Indians won the title the next day in Boston, and Paige had played a major part in their season. "He went 6–1 for the year; he helped us as a starting pitcher," Eddie Robinson, the Indians' first baseman, said in 2019. "He was a delight to have on the team." (The first Black pitcher to play in the World Series was technically Dan Bankhead of the 1947 Dodgers, but he appeared as a pinch-runner and did not pitch.)

Juan Marichal

The only World Series appearance of Juan Marichal's career ended in the batter's box. In 1962, Marichal was pitching a shutout in Game 4 when he came to bat against Whitey Ford in the fifth inning with runners at the corners and one out. With a full count, the Giants called for a suicide squeeze, leaving Marichal helpless when Ford's pitch missed, down and in. "It was a bad pitch," Marichal told reporters later, "but I couldn't let it go by because [Tom] Haller was coming from third." The Giants won the game, but the finger injury knocked out Marichal from another possible start. He would finish his career with the 1974 Red Sox, who won the pennant the next season, and the 1975 Dodgers, who had won it the year before.

Nolan Ryan

Nolan Ryan was just 22 years old, with seven no-hitters and more than 5,000 strikeouts ahead of him, when he took the mound for the Mets at Shea Stadium with two outs in the seventh inning of Game 3 in 1969. Gary Gentry had walked the bases loaded with a 4–0 lead, bringing up Baltimore's Paul Blair as the tying run. Ryan fired an

0–2 fastball and Blair slashed it to deep right center. Center fielder Tommie Agee ranged far into the gap, diving on the warning track for his second dazzling catch of the day. When Blair came up again, with two outs and the bases loaded in the ninth, Gil Hodges met at the mound with Ryan, who insisted he still felt strong. Again, the count went to 0–2—but this time, after two fastballs, Ryan knew what to do. "I wasn't going to make the same mistake twice," he wrote in his book, *Throwing Heat*. "I went into my windup and threw probably as good a curveball as I have ever thrown." Blair flinched as his knees buckled. Called strike three, game over.

Trevor Hoffman

In Game 3 of the 1998 World Series, Padres manager Bruce Bochy did something he hadn't done all season: he called on Trevor Hoffman in the eighth inning for a six-out save. The Padres held a one-run lead on the Yankees, who had won the first two games in the Bronx, and Randy Myers had walked the leadoff man. After an out and another walk, Hoffman faced Scott Brosius. Pitching coach Dave Stewart told Hoffman to be aggressive—and Brosius pulverized an 89-mile-an-hour fastball to straightaway center for a three-run homer. Hoffman is at peace with the outcome, but he'll always wonder what would have happened if he had thrown his signature changeup in the biggest moment of his career. "That's probably the optimal time that I should have thrown it," he says, "and I didn't." The Yankees completed a sweep the next night.

THREE WHO PLAYED WITHOUT PLAYING

Jim Thorpe, 1917
Howard Battle, 1999
Mike Fontenot, 2010

In the eighth inning of Game 2 of the 2010 World Series, the Giants announced the left-handed-hitting Mike Fontenot as a pinch hitter. Then the Rangers replaced their right-handed pitcher with a lefty.

Fontenot went back to the bench, and the Giants used a right-hander, Aaron Rowand, instead.

That was the extent of Fontenot's World Series experience. He did not play again in the Giants' five-game victory, yet because he was used—if only as a decoy—he gets credit for one game. It's an odd sort of historical purgatory.

"I mean, I had an appearance, my name's in the box score," Fontenot told me the next spring, with a laugh. "Yeah, I didn't play any. But that's fine. It was an awesome experience. I wouldn't give it up for anything."

Sure, I pressed, but what would you tell people? Did you really, you know . . . play? Fontenot thought for a moment.

"I don't know what I'd tell them," he finally said. "I didn't get out or anything. I could make up something like, 'Yeah, I hit a missile and the guy caught it.' But then I'd be 0-for-1. I'm not, so . . ."

He trailed off, not really completing the thought. "I'm not worried about that too much," he said.

Fair enough—Fontenot got a championship ring and a quirky distinction as the only player to participate in a World Series for the winning team without actually playing. Two others have done it for losing teams, including Jim Thorpe, possibly the greatest all-around athlete of the twentieth century.

Thorpe—Olympic gold medalist in the decathlon and pentathlon, Hall of Famer in pro and college football—played six years in the majors, mostly with the Giants, with a .252 career average. He batted right-handed, and the White Sox started only one lefty in the 1917 World Series: Reb Russell, who got the call for Game 5 at Comiskey Park. John McGraw put Thorpe in his lineup, batting sixth and playing right field, but by the time Thorpe came up in the top of the first inning, Russell had already left the game. With two outs, a runner on, and righty Eddie Cicotte on the mound, McGraw yanked Thorpe for a lefty, Dave Robertson.

In both Giants examples, the strategy worked: Rowand lashed a two-run triple, and Robertson singled in a run. Poor Howard Battle was not so lucky for the Braves in 1999. His replacement, Keith Lockhart, made an out—and Battle never appeared in the majors again.

ONE MORE, PLEASE . . .

The Phillies brought the winning run to the plate at the end of my first World Series game in 1983. Joe Morgan lined out to second base, but if he'd hit a home run, it would have tied the series at two apiece and ensured another start for my baseball hero, Steve Carlton. Instead, the Orioles wrapped it up in Game 5 the next day.

One more homer, one more win, one more start. For all the highlights we get to see in the World Series, we're often left yearning for just one more . . . something, like these five:

One more Sandy Koufax start in 1966

The great Koufax never pitched again after losing Game 2 of a four-game sweep by the Orioles. The Dodgers made six errors, three by center fielder Willie Davis, blinded by the bright L.A. sky. "Willie, never let it be unsaid, had his moment in the sun," wrote Jim Murray in the *Los Angeles Times*. "Alas, so did the ball." Koufax deserved a better ending.

One more Willie Mays at-bat in 1973

The World Series MVP award is named for Willie Mays, and the winner gets a bronze statuette of his over-the-shoulder catch against Cleveland in 1954. That's the best way to depict the Fall Classic version of Mays, because he didn't do much at the plate, batting .228 with no homers. Yet what if Mays had gotten one more chance—with a championship at stake, no less? It could have happened, if only Yogi Berra had let him do it in 1973. In Game 7, with the Mets down to their last out in the bottom of the ninth inning in Oakland, Gene Tenace made an error at first base, allowing a run to score and bringing up Wayne Garrett as the tying run. The A's then replaced Rollie Fingers (who'd already gotten 10 outs) with a lefty, Darold Knowles, who would have the matchup edge on the left-handed Garrett. It had been a rough postseason for Garrett, who was 7-for-52, but he'd homered twice in the World Series, and another long ball would tie Game 7. Berra, the Mets' manager, just happened to have a righty hitter with 660 homers on his bench. But Mays was 42 years old by then and hadn't gone deep in two months. As cinematic as the moment could have been, Berra left Mays on the bench as Garrett popped out, ending both the World Series and the breathtaking career of Willie Mays.

One more healthy month for Tom Seaver in 1986

Seaver made his last appearance on September 19, 1986, for the Red Sox in Toronto, when he felt something snap in his knee. Ron Taylor, Seaver's teammate on the Miracle Mets of 1969, was the Blue Jays' team doctor and diagnosed a sprained ligament. It never got better, causing Seaver to miss the World Series against his old team. There would have been room for Seaver on the roster, too—he had a respectable final season for Boston, with a 3.80 ERA in 16 starts, and the Red Sox carried two pitchers (Tim Lollar and Sammy Stewart) who never got into a game.

One more Game 7 at Yankee Stadium in 2003

No postseason has ever had three Game 7s, but this should have been it. The Marlins had shocked the Cubs in a seven-game NLCS, and the Yankees had done the same to Boston in the ALCS. But Florida wrapped up the World Series in six behind Josh Beckett, and the original Yankee Stadium never hosted another Fall Classic. A seventh game in 2003, with Mike Mussina starting for the Yankees and Roger Clemens lurking in relief, would have been so much fun.

Ninety more feet for Alex Gordon in 2014

When Gordon's two-out single squirted away from the Giants' outfielders with two outs in the ninth inning of Game 7, it seemed for an instant as if he might try to circle the bases and score the tying run. The third base coach, Mike Jirschle, held him up, and Brandon Crawford likely would have nailed Gordon at the plate to end the World Series.

"The hardest part of making that play was picking the throw from [left fielder] Juan Perez," Crawford said in 2022. "Once I got it, I felt like I was ready to throw. Believe me, I've watched the replay as much as anybody, and I don't think he was far enough to make it, unless I made a terrible throw. But I trust my arm." Maybe so, but Gordon wishes he'd blown through that stop sign.

"Oh, absolutely," he told me at his last spring training camp, in 2020. "Even if I would have ended the game on a close play like that or a replay, or if I would have run over Buster Posey at home plate, who knows what would have happened? It would have been a crazy way to end it, either win or lose." Would he have really run over Posey, who had famously been injured on a collision at the plate? Maybe not. "I love Buster, so I wouldn't do it," Gordon conceded. "I'd try to slide around him. That rule is named for him!"

And one that thankfully didn't happen . . .

One more look at the final out in 2005: The White Sox were one out away from a sweep in Houston, but the Astros had the tying run on second. Orlando Palmeiro smacked a high chopper over the mound, and Juan Uribe dashed in from shortstop to glove it on the grass. Uribe fired to first as Palmeiro crossed the bag and made a desperate safe signal with his arms. Umpire Gary Cederstrom called him out, ending the World Series and giving the White Sox their most exhilarating moment in 88 years—one that would have been painfully awkward with a replay review. Would Astros manager Phil Garner really have challenged the play? "Sure I would have," he told me. "I don't remember if he was out or safe, but certainly, in a 1–0 ballgame, I'd have contested it if I had the ability to do it." Thankfully, replay did not come to the World Series until 2009, and has never been used on the final out. But that day is coming.

THE TEN GREATEST WORLD SERIES EVER

Well, friends, we've come this far.
It's time to rank the best of the best.

#10: 1926, Cardinals over Yankees in 7—Babe Ruth, Lou Gehrig, and nine other Hall of Famers starred as the Cardinals won their first championship behind Ol' Pete Alexander—with a surprise twist at the end.

#9: 1957, Braves over Yankees in 7—In a showcase for inner-circle Hall of Famers (Hank Aaron, Whitey Ford, Mickey Mantle, Warren Spahn, and Eddie Mathews, who hit a walk-off homer in Game 4), it was Lew Burdette who shone brightest. His third victory, a Game 7 shutout, gave Milwaukee its only World Series crown.

#8: 1972, A's over Reds in 7—A lower-profile series, but close throughout and perhaps the first with truly modern managing styles. A record six games were decided by one run, and no pitcher threw a complete game.

#7: 1988, Dodgers over A's in 5—Never has a World Series packed so much greatness into five games: two walk-off homers, two Orel Hershiser gems, and a fascinating fourth game that turned the series. An underdog script made for Hollywood.

#6: 1960, Pirates over Yankees in 7—Memorably weird, with four close wins by the Pirates and three blowout wins by the Yankees. Fun fact: the kid who picked up Bill Mazeroski's walk-off homer in Schenley Park, behind Forbes Field, lost it in a pickup game with his buddies the next spring.

#5: 2001, Diamondbacks over Yankees in 7—Lead changes in the bottom of the ninth in Games 4, 5, and 7, set against the emotional backdrop of 9/11, with the Diamondbacks ending a dynasty by beating the great Mariano Rivera.

#4: 1924, Senators over Giants in 7—A classic bookended by 12-inning games; the first a loss by Walter Johnson, the second a win. In the clincher, bad-hop hits eluded the youngest player in World Series history, Giants third baseman Freddie Lindstrom, to tie it in the eighth and win it in the twelfth.

#3: 1912, Red Sox over Giants in 8 (including a tie)—Boston and New York, Fenway Park and the Polo Grounds, Snodgrass and Speaker and Smoky Joe Wood. A tenth-inning comeback off Christy Mathewson, winner-take-all. A series for the ages.

#2: 1975, Reds over Red Sox in 7—This had everything: transcendent performances, controversies, breathtaking visuals, a Luis Tiant shutout in Game 1, and then six comeback wins in a row. First of two titles for the Big Red Machine, an all-time great team.

#1: 1991, Twins over Braves in 7—Worst-to-first teams, pulsating ballparks, and five games decided in the winning team's last at-bat. Games 6 and 7 both went to extra innings for the first time ever, and Hall of Famers did Hall of Fame things: first a walk-off homer by Kirby Puckett, then a 10-inning shutout by Jack Morris.

Acknowledgments

Every baseball needs 108 stitches. Every World Series winner needs 108 outs: four victories, 27 outs in each—more are needed if the games go extra innings, of course, but you can't win a title without those 108. Likewise, you can't write a book about the history of the World Series without a lot of folks tying it all together—many more than 108, in fact.

This is my second collaboration with my editor at Doubleday, Bill Thomas, whose encouragement and wisdom have been invaluable. My agent, David Black, is a tireless, trusted advocate and confidant. Thank you both for helping me achieve a lifelong goal—twice.

In researching this book, I tried not to cover the same old ground—as sacred as it is—that would already be familiar to fans. I needed a lot of insights from folks who've been out of the game for a while, and many people were kind enough to find them and make the connection for me. Thank you to Fernando Alcalá, John Blake, Dina Blevins, John Blundell, Peter Botte, Rob Butcher, Greg Casterioto, Matt Chisholm, Bonnie Clark, Pat Courtney, Jerry Crasnick, Maria Cresswell, Chris Dahl, Maureen Dowd, Gordon Edes, Lorraine Fisher, Richard Griffin, Paul Hagen, Dan Hart, Jay Horwitz, Joe Jareck, Lee Jenkins, Kevin Kernan, Mark Langill, Mike Lupica, Warren Miller, Dustin Morse, Donald Muller, Christine Negley, Jesus Ortiz, Jeff Pearlman, Eduardo Pérez, Ed Randall, John Shea, Mike Swanson, Mike Teevan, Chuck Torres, Jim Trdinich, Julie Vavruska, Ben Walker, and Casey Wilcox.

I actually started on this book long before I even knew it, gathering

World Series anecdotes and memories since my teenage years. I published a little baseball magazine then, and my hometown Phillies gave me press passes. (Thank you, Larry Shenk!) Sometimes I'd talk to players about the World Series I had watched as a little kid.

Bob McClure told me he could never bring himself to wear his 1982 AL championship ring; he'd lost Game 7 for the Brewers when his high school teammate, the Cardinals' Keith Hernandez, singled for the go-ahead hit. McClure was 40 when we spoke, the oldest player in the National League, still chasing a championship that never came.

Then there was Gary Carter, nearing the end of his Hall of Fame career, describing how he prayed on his way to the plate in 1986, with two outs and the bases empty, down by two in the bottom of the tenth inning of Game 6 for the Mets:

> The biggest thing that was going through my mind is that I reflected back upon my days in the alleyway dreaming about this. You always think World Series, bottom of the ninth, two outs, that kind of stuff. And then, I felt an extreme presence and I knew that our good Lord was with us. I felt like when I went up to the plate, I was not going to make the last out.

Who knows what the Almighty had to do with it, but Carter believed, and his state of mind mattered. And while he'd surely told that story many times, it was captivating to hear it in person, one-on-one, all wide-eyed, boyish enthusiasm from a famous grown-up in my baseball card collection. Moments like that made me want to be a baseball writer, and I'm grateful to everyone who has shared their memories with me.

I'm also very proud to work for a newspaper that has assigned me to cover the World Series every year, even in the decade before I became the national baseball writer. In 22 years at *The New York Times*, I've missed only two World Series games: the final two in Arizona in 2001, for my daughter Lily's christening. So many colleagues have made life easier for me in covering all those games, but special thanks to Neil Amdur, Randy Archibold, Jack Curry, Terri Ann Glynn, Ben Hoffman, Tom Jolly, Scott Miller, Carl Nelson, Buster Olney, Joel Petterson,

Jay Schreiber, Ben Shpigel, Jason Stallman, Fern Turkowitz, George Vecsey, James Wagner, and David Waldstein.

Thanks to my friends in Cooperstown, especially Bill Francis, Chris and Jen Hulse, Jeff Idelson, Jeff Katz, Cassidy Lent, Bruce Markusen, Tim Mead, Craig Muder, Josh Rawitch, Jon Shestakofsky, and Tom Shieber; my pals at MLB Network Radio, for letting me prove on the air that I can name the starting pitchers for every World Series game in my lifetime; and to cherished friends and role models in the game, especially Peter Gammons, Derrick Goold, Dan Shaughnessy, Jayson Stark, and the late David Montgomery.

Growing up, my friends and I would actually practice how to celebrate the last out of the World Series—or maybe it was just an exercise in dogpiling at recess. Either way, I love them like brothers. That's saying something, because I really love my brothers, Tim and Dave, and my parents, John and Mimi, to whom this book is dedicated.

I've come to believe that home field advantage means next to nothing in the World Series; more often than not, the winning team clinches on the road. But it sure means a lot in life, and I'm blessed to have Jen, Lily, Mack, Caroline, and Rory as my home team. I love them more than baseball, though now I can confess it: I always root for the World Series to go seven games, even if I have to miss Halloween.

Tyler Kepner
Spring 2022
Wilton, Connecticut

Bibliography

The primary sources for this book were the many hours of interviews I conducted, in person and by phone, from May 2019 through May 2022, as well as those I did before research on this book began. I also utilized the archives at Newspapers.com, *The New York Times,* and *The Sporting News;* player biographies from the Society of American Baseball Research; the indispensable Baseball-Reference.com; and the extensive clip files at the Giamatti Research Center at the National Baseball Hall of Fame in Cooperstown, New York. These books from my personal library were all helpful:

Amore, Dom. *A Franchise on the Rise: The First Twenty Years of the New York Yankees.* New York: Sports Publishing, 2018.

Anderson, Sparky, with Dan Ewald. *Sparky!* New York: Prentice Hall Press, 1990.

Angell, Roger. *Late Innings.* New York: Ballantine Books, 1982.

———. *The Summer Game.* New York: Viking Penguin, 1972.

Armour, Mark L., and Daniel R. Levitt. *In Pursuit of Pennants.* Lincoln: University of Nebraska Press, 2015.

Black, Martha Jo, and Chuck Schoffner. *Joe Black: More Than a Dodger.* Chicago: Academy Chicago Publishers, 2015.

Cook, Kevin. *Electric October.* New York: Henry Holt, 2017.

Darling, Ron. *The Complete Game.* New York: Vintage Books, 2009.

Dellinger, Susan. *Red Legs and Black Sox: Edd Roush and the Untold Story of the 1919 World Series.* Cincinnati: Emmis Books, 2006.

Dorfman, H. A., and Karl Kuehl. *The Mental Game of Baseball.* Lanham, Md.: Diamond Communications, 1989.

Elliott, Richard. *Clem Labine: Always a Dodger.* Conneaut Lake, Pa.: Page Publishing, 2015.

Gammons, Peter. *Beyond the Sixth Game.* New York: Houghton Mifflin, 1985.

Gibson, Bob, and Reggie Jackson, with Lonnie Wheeler. *Sixty Feet, Six Inches.* New York: Doubleday, 2009.

Golenbock, Peter. *Bums: An Oral History of the Brooklyn Dodgers.* New York: G. P. Putnam's Sons, 1984.

Goold, Derrick. *100 Things Cardinals Fans Should Know & Do Before They Die.* Chicago: Triumph, 2019.

Grimm, Charlie, with Ed Prell. *Jolly Cholly's Story: Baseball, I Love You!* Chicago: Henry Regnery Company, 1968.

Halberstam, David. *October 1964.* New York: Villard Books, 1994.

———. *The Teammates.* New York: Hyperion, 2003.

Herzog, Whitey, and Jonathan Pitts. *You're Missin' a Great Game.* New York: Simon & Schuster, 1999.

Honig, Donald. *The October Heroes.* New York: Simon & Schuster, 1979.

Hornig, Doug. *The Boys of October.* New York: McGraw-Hill, 2003.

Jackson, Reggie, with Kevin Baker. *Becoming Mr. October.* New York: Doubleday, 2013.

James, Bill. *The Bill James Guide to Baseball Managers.* New York: Scribner, 1997.

Joseph, Dan. *Last Ride of the Iron Horse.* Mechanicsburg, Pa.: Sunbury Press, 2019.

Kahn, Roger. *The Boys of Summer.* New York: HarperCollins, 1971.

Koppett, Leonard. *The Man in the Dugout.* New York: Crown, 1993.

Kuhn, Bowie. *Hardball: The Education of a Baseball Commissioner.* New York: Random House, 1987.

Leavy, Jane. *The Big Fella: Babe Ruth and the World He Created.* New York: HarperCollins, 2018.

Leerhsen, Charles. *Ty Cobb: A Terrible Beauty.* New York: Simon & Schuster, 2015.

Lewis, Michael. *Moneyball: The Art of Winning an Unfair Game.* New York: W. W. Norton, 2003.

Leyritz, Jim, with Douglas B. Lyons and Jeffrey Lyons. *Catching Heat: The Jim Leyritz Story.* Deerfield Beach, Fla.: Health Communications, 2011.

Macht, Norman L. *Connie Mack and the Early Years of Baseball.* Lincoln: University of Nebraska Press, 2007.

Madden, Bill. *Pride of October: What It Was to Be Young and a Yankee.* New York: Warner Books, 2003.

Maraniss, David. *Clemente: The Passion and Grace of Baseball's Last Hero.* New York: Simon & Schuster, 2006.

Masur, Louis P. *Autumn Glory: Baseball's First World Series.* New York: Hill and Wang, 2003.

Mays, Willie, and John Shea. *24: Life Stories and Lessons from the Say Hey Kid.* New York: St. Martin's Press, 2020.

McGraw, Tug, with William C. Kashatus. *Was It As Good for You?* Media, Pa.: McGraw and Company, 2000.

McKeon, Jack, and Kevin Kernan. *I'm Just Getting Started.* Chicago: Triumph Books, 2005.

Menefee, Curt, with Michael Arkush. *Losing Isn't Everything.* New York: Dey Street Books, 2017.

Peary, Danny. *We Played the Game.* New York: Hyperion, 1994.

Posnanski, Joe. *The Machine.* New York: HarperCollins, 2009.

Puckett, Kirby, and Mike Bryan. *I Love This Game! My Life and Baseball.* New York: HarperCollins, 1993.

Ritter, Lawrence S. *The Glory of Their Times.* New York: William Morrow, 1966.

Ryan, Bob. *When Boston Won the World Series.* Philadelphia: Running Book Press, 2002.

Schmidt, Mike, with Glen Waggoner. *Clearing the Bases.* New York: Harper-Collins, 2006.

Shamsky, Art, and Erik Sherman. *After the Miracle: The Lasting Brotherhood of the '69 Mets.* New York: Simon & Schuster, 2019.

Shapiro, Michael. *The Last Good Season.* New York: Doubleday, 2003.

Sherman, Erik. *Two Sides of Glory: The 1986 Boston Red Sox in Their Own Words.* Lincoln: University of Nebraska Press, 2021.

Smith, Red. *To Absent Friends.* New York: Atheneum, 1982.

Snell, Roger. *Root for the Cubs: Charlie Root & the 1929 Chicago Cubs.* Nicholsville, Ky.: Wind Publications, 2009.

Sowell, Mike. *One Pitch Away.* New York: Macmillan, 1995.

Stark, Jayson. *Wild Pitches.* Chicago: Triumph, 2014.

Swoboda, Ron. *Here's the Catch.* New York: St. Martin's Press, 2019.

Terry, Ralph, with John Wooley. *Right Down the Middle: The Ralph Terry Story.* Tulsa, Okla.: Mullerhaus Publishing Arts, 2016.

Tewksbury, Bob, and Scott Miller. *Ninety Percent Mental.* New York: Da Capo Press, 2018.

Torre, Joe, and Tom Verducci. *The Yankee Years.* New York: Doubleday, 2009.

Vaccaro, Mike. *The First Fall Classic.* New York: Doubleday, 2009.

Verducci, Tom. *The Cubs Way.* New York: Crown Archetype, 2017.

Wallace, Joseph. *World Series: An Opinionated Chronicle.* New York: Harry N. Abrams, 2003.

Weber, Bruce. *As They See 'Em: A Fan's Travels in the Land of Umpires.* New York: Scribner, 2009.

Weisberger, Bernard A. *When Chicago Ruled Baseball: The Cubs–White Sox World Series of 1906.* New York: William Morrow, 2006.

Wolf, Thomas. *The Called Shot.* Lincoln: University of Nebraska Press, 2020.

Index

Illustration Credits

Page 3: (top) Robert Sullivan/AFP via Getty Images; (middle) John Iacono/ *Sports Illustrated* via Getty Images; (bottom) AP Photo/Eric Gay

Page 4: (top) Michael Chritton/*Akron Beacon Journal*/TNS/Alamy Live News; (bottom) Robert Beck/*Sports Illustrated* via Getty Images

Page 5: (top) Reuters/Pool/David J. Phillip; (bottom) Bill Greene/*The Boston Globe* via Getty Images

Page 6: (top left) AP Photo; (top right) Reuters/Pool/Paul Sancya; (bottom) Bettmann/Getty Images

Page 7: (top) John Biever/*Milwaukee Journal* via Gannett; (bottom) FLHC DC1/Alamy Stock Photo

Page 8: (top left) Reuters/Jessica Rinaldi; (top right) Reuters/Pool/David J. Phillip; (bottom) Reuters/Mike Segar